CLIMATE CHANGE, COMING SOON TO A COURT NEAR YOU

CLIMATE LITIGATION IN ASIA AND THE PACIFIC AND BEYOND

DECEMBER 2020

ASIAN DEVELOPMENT BANK

Notes:
In this publication, "$" refers to United States dollars unless otherwise stated.
ADB recognizes "China" as the People's Republic of China, "Ceylon" as Sri Lanka, "Vietnam" as Viet Nam, and "Orissa" as Odisha.
All photos are by ADB, unless otherwise specified.

Cover design by Gayle Certeza, Daniel Desembrana, and John Michael Casipe.

Printed on recycled paper

CONTENTS

FIGURES AND BOXES

FIGURES

BOXES

> We should include courts in the climate change picture because we have no other option. No substitute exists for the court system. If judges are in charge of deciding all sorts of conflicts about life, death, love, human rights, and national security, it makes no sense to leave climate change outside the courtroom.
>
> —*Justice Antonio Herman Benjamin*

Photo by Ariel Javellana/ADB.

FOREWORD

CLIMATE CHANGE AND JUDGES

Climate change poses the most urgent existential challenge of our lifetime—not only for humanity's survival and protection of the planet's biodiversity, but also for the proper functioning of the Environmental Rule of Law. Our global climate's accelerating volatility—with its adverse impacts on ecosystems, vast landscapes, and human health and dignity—is transforming how lawyers and judges address Environmental Law's traditional principles, objectives, instruments, and institutions. From an institutional point of view, the climate crisis fundamentally affects the way we perceive the role of courts in natural resource disputes.

Judges are trained and work in boxes of legal knowledge, practical expertise, and jurisdiction. The "little world" of a judge is one of unavoidable boundaries: political and judicial arenas that fragment ecological spaces instead of respecting them.

Climate change profoundly modifies these ancient premises and rattles judges' comfort zones. Some perceive the subject matter of climate protection—the atmospheric common good, ecosystem services, and intergenerational values—as extending beyond the jurisdiction of local courts. In fact, judges may feel that climate issues reside outside the sovereign borders of national courts. Particularly in respect to the planet's climate, the material good—the atmosphere as a whole—is one that just a few decades ago, following the lessons of Roman law, was considered alien to the categories addressed by domestic legislation.

It is also disturbing to judges that, while those who need protection and would benefit from judicial measures taken to address climate change are spread across the world, only a fraction might live within their jurisdiction. The same applies to the causes of climate change—perpetrated in large part by seemingly faraway activities and actors. Even more complicated for the generalist judge is the inability to see, touch, hear, or directly know the subject of the case. Although intangible categories are not unknown in the judicial context, the more this "physicality" is weakened or dissipated, the more ordinary judges begin to think that the conflict should be decided by someone else or somewhere else.

The climate crisis poses even greater judicial complication when we realize that many countries still do not have comprehensive or effective environmental laws. In others, judges may lack jurisdiction over the whole spectrum of environmental matters. Or, worse, when they can exercise authority, judges may lack the independence, knowledge, or integrity to discharge their responsibilities properly. In other words, although the biodiversity and climate change crises are universal, environmental law and adequate access to courts and justice are not. People in developed countries with robust democratic systems take fair and effective environmental adjudication for granted. For a large portion of the world, however, fundamental access to justice cannot be assumed. Sadly, those large areas are frequently home to rich biodiversity hot spots and tropical forests in desperate need of judicial enforcement.

Therefore, we may fairly raise the question: should we expect—and trust—courts to address climate change? Despite the above difficulties, my qualified answer is yes, for at least four pragmatic, legal, ethical, and policy and/or institutional reasons.

First, the pragmatic argument. We should include courts in the climate change picture because we have no other option. No substitute exists for the court system. If judges are in charge of deciding all sorts of conflicts about life, death, love, human rights, and national security, it makes no sense to leave climate change outside the courtroom. This assumption does not mean that we do not recognize the enormous differences between climate and "regular" environmental cases. However, the lack of other or better alternatives makes courts an inevitable choice.

Second, it would not be reasonable to entrust Environmental Law to judges, as we already do globally, without including climate change. At the end of the day, many key parts of nature—biomes, ecosystems, species, and genetic diversity—and the human environment will be directly and perhaps irreversibly affected by climate change. For obvious reasons, the exclusion of climate cases would handicap and ossify environmental jurisdiction, transforming it into a body without its heart and preventing the legal system's evolution in a world of rapid transformations. Climate change is already affecting and will continue to affect not just Environmental Law. It will also impact most, if not all, legal disciplines that compose the conventional field of judicial intervention—from constitutional to tax and insurance law, from civil and administrative liability to criminal law, and from family to international and civil procedure law. In other words, if climate change is not allowed to enter the courtroom through the front door (Environmental Law), it will undoubtedly invade the judicial sanctum through the back door.

Third, except for a few areas of law (contracts, for example), judges are merely part of the solution for social problems; even then, they are not the only or even the best option. Courts do not replace the constellation of actors and measures in the climate change domain—both national and international. They complement whatever is in place. Some judges may see this role as a second-class type of judicial intervention, one filled with humility (not a widespread characteristic in the profession) as opposed to the ordinary exercise of jurisdiction in which judges have the final and most authoritative word on any complaint brought before them. That misguided but understandable sentiment fails to grasp judges' role in contemporary society as one that is not uniform for all aspects of human conflicts.

Fourth, the position of judges in climate adaptation is much less daunting than in climate mitigation. Take, for instance, the thousands of cases around the world where judges are already dealing with permits, environmental impact assessments, protected areas, deforestation, water resources, wetlands, and desertification. Is it really defensible to keep addressing those legal issues without taking into account the impacts of climate change? Can a judge decide an objection to a permit for building a hotel resort in the middle of endangered mangroves without considering sea level rise due to climate change? Or adjudicate a case of significant deforestation in a region that is already suffering from growing water stress?

None of these reasons ignore or reduce the relevance of legitimate counterarguments that advocate that climate change policy issues should be fought outside the courtroom. Climate change is not the only or the first highly technologically or economically complex issue facing the courts. Software and DNA cases are common nowadays in many countries. Climate change is no more politically charged than national security, torture, discrimination, abortion, immigration, corruption, same-sex marriage, or election disputes. Even war and peace are not entirely beyond the judicial realm.

It is also worthwhile mentioning that, in light of general or specific legislation dealing with the subject, including constitutional provisions, judges do not make climate change law. They apply (within the limits of the separation of powers) norms discussed and approved by legislative bodies or enacted by administrative authorities. Under these circumstances, it is not *judicial lawmaking*, but rather *judicial law implementation*. Once clear and detailed policies—that go much further than vague, conditional and noncommittal statements of public intentions—are legislated, they become legal policies that can and should be enforced by judges. Otherwise, what would be the purpose of legislating? Therefore we should here make a distinction between *activist environmental judges* and *activist environmental legislation* (or legislators).

Thus, with a qualified yes, I respond to the initial question I have posed. It is qualified because it comes with one major and several secondary requirements, especially if we want to have judges involved in responding to the climate change crisis adequately. Let me focus on the primary requirement only. In general, judges are still not fully aware of the existential threat that the climate crisis poses to humanity as a whole and every person on the planet, in every jurisdiction. Judges tend to ignore that environmental law regimes they use in their daily practice already include contact points that allow for easy connection to the climate change dimension. In other instances, new and specialized laws have been passed, but remain unknown to or insufficiently understood by judges and therefore endure as untouched laws in the books. Finally, bound by their training and jurisdictions, judges are prone to feel isolated as professionals—a state of mind that discourages innovation and the kind of learning from each other that greater interaction and communication could bring. From the judges' perspective, the most effective medicine for this complex set of attributes and attitudes, which impair their ability to confidently manage climate change litigation, is *judicial education*.

And judicial education has been precisely the road chosen by the Asian Development Bank (ADB) in its work with judges from this immense and diverse part of the world. It has been a most successful journey, one that developed a judicial community around Environmental Law. The present reports are testimony to such an initiative and a component of the broader series of successful ADB endeavors in the Environmental Rule of Law universe. As the first publication of its kind with a focus on judges, this report series will greatly benefit those who already know the subject. It will also particularly serve the many for whom climate change is (until now) a remote area of law.

On behalf of the *Global Judicial Institute on the Environment*, I offer my effusive congratulations to ADB's extraordinary team and the distinguished coauthors of this innovative report series.

ANTONIO HERMAN BENJAMIN
Justice, National High Court of Brazil
Lead founding member of the Global Judicial Institute on the Environment
6 November 2020

> **Climate change is a global challenge.**
> While the emphasis on the Paris Agreement is on nationally determined contributions, to be enforced by national legal measures, the problems are common to all, and we all have much to learn from each other.
>
> —*Lord Robert Carnwath*

FOREWORD

I am delighted to welcome this important series of reports on climate litigation and legal frameworks.

It was in 2002 that the Global Judges' Symposium in Johannesburg affirmed the vital role of an independent judiciary and judicial processes in interpreting and enforcing environmental laws, and called for a UNEP-led programme of judicial training and exchange of information on environmental law. Since then, as member of the UNEP judicial advisory group, I have taken part in numerous judicial conferences on environmental law in different parts of the world. Since 2010, the Asian Development Bank has taken a lead in encouraging judicial interchange and training through its Law and Policy Reform Programme, including a series of judicial conferences in the Asia and Pacific region, in which I have been honoured to participate. The cases collected in this study are testament to the richness of the contribution of judges from that part of the world.

Climate change is a global challenge. While the emphasis on the Paris Agreement is on nationally determined contributions, to be enforced by national legal measures, the problems are common to all, and we all have much to learn from each other. Two of the most significant climate change cases in recent years—the *Urgenda* case in Holland and the *Leghari* case in Pakistan—came from countries with widely differing legal systems. But the principle they established is universal—that effective action on climate change is a human right and fundamental constitutional responsibility of governments everywhere. As was said in 1993 by the Philippines' Supreme Court in the famous *Oposa* case, rights to a balanced and healthful ecology are "basic rights" which "predate all governments and constitutions" and "need not be written in the Constitution for they are assumed to exist from the inception of humankind."[a]

I congratulate the Asian Development Bank team responsible for these remarkable reports. I have no doubt that they will be of immense value to all those involved in giving legal force to the Paris commitments, whether as judges, legislators, or legal professionals.

LORD ROBERT CARNWATH
Commander of the Royal Victorian Order (CVO)
Former Justice of the Supreme Court of the United Kingdom
April 2020

---

[a]   *Oposa v. Factoran*, G.R. No. 101083, 30 July 1993.

> "This report chronicles green and climate jurisprudence that emerged over the years and is a testament to ADB's tireless effort over a decade in building a judicial coalition.
>
> — *Justice Syed Mansoor Ali Shah*

Photo by Syed Muhammad Rafiq/ADB.

FOREWORD

Unbridled human desire, supported by unsustainable development over centuries, has disrupted the rhythm of nature. Defiling of the local environment slowly snowballed into a threat for the entire planet as carbon emissions sullied the atmosphere. Humanity's disruption of Earth's system is climate change.

Any remedial response to this global challenge can only be through the collective coordination of humankind. Nationalism needs to give way to global cooperation and solidarity. While nations of the world try to coalesce to combat this challenge, politics and powerful vested interests continue to hamper such a consensus. Nations have been unable to implement their international commitments to meet this most serious existential threat. Dissatisfied citizenry of the world has been compelled to consider other options to combat this challenge. Some of them have knocked at the doors of the courts of justice to fight climate change by making their governments answerable and accountable and by seeking climate justice.

Courts, unlike other limbs of government, are not elected and have no constituencies or voters or political agendas to tow. They are not swayed by politics or other vested or corporate interests, but are guided by ethos of justice and fair play. They function within the frame of constitutionalism and the rule of law. This gives the courts of the world a common language to communicate. It is, therefore, easy to build a global judicial consensus on climate justice. The Asian Development Bank (ADB) realized this and put together a judicial environmental coalition in Asia and the Pacific in 2010. Since then, "green" judges in Asia and the Pacific have met and shared ideas in a series of roundtables and knowledge-sharing events. This unique congress of judges from different jurisdictions debated and dialogued to evolve innovative and avant-garde judicial techniques to safeguard the environment. These judges put these ideas to work and produced far-reaching jurisprudence that has touched the soul of the planet.

Several judiciaries from Asia have a rich tradition in public interest litigation and enforcement of constitutional human rights and, therefore, did not take long to absorb environmentalism in its fold. The jurisprudence that evolved showcased a new judicial technique of forming judicial commissions comprising environmental scientists, experts, and members of the civil society to sit face to face with the government and evolve sustainable solutions. The overarching environmental judicial approach of this period remained inquisitorial and consensus-based.

These judges were ready with their jurisprudence and sharpened tool kit when climate change walked into their courtroom. Climate litigation brought with it a host of new issues that slowly overshadowed the erstwhile environmental litigation. Climate change cut across sectors which were not earlier part of

the environmental checklist. Climate litigation has to embrace multiple new dimensions like Health Security, Food Security, Energy Security, Water Security, Human Displacement, Human Trafficking, and Disasters Management. Climate Justice covers agriculture, health, food, building approvals, industrial licenses, technology, infrastructural work, human resource, human and climate trafficking, disaster preparedness, health, etc.

Most countries from Asia and the Pacific do not significantly contribute to climate change but suffer at the hands of it. Adaptation, as opposed to mitigation, has a totally different judicial response. Climate change, therefore, has a much broader meaning for the judiciaries of Asia and the Pacific. Adaptation entails issues that, facially, might not appear to be climate related but, upon deeper probe, show a causal link with climate change. The jurisprudence on climate justice emerging from the developed economies is more focused on mitigation and review of governmental decisions to curb emissions. On the whole, jurisprudence evolved by the courts has played a key role in fashioning climate governance and effectively combating climate change.

This report chronicles green and climate jurisprudence that emerged over the years and is a testament to ADB's tireless effort over a decade in building a judicial coalition. The Asian Judges Network on Environment helped the judges meet, discuss, and share ideas, which contributed to developing judicial inventiveness that emerged from Asia and the Pacific. The report is an invaluable exposé of judicial innovation and a valuable source for judiciaries around the world.

As I close this foreword, the coronavirus disease (COVID-19) pandemic has stalled the wheels of human activity and has caged humans with self-isolation and global lockdown. Weeks into it, I see blues skies out of my window, greener pastures, clean air, less noise, singing of the birds, and a general sense of relief on the face of nature. I guess the lesson for humankind is to back up and learn to coexist with nature. A new world is taking shape as I write this. A world that requires us to shed our old ways and move to a new normal. This report and the rich jurisprudence it puts out on display will help us fight and defy going back to the pre-corona world of greed, avarice, mindless consumerism, and unchecked carbon emissions.

I wish this report a huge success.

SYED MANSOOR ALI SHAH
Justice
Supreme Court of Pakistan
Islamabad
20 April 2020

> "ADB is committed to supporting the global climate agenda, including by developing the capacity of judicial systems within Asia and the Pacific to play their vital role.
>
> —*Thomas M. Clark*

PREFACE

J udges are vital development partners for institutions promoting a sustainable and inclusive future, with an indispensable role to play in climate governance in Asia and the Pacific. This work is for them.

The Office of the General Counsel within the Asian Development Bank (ADB) started judicial capacity development on environmental law in 2010 as part of its Law and Policy Reform Program. ADB chose to work with judges for three principal reasons. First, judges form a distinct, independent, and critical branch of government; yet, development partners frequently overlook the benefits of judicial capacity building. Second, judges play a significant role in advancing the rule of law and as guardians of justice in Asia and the Pacific. Third, despite these critical responsibilities, judges need greater resources and opportunities for professional development, information sharing, and judicial networking.

Initially, ADB's program focused on judicial trainings on environmental protection issues, more narrowly, without inclusion of climate mitigation and adaptation. Then, over the past decade, global awareness of climate change and of the need for concerted action to address it surged. Countries expanded their domestic legal and policy frameworks to address climate impacts, and came together in global fora to coordinate this response, most notably by signing the Paris Agreement in 2015. Driven by the need to protect themselves, their children, and their environment from climate change, people turned more to litigation to address climate change, under a variety of theories. With these shifts, ADB expanded the focus of its judicial capacity building program to incorporate climate change and sustainable development.

In our work with judiciaries over the last 10 years, ADB has seen the extraordinary potential of judicial capacity building, along with the huge gaps that remain to be filled.

- Issuing judgments advancing environmental protection can see judges labeled "anti-development." This label isolates and demotivates judges and can hamper them from addressing the serious legal and constitutional issues that may be implicated by climate change. For such judges, we created the Asian Judges Network on Environment (AJNE), a platform to connect judges and legal professionals, facilitate the sharing of knowledge and legal developments on a regional and global level, and boost motivation. ADB also launched annual conferences on environmental and climate law to share best practices. We complemented that work with assisting on targeted national judicial reforms in almost all host countries.
- During the annual judicial conferences, Asian and Pacific judges debated and developed the concepts of environmental and climate justice for the region. These sessions helped develop shared judicial language and frameworks to assess climate issues, and gave impetus to the development of seminal jurisprudence across the region. Despite these successes in the region, broader global audiences are often not aware of the phenomenal work that Asia and Pacific judiciaries do for lack of international reporting.

The Law and Policy Reform Program realized that ADB could, with these reports, both provide practical support to judges facing complex climate litigation as well as showcase climate jurisprudence from Asia and the Pacific to a broader audience.

In service of these overarching objectives, this report series seeks to (i) share environmental and climate jurisprudence from Asia and the Pacific, contributing to global knowledge on regional climate law and litigation; (ii) provide a comprehensive benchbook and tool kit for judges, especially those from Asia and the Pacific, to facilitate decision-making in this ever-evolving field of law; (iii) capture the results of ADB's judicial capacity development work—the legacy of ADB's work to date; and finally, (iv) acknowledge the prodigious work done by the judiciaries of Asia and the Pacific—ADB applauds their dedication and progress.

ADB was pleased to collaborate with the Sabin Center for Climate Change Law on this project. Michael Burger, Ama Francis, and the team at Sabin provided extraordinary support for ADB, contributing authoritatively on climate litigation around the world in Report Two, supplementing ADB's own research, and drafting the national legal frameworks report.

With pleasure, I acknowledge and introduce ADB's young and extraordinarily smart team of researchers and authors. Seventeen researchers gathered laws and cases from the 32 countries covered by these reports. Gregorio Rafael P. Bueta and Francesse Joy J. Cordon-Navarro contributed to and assisted with reviewing the reports. Maria Cecilia T. Sicangco wrote the report on international climate change legal frameworks and assisted with reviewing and editing these reports.

Many thanks to Irum Ahsan who led this initiative. Irum headed the Law and Policy Reform team between 2017 and 2020, under the guidance of ADB's former Deputy General Counsel Ramit Nagpal. Her energy, drive, and creativity have created a flagship program for ADB. I thank Briony Eales, who steered this initiative tirelessly over the last 3 years, working with researchers and authors, and juggling work with a young child. She worked with the researchers; wrote about climate science, climate litigation, and climate laws; and created a synthesized and cohesive series of reports.

The team diligently works on strengthening the rule of law, a key driver for robust and sustainable economic development. This will be vital work over the coming years. The global efforts to mitigate climate change and address its harmful impacts must only intensify in the near future, especially in Asia and the Pacific. The region is too large, diverse, and globally significant not to be at the center of these efforts. ADB is committed to supporting the global climate agenda, including by developing the capacity of judicial systems within Asia and the Pacific to play their vital role.

We look forward to our continued work with the region's judiciaries to strengthen climate justice and the rule of law.

Thomas M. Clark

THOMAS M. CLARK
General Counsel
Office of the General Counsel
Asian Development Bank

ACKNOWLEDGMENTS

Climate Change, Coming Soon to a Court Near You is a flagship publication series of the Law and Policy Reform Program under the Office of the General Counsel of the Asian Development Bank (ADB). The reports would not have been possible without the vision and leadership of Irum Ahsan, project team leader, and currently advisor, Office of the Compliance Review Panel.

A team of lawyers, led by Briony Eales, wrote this report, Climate Change Litigation in Asia and the Pacific and Beyond. We thank Ama Ruth Francis, Michael Burger, Romany Webb, Jessica Wentz, and Dena Adler of the Sabin Center for Climate Change Law, along with Gregorio Rafael P. Bueta and Francesse Joy J. Cordon-Navarro for writing this report. We also thank Maria Cecilia T. Sicangco for assisting with the review of this report.

We thank the team of researchers who made this report possible: Afghanistan, Rohullah Azizi; Bangladesh, Asif Nazrul; Bhutan, Kuenzang Tshering; Cambodia, Phanna Sok; India, Padma Priya; Indonesia, Andri Wibisana; the Lao People's Democratic Republic, Nang Nalinthone; Malaysia, Judge Wan Fadhilah Nor binti Wan Idris; Maldives, Malcolm Simmons; Myanmar, Khin Thandar; Nepal, Padam Bahadur Shrestha; the Pacific developing member countries, Maria Goreti Muavesi; Pakistan, Angbeen Atif Mirza; the People's Republic of China, Allen Smith; the Philippines, the Supreme Court of the Philippines; Sri Lanka, Wardani Karunaratne; Thailand, Chacrit Sitdhiwej; and Viet Nam, Tran Thi Huong Trang.

Tara Mitchell and Hammed Bolotaolo gave instrumental editorial advice on this report. Judy T. Yñiguez handled typesetting and graphics generation. The cover artwork was designed by Gayle Certeza, Daniel Desembrana, and John Michael Casipe, guided by Anthony Victoria. Levi Rodolfo Lusterio and Jess Alfonso Macasaet proofed the draft layout.

Support for printing and publishing the report was provided by the Printing Services Unit of the ADB Office of Administrative Services and by the ADB Department of Communications' publications and web teams. We are grateful to Anna Sherwood and colleagues in the Department of Communications for their guidance on design and publishing. Noren Jose advised on ADB style and legal citations.

We express gratitude to former ADB General Counsel Christopher Stephens and former Deputy General Counsel Ramit Nagpal for supporting these reports from their inception. We also thank the present General Counsel Thomas M. Clark for his support in completing this publication.

ABBREVIATIONS

ACCC	Australian Competition and Consumer Commission
ADB	Asian Development Bank
BELA	Bangladesh Environmental Lawyers Association
CHR	Commission on Human Rights (Philippines)
CO$_2$	carbon dioxide
CO$_2$e	carbon dioxide equivalent
ECHR	European Convention on Human Rights
EIA	environmental impact assessment
EIS	environmental impact statement
EPA	Environmental Protection Agency
EU	European Union
FAO	Food and Agriculture Organization of the United Nations
FPIC	free, prior, and informed consent
FSM	Federated States of Micronesia
GHG	greenhouse gas
ICJ	International Court of Justice
IPCC	Intergovernmental Panel on Climate Change
km	kilometer
LDA	Lahore Development Authority
MRGO	Mississippi River Gulf Outlet
MTUC	Malaysian Trades Union Congress
MSW	municipal solid waste
MW	megawatt
NDC	nationally determined contribution
NEPA	National Environmental Policy Act (United States)
NGO	nongovernment organization
NGT	National Green Tribunal (India)
ppm	parts per million

PRC	People's Republic of China
RDA	Road Development Authority (Sri Lanka)
REIA	reverse environmental impact assessment
SDG	Sustainable Development Goal
UK	United Kingdom
UN	United Nations
UNFCCC	United Nations Framework Convention on Climate Change
UNICEF	United Nations Children's Fund
US	United States
VCAT	Victorian Civil and Administrative Tribunal
WALHI	Wahana Lingkungan Hidup Indonesia
WTE	waste-to-energy

Sea abundance. Fisherfolk across the Pacific rely on their local fish stocks for nutrition and livelihood (photo by Eric Sales/ADB).

EXECUTIVE SUMMARY

Climate Change: A Clarion Call for Judges

It is 2020 and the world is at a crossroads on climate change.

The Paris Agreement aims to limit global warming to 1.5°C–2°C above preindustrial temperatures. Current international climate responses will not meet these targets. Thus, urgent and widespread action is indispensable. Recent Intergovernmental Panel on Climate Change reports showed a significant difference in the degree of impact between 1.5°C and 2°C of warming. Indeed, the 1.5°C goal is the safest for most of Asia and the Pacific.

And then the coronavirus disease (COVID-19) pandemic entered the equation, shutting down economies and claiming almost 1,163,459 lives by 28 October 2020. Its devastating impacts leave the world struggling to rebuild. After COVID-19, the world must choose the path toward a safer, inclusive, dignified, and resilient future.

Frustrated by government inaction and threatened by climate change impacts on their lives and human rights, global citizens are taking the fight for climate justice to the courts. Climate litigation is demanding that judges play a role in climate governance.

Asian courts have issued groundbreaking climate decisions. Their approaches diversify the global discourse on climate jurisprudence and are worth sharing. For other judges in Asia and the Pacific, climate change is coming soon to your courts.

The Asian Development Bank (ADB) has worked with courts in Asia and the Pacific for over 10 years to build networks and support judges with environmental and now climate change decision-making. This report series captures the wisdom gained over the last 10 years and provides resources for judges, decision-makers, and lawyers involved in climate litigation.

Why These Reports?

Climate Change, Coming Soon to a Court Near You is a series of four reports on climate law, policy, and litigation. Climate litigation is growing in Asia and the Pacific, so judges and quasi-judicial decision-makers must have access to climate law resources.

Cases from high-income countries dominate global literature about climate litigation. These countries have different mindsets, legal and policy frameworks, and climate change challenges. Although judges from Asia and the Pacific have much to gain from reading this literature, they also need perspectives and approaches closer to home from peers working with similar challenges.

Most Asia and the Pacific countries have low emissions and are incredibly susceptible to climate change. The region therefore focuses on climate adaptation and resilience—activities supported by ecosystem resilience and biodiversity.

Unfortunately, weak environmental governance is common in Asia and the Pacific, creating cascading effects in this era of climate change. Frail ecosystems and biodiversity offer communities less protection from the impacts of climate change, e.g., healthy mangrove forests protect humans and other species from storm surges. Ecosystems are also more easily damaged by climate change. Unchecked environmental degradation leaves indigenous, agrarian, and island communities even more vulnerable to death, homelessness, and displacement. Judiciaries in the region benefit from understanding the role of ecosystem protection, biodiversity, and sustainable development in boosting local climate resilience. Hence, these reports outline links between environmental protection, biodiversity, and climate change.

Prioritizing environmental protection and low-emission development is challenging in Asia and the Pacific, a region dominated by low to lower middle-income countries with development objectives. Judges who do that are often labeled "anti-development," isolating them from their peers. Judges need access to resources and networks that boost their knowledge, and to information that proves that balanced and appropriate environmental and climate protection makes business sense and aligns with national climate commitments.

Judicial knowledge about climate change, legal frameworks, and relevant legal principles are fundamental to a strong rule of law. Many core principles in climate law stem from environmental law, a field that a few judges in Asia and the Pacific have studied or practiced.

Resource limitations, ad hoc publication of laws, and language barriers in Asia and the Pacific also make it difficult for judges to maintain current knowledge about climate law, climate science, and local climate change impacts, diminishing judicial effectiveness. These reports seek to overcome some of these barriers by synthesizing climate information and achievements and weaving a regional perspective into the global discourse on climate law.

Report Series Structure

Within this series are four reports:

- **Report Series Purpose and Introduction to Climate Science:** a brief introduction to climate change and climate science
- **Climate Litigation in Asia and the Pacific and Beyond:** a comparative analysis of climate litigation in Asia and the Pacific and the rest of the world
- **National Climate Change Legal Frameworks in Asia and the Pacific:** analyses of the national climate change policy and legal frameworks in ADB developing member countries in South Asia, Southeast Asia, and the Pacific and the People's Republic of China, with tables to highlight constitutional provisions relevant to climate change and a discussion of trends in climate law
- **International Climate Change Legal Frameworks:** a ready reference to key international climate change instruments and soft law, with tables showing treaty commitments by country

ADB has specifically designed these reports for judges, quasi-judicial decision-makers, lawyers from Asia and the Pacific, and those interested in Asian and Pacific climate law.

Key Takeaways

Litigation

Climate litigation is growing—in Asia and the Pacific and around the world. Most climate lawsuits in Asia target government respondents, seeking climate action or challenging decisions with climate impacts. The number of cases against governments based on treaty obligations, particularly the Paris Agreement, is increasing, and so is litigation against private entities.

Litigation preferences reflect domestic legal frameworks, with litigants looking for appropriate hooks to support their claims. Of the countries surveyed in this report, 25% have adopted framework climate legislation—economy-wide framework climate change law. The other states use climate policies and existing laws to achieve their goals. Unclear or incomplete legal and policy frameworks combined with weak enforcement frequently lead litigants to sue for violations of constitutional rights.

Petitioners in Asia favor constitutional litigation because it (i) has been used successfully in environmental litigation, (ii) allows direct access to superior courts, (iii) provides a legal basis for a claim where the existing legal and policy framework is incomplete, and (iv) is easier for petitioners to demonstrate standing where a constitutional right has been breached. The preference for rights-based litigation reflects a global trend. Roughly one-third of all climate litigation outside the United States hinges on fundamental, human, and constitutional rights.

Most lawsuits target climate mitigation—the reduction of greenhouse gas emissions. However, litigation seeking climate change adaptation is growing and frequently emerges as a silent issue in Asian environmental lawsuits. In various cases, neither the parties nor the court identified climate change as an issue, but the case outcomes had co-benefits for climate resilience and, therefore, adaptation. These reports treat such cases as climate cases.

Climate litigation in Pacific courts remains rare, which does not reflect the existential nature of the climate threat in the Pacific.

Pacific islanders are more likely to rely on customary dispute resolution to resolve local conflicts, reducing the likelihood of litigation. Pacific nations know that their contribution to climate change is negligible. Lawsuits against national governments are also counterproductive if the state has limited resources to respond. Therefore, Pacific islanders are more likely to pursue human rights petitions in United Nations bodies or engage in transnational litigation, e.g., the climate migration cases filed in Australia and New Zealand.

Women, children, indigenous communities, and older adults—people who are particularly vulnerable to climate change—have also been active in domestic and international climate litigation.

National Legal and Policy Frameworks

Legal and policy frameworks are growing in Asia and the Pacific as governments plan for low-emission and resilient growth and ramp up climate responses in line with the Paris Agreement.

National legal and policy frameworks help drive global climate action. The period preceding the Paris Agreement (2009–2015) saw the most intense adoption of domestic laws and policies globally. This factor underscores the relationship between bolstering national climate action and driving forward the global agenda. Only collaborative, widespread, and urgent local responses can limit climate change, requiring quality national legal and policy frameworks backed up by well-informed judiciaries supporting implementation.

Legal and policy commitments need strengthening across the region. Most procedures for environmental impact assessments do not expressly require consideration of climate change. Laws requiring proponents to account for climate effects on a project and incorporate climate durability into its design are rare, undermining climate-resilient development. A few laws cover climate change and oceans.

Climate impacts, the Paris Agreement, technology, and markets will shape domestic climate laws and policies, as governments seek to keep up with changes.

Courts in Asia and the Pacific are shaping national legal and policy frameworks with their decisions. Further, given the existential crisis presented by climate change, courts have been willing to assess whether national laws and policies meet international climate commitments.

International Legal and Policy Frameworks

COVID-19 put much of 2020 on hold, including meetings central to the Paris Agreement implementation. The 26th Session of the Conference of the Parties to the United Nations Framework Convention on Climate Change was postponed until 2021, delaying agreement on a carbon trading mechanism, common time frames for reporting under the agreement, and ramping up climate finance and technology transfers.

The Paris Agreement is mainly silent on oceans and aviation. However, the adoption of domestic laws and policies in the 6 years leading up to the Paris Agreement showed the power of national legal frameworks to shape global action.

Judges Can Contribute to Better Climate Outcomes

Judges' role in government makes them gatekeepers, even climate emergency managers. Judges are central to

- holding governments accountable for meeting policy commitments and complying with legal obligations on climate change, the environment, and sustainable development, and thereby shaping legal and policy frameworks;
- admitting relevant and credible scientific evidence for climate change in courtrooms and making judicial findings of fact about climate change, which can elevate the national discourse on climate change (indeed, courts have successfully incorporated international scientific consensus, synthesized by the Intergovernmental Panel on Climate Change, into domestic legal common ground, ensuring that advancements in climate science filter into local law); and
- balancing outcomes and protecting citizens' fundamental, constitutional, and other legal rights, frequently closing the gaps through which people and ecosystems fall.

These functions demonstrate that judges have a vital role in climate governance in Asia and the Pacific. Supporting judges to respond to climate litigation contributes to better quality climate governance.

Moving Forward

Today's judges are being asked to decide on the burning issue of our generation—climate change. It is a challenge that threatens to eclipse all others in modern history.

As Albert Einstein once said, "We cannot solve our problems with the same thinking we used when we created them." Significant judicial advancements have often rested on the shoulders of jurists who were willing to apply new consciousness and imagination to existing principles to resolve society's pressing problems. We need new perspectives to create climate justice. Justice will only be fair if it considers diverse perspectives and rights—those of women, children, elders, indigenous peoples, the differently abled, and future generations, as well as those of the traditional power structures.

These reports are for those who must adjudicate climate litigation in Asia and the Pacific. ADB lauds the advancements that Asia and the Pacific judiciaries have made in environmental and climate justice and sustainable development. The authors hope that this jurisprudence brings diversity and a fresh perspective to the global discourse on climate law.

As for climate justice, more work is needed. Emissions continue to rise, and global commitments do not yet have the world on track to limit global warming to well below 2°C above preindustrial temperatures. Gaps persist in climate change legal and policy frameworks, allowing action to stagnate. To promote climate justice in Asia and the Pacific, judges can assess these gaps. They can ask, do these frameworks support the overarching 1.5°C–2°C temperature goal under the Paris Agreement?

These reports encourage judiciaries to equip themselves with knowledge about climate science and law because litigation demands that judges take part in reckoning climate justice. The future rests heavily on each of us. Those able to make powerful decisions must choose action. This work is in the service of judges and decision-makers. We hope it lights the way, a little.

Photo by Eric Sales/ADB.

Mangroves growing in Tarawa, Kiribati. Mangroves are immensely important across Asia and the Pacific for sequestering carbon and protecting coastal communities from water-related disasters (photo by Eric Sales/ADB).

INTRODUCTION

Climate Change is a defining challenge of our time and has led to dramatic alterations in our planet's climate system. . . . On a legal and constitutional plane this is [a] clarion call for the protection of fundamental rights of the citizens. . ., in particular, the vulnerable and weak segments of the society who are unable to approach this Court.[1]

Since the first industrial revolution, human emissions of greenhouse gases (GHG) have warmed Earth and caused dramatic shifts in its climate. These climatic shifts are resulting in destructive weather patterns like drought and flooding, and phenomena like sea level rise and ocean acidification. Climate change affects ecosystems, agriculture, water, and human settlements, and will continue to do so to a greater degree unless the global community takes urgent action.[2] When people can no longer grow food, access clean water, or live in their homeland, they suffer grave injustice and deep-seated impacts on their human rights.[3]

People have many responses to the deprivation of their rights. One reaction is seeking justice in a court of law. A good justice system upholds the rule of law and is responsive to people who want to protect their rights. A sound justice system balances the rights of all within its ambit.

This report series—*Climate Change, Coming Soon to a Court Near You*—recognizes the inevitability of increased litigation in the face of growing climate change impacts. Judges in Asia and the Pacific need tools to advance justice in this era of climate change. This document supports judicial responses to climate change by enhancing judicial tool kits with knowledge.

Asian courts have written dynamic judgments on climate change. Judicial action has, at times, driven national climate action and shaped domestic climate governance. These judicial approaches are worth sharing and have much to add to the global discourse on climate jurisprudence.

The world often overlooks the capacity of judges to contribute to global climate action. In 2018, Justice Syed Mansoor Ali Shah, Justice of the Supreme Court of

---

[1] *Leghari v. Federation of Pakistan*, PLD 2018 Lahore 364. p. 5.

[2] For a discussion of the impacts of climate change, see Report One. Also see Intergovernmental Panel on Climate Change (IPCC). 2018. Summary for Policymakers. In V. Masson-Delmotte et al., eds. *Global Warming of 1.5°C. An IPCC Special Report*. In press.

[3] United Nations Environment Programme and Columbia University, Sabin Center for Climate Change Law. 2015. *Climate Change and Human Rights*. Nairobi.

Pakistan opened the Asia Pacific Judicial Colloquium on Climate Change. After highlighting the robust role of Pakistan's judiciary in shaping national climate governance, he observed:

> Judiciary as an institution or an actor has not been considered as an integral part of the climate change debate. International negotiations or international platforms do not include the judiciary as a major stakeholder or as a major policy player. I urge the international organizations here to look into this aspect. Our efforts to combat climate change might remain incomplete without taking the judiciary along.[4]

With this information, the Asian Development Bank (ADB) hopes to include judges and their judicial achievements in the global discourse on climate action because—we can all be sure of this—climate change is coming soon to a courtroom near you.

Report Structure

This report reviews climate litigation in six thematic areas and contrasts approaches in Asia and the Pacific with jurisprudence from other parts of the world. It discusses climate litigation involving

  (i)   rights-based litigation against governments,
  (ii) permitting and judicial review,
  (iii) private parties,
  (iv) adaptation,
  (v)   vulnerable people, and
  (vi) transboundary litigation.

One of the most comprehensive analyses to date of climate litigation in Asia and the Pacific, this document allows ADB to showcase regional judicial approaches. It also supports the cross-fertilization of ideas on climate jurisprudence.

ADB collaborated with Columbia University's Sabin Center for Climate Change Law in drafting this report. ADB wrote the sections on Asia and the Pacific litigation, and the Sabin Center for Climate Change Law wrote the sections discussing approaches from the rest of the world. Given ADB's intent to support Asia and the Pacific judiciaries and to showcase their work, the discussions regarding Asia and the Pacific cases have more detail than the case discussions from the rest of the world.

---

[4]   S.M.A. Shah J. 2018. *Environmental and Climate Justice—A Perspective from Pakistan*. Remarks given at the Asia Pacific Judicial Colloquium on Climate Change: Using Constitutions to Advance Environmental Rights and Achieve Climate Justice. Lahore. 26–27 February. p. 6.

Rights-Based Litigation Against Governments

Suing governments has been the most common type of climate suit, and such cases typically fall into one of four types of suits:

(i)   rights-based action founded on human rights or natural rights,

(ii)   rights-based action founded on constitutional rights,

(iii)   claims based on statutory or policy rights, and

(iv)   lawsuits seeking governmental compliance with Paris Agreement commitments.

Climate cases in Asia, especially South Asia, often raise claims based on international and domestic human rights, often secured through national constitutions. In such cases, petitioners argue that climate change or environmental damage impairs their constitutional right to life. Petitioners in South Asia have also favored constitutional writs because such claims grant immediate access to higher-level courts, shortening the litigation time frames.

Following instrumental decisions from courts in India, courts across Asia have expanded constitutional rights—especially the right to life—to include a right to a clean and functioning environment.[5] These decisions recognize that environmental damage deprives citizens of their capacity to live fully and with dignity. Like environmental damage, climate change threatens to deprive people of food, water, health, security, education, and their home. Each of us has a human right to these necessities. Therefore, climate change threatens human rights and constitutional rights, depending on a nation's constitution.

Lawsuits seeking to enjoin the implementation of statutory or policy commitments rely on courts' inherent power to interpret and enforce the law. Since the enactment of the Paris Agreement, numerous cases have argued that governments must actively reduce national GHG emissions or ramp up initiatives to improve national resilience to climate change impacts.

Standing to sue is an issue that cuts across attempts to use courts to force government action. It is especially tough for petitioners to sue a government for climate action or inaction in jurisdictions that do not have relaxed rules of standing. We, therefore, include case examples of various jurisdictions' approaches to standing in climate change and environmental cases.

Permitting and Judicial Review

Actions seeking judicial review of government permitting decisions or project approvals are a rich source of climate law. These cases frequently target procedural aspects of government decision-making processes, particularly in

---

[5]   For example, see *Virender Gaur and Ors. v. State of Haryana and Ors.*, (1995) 2 SCC 577.

environmental impact assessments (EIAs). For this reason, this type of litigation tends to start in lower courts or tribunals.

This report classifies permitting and judicial review cases as those challenging

  (i)   fossil fuels—"leave it in the ground" cases,
  (ii)   energy production,
  (iii) transportation policies or decisions,
  (iv)   decisions impacting water and aquatic environments, and
  (v)   decisions relating to land use and forests.

"Leave it in the ground" cases argue that mining fossil fuels or using them to generate electricity increases atmospheric GHG, contributing to global warming. Clean energy production has also been a source of litigation. Residents have adopted "not in my backyard" arguments to resist nuclear, wind, solar, and waste-to-energy projects in their communities. Litigants have also targeted the transport sector, arguing that governments should pursue projects or policies that reduce emissions within the industry.

Asia and the Pacific countries are predominantly agrarian societies. More than 60% of their population relies on agriculture for income.[6] Therefore, a low-carbon and resilient agriculture sector is essential. Concerned citizens have challenged government inaction on forestry emissions due to deforestation and forest fires—a topical issue following the 2019–2020 global wildfires.

Cases Against Private Entities

Private entities are increasingly subjected to climate suits. In the post-Paris Agreement world, climate change risk is one of the critical risks for economic markets and the private sector.[7] Suits against private entities include

  (i)   human rights-based claims;
  (ii)   torts-based claims, frequently those based on the torts of negligence and nuisance;
  (iii) wrongful damage to forest cases in Indonesia;
  (iv)   enforcement action, with governments requiring regulatory compliance or imposing sanctions for noncompliance; and
  (v)   cases involving carbon credits.

Claims based on human rights are growing in popularity. In 2018, Philippine petitioners lodged the world's first complaint in a national human rights commission. They asked the Philippine Commission on Human Rights to

---

[6]   ADB and International Food Policy Research Institute. 2009. *Building Climate Resilience in the Agriculture Sector of Asia and the Pacific*. Manila. p. xiii.

[7]   M. Carney. 2018. *A Transition in Thinking and Action*. Remarks given at International Climate Risk Conference for Supervisors, De Nederlandsche Bank. Amsterdam. 6 April.

investigate whether climate change impacts human rights and, if so, whether the world's largest GHG emitters have responsibility for climate change.[8] In December 2019, the commission found that large fossil fuel companies have contributed to anthropogenic climate change and can be held liable for the human rights impacts under domestic laws.[9] The commission warned corporations of the risk of criminal prosecution for acts of climate denial and obstruction.[10]

In the United States, subnational governments and private parties have sued fossil fuel companies, seeking emissions reductions and compensation for the cost of responding to past and anticipated climate change impacts. Meanwhile, the Australian Competition and Consumer Commission has sued companies breaching the national consumer law by greenwashing—falsely claiming that a project or product is "green" or has a reduced carbon footprint.

In Southeast Asia, intense storms have created havoc for noncompliant companies. Failure to meet regulatory safety standards, for example, has resulted in flooding and created exposure to administrative sanctions for regulatory noncompliance.

Indonesia has pioneered innovative litigation in response to deforestation and wildfires, a significant source of its carbon emissions.[11] The Supreme Court of Indonesia imposed liability on companies for wrongfully clearing trees and peatland and starting wildfires. Reasoning that government-issued land use agreements obligated licensees to protect trees and peatland within their license area, the court ordered wrongdoers to pay compensation. The orders included compensation for carbon emissions from burning the peatland and trees.

Within the Pacific, plaintiffs unsuccessfully argued that they should be entitled to recover the value of carbon credits as a component of economic loss. We expect carbon credit litigation will become more popular when parties to the Paris Agreement adopt rules for trading carbon credits under a sustainable development mechanism.[12]

[8] Government of the Philippines, Commission on Human Rights. 2018. PHL at the Forefront of Seeking Climate Justice with CHR's Landmark Inquiry on the Effects of Climate Change to Human Rights. Press Release. 28 March.

[9] J. Paris. 2019. CHR: Big Oil, Cement Firms Legally, Morally Responsible for Climate Change Effects. *Rappler*. 11 December; and T. Challe. 2020. Philippines Human Rights Commission Found Carbon Majors Can Be Liable for Climate Impacts. *Sabin Center for Climate Change Law, Climate Law Blog*. 10 January.

[10] Center for International Environmental Law. 2019. Groundbreaking Inquiry in Philippines Links Carbon Majors to Human Rights Impacts of Climate Change, Calls for Greater Accountability. News release. 9 December.

[11] D. Dunne. 2019. The Carbon Brief Profile: Indonesia. *Carbon Brief*. 27 March.

[12] *Paris Agreement*, Paris, 12 December 2015, *United Nations Treaty Series*, No. 54113, art. 6; S. Evans and J. Gabbatiss. 2019. COP25: Key Outcomes Agreed at the UN Climate Talks in Madrid. *Carbon Brief*. 15 December.

Adaptation Cases

Adaptation plays a pivotal role in climate action in Asia and the Pacific and presents a potential growth area in regional climate litigation. The authors, therefore, opt to dedicate one part of this document to adaptation cases, which covers three kinds of adaptation lawsuits:

(i)   failure to adapt cases;
(ii)   lawsuits arguing that EIAs should take into account the impacts of climate change on a project, i.e., project design should be climate resilient; and
(iii) cases challenging adaptation action.

In failure-to-adapt cases, litigants allege that their government should plan for climate disasters or implement adaptation measures. Specifically, litigants assert that their government must make society, ecosystems, and infrastructure more resilient to the impacts of climate change. These cases are rare in Asia and the Pacific. It is more common to see environmental lawsuits seeking to protect ecosystem function. Even though these cases do not explicitly refer to climate change, they have benefits for climate action and, therefore, fall under the expanded definition of climate case under this report.

The authors anticipate that adaptation litigation will grow across Asia and the Pacific as climate change impacts and ensuing disasters intensify. Additionally, given the importance of environmental protection to climate adaptation, this document highlights some connections between biodiversity protection and climate change.

People Who Are Vulnerable to Climate Change

Across the globe, some people are "socially, economically, culturally, politically, institutionally, or otherwise marginalized," making them "especially vulnerable to climate change."[13] This section explores some of the current climate litigation involving vulnerable people, including

(i)   migration,
(ii)   post-disaster lawsuits,
(iii) participatory rights,
(iv)   indigenous peoples,
(v)   women and climate change, and
(vi)   children and climate change.

---

[13] IPCC. 2014. Summary for Policymakers. In C.B. Field et al., eds. *Climate Change 2014: Impacts, Adaptation, and Vulnerability. Part A: Global and Sectoral Aspects. Contribution of Working Group II to the Fifth Assessment Report of the Intergovernmental Panel on Climate Change.* Cambridge, United Kingdom and New York, NY, United States: Cambridge University Press. p. 6.

Vulnerable groups have unique perspectives and specialized knowledge that enhance climate change planning and responses. For example, around 80% of the world's biodiversity sits within the ancestral lands of 370 million indigenous peoples, many of whom have long fought deforestation.[14] The very factors that marginalize vulnerable groups—poverty and unequal access to resources and rights—also exclude them from participating in climate change mitigation and adaptation planning. The Intergovernmental Panel on Climate Change (IPCC) defines mitigation as "a human intervention to reduce greenhouse gas emissions or enhance sinks of."[15]

This thematic area explores issues that judges ought to consider when dealing with climate litigation involving vulnerable groups. Recognizing the right of vulnerable groups to participate in climate change mitigation and adaptation planning, post-disaster management, and disaster risk reduction is vital to ensuring just outcomes and the realization of sustainable development goals.[16]

Addressing Transboundary Harm

Climate change is a global problem in effect and causation. Unsurprisingly, interested groups now threaten transboundary litigation before the International Court of Justice (ICJ).[17] This section briefly explores cases from the ICJ, considering the obligation of states to avoid causing transboundary harm.

In India, the National Green Tribunal considered the obligation of its central government to engage with a foreign government to alleviate cross-border pollution. This innovative transboundary approach within the domestic context demonstrates the capacity of courts in Asia to prod their national government into action.

Defining Climate Litigation

Climate change litigation is defined broadly in this report as any case that is brought before judicial courts and administrative or specialized tribunals that (i) raises climate change as a central issue; (ii) raises climate change as a peripheral issue; or (iii) does not explicitly raise climate change but has ramifications for climate change mitigation or adaptation efforts, e.g., recognition of intergenerational responsibility. The figure shows the three elements of the definition.

---

[14] World Bank. Indigenous Peoples; and L. Etchart. 2017. The Role of Indigenous Peoples in Combating Climate Change. *Palgrave Communications.* 3 (17085).

[15] A sink is a "reservoir (natural or human, in soil, ocean, and plants) where a greenhouse gas, an aerosol or a precursor of a greenhouse gas is stored." IPCC. 2018. Annex I: Glossary. In V. Masson-Delmotte et al., eds. *Global Warming of 1.5°C. An IPCC Special Report.* In press. p. 554 and 558.

[16] See Committee on the Elimination of Discrimination against Women. 2018. *General Recommendation No. 37 on Gender-Related Dimensions of Disaster Risk Reduction in the Context of Climate Change.* CEDAW/C/GC/37. 7 February.

[17] I. Caldwell. 2019. I am Climate Justice (ICJ) Movement. *GreenLaw.* 22 November; E. Wasuka. 2019. Students Want International Court of Justice to Rule on Climate Change. *ABC Radio Australia.* 29 July; Yale Law School. 2013. Climate Change and the ICJ: Seeking an Advisory Opinion on Transboundary Harm. News release. 12 September.

Figure 1: Report Definition of Climate Change

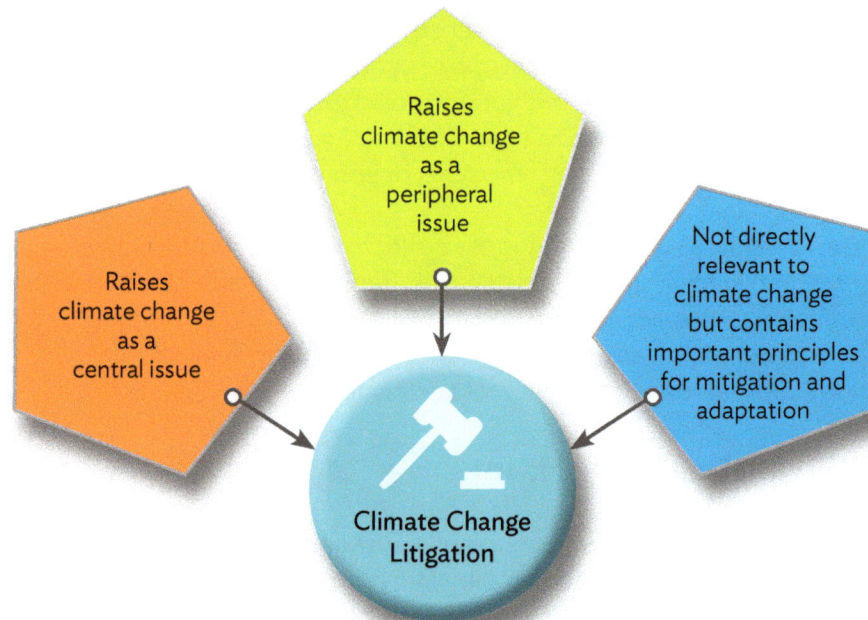

Raises climate change as a peripheral issue

Raises climate change as a central issue

Not directly relevant to climate change but contains important principles for mitigation and adaptation

Climate Change Litigation

Source: Asian Development Bank Team.

Two Key Considerations for Defining Climate Litigation Broadly

Previous authoritative works on this topic have limited the scope of climate litigation to those "cases brought before administrative, judicial and other investigatory bodies that raise issues of law or fact regarding the science of climate change and climate change mitigation and adaptation efforts."[18] Setting a clear and more limited definition of climate litigation is useful where the work seeks to define an emerging field of law and canvass recent developments and trends. This definition is also sufficiently broad to accommodate cases that do not specifically plead climate change as an issue.

However, such a definition felt too constricted to accommodate ADB's objectives for this knowledge product. This document was designed to support judiciaries in Asia and the Pacific by sharing knowledge and ideas about how to respond to

---

[18]   United Nations Environment Programme. 2017. *The Status of Climate Change Litigation: A Global Review*. Nairobi. p. 10. See also M. Wilensky. 2015. Climate Change in the Courts: An Assessment of Non-U.S. Climate Litigation. *Duke Environmental Law & Policy Forum*. 26 (1). pp. 131–179; and D. Markell and J.B. Ruhl. 2012. An Empirical Assessment of Climate Change in the Courts: A New Jurisprudence or Business as Usual? *Florida Law Review*. 64 (1). p. 27. In contrast, Osofsky and Peel advocate for a broader definition of climate change litigation in H.M. Osofsky and J. Peel. 2013. The Role of Litigation in Multilevel Climate Change Governance: Possibilities for a Lower Carbon Future? *Environmental and Planning Law Journal*. 30 (4). pp. 303–328.

climate change when it appears in the courtroom, and to showcase the valuable work done by Asia and the Pacific courts. A narrower definition would have inhibited this report from addressing two crucial issues:

(i) Cases about biodiversity and ecosystem resilience are often omitted from discussions about climate litigation. Yet, building biodiversity and ecosystem resilience are indispensable components of climate action in Asia and the Pacific.

(ii) Climate change and the requisite adaptive responses have the potential to touch all aspects of society. Therefore, across Asia and the Pacific, climate justice requires judges to consider whether the case before them has ramifications for climate change.

Consideration 1: Building Biodiversity and Ecosystem Resilience Support Adaptation

Asia and the Pacific is home to some of the world's most climate-vulnerable countries, and most have not been substantial carbon emitters.[19] These countries must now focus on climate adaptation—the process of adjusting to "actual or expected climate and its effects."[20] In particular, "incremental adaptation...maintains the essence and integrity of a system or process at a given scale" (footnote 20).

Maintaining clean environments and ecosystem integrity is challenging in Asia and the Pacific. Weak natural resource management and corruption have damaged biodiversity and ecological systems, undermining their adaptive capacity.[21]

Judiciaries across Asia and the Pacific have risen to the challenge, relying on constitutional protections to safeguard the environment. To ensure the implementation of decisions, judges pioneered writs of continuing mandamus and established commissions to advance climate action. Judiciaries in Asia and the Pacific have written insightful decisions promoting environmental justice across the region. Decisions protecting ecosystems frequently have co-benefits for climate action. For example, a decision that protects mangrove forests can also protect coastal communities from storm surges.

Environmental litigation in Asia and the Pacific may not explicitly raise climate change as an issue of law or fact. A narrow definition of climate change litigation might exclude pure environmental cases where they do not specifically raise issues of law or fact regarding climate change. It—the narrow definition—ignores excellent regional jurisprudence that provides tools and guidance for climate change-related

---

[19] D. Eckstein et al. 2019. *Global Climate Risk Index 2020: Who Suffers Most from Extreme Weather Events? Weather-Related Loss Events in 2018 and 1999 to 2018.* Berlin: Germanwatch e.V.; and ADB. 2017. Climate Change in Asia and the Pacific. Infographic. 28 November.

[20] IPCC. 2018. Annex I: Glossary. In V. Masson-Delmotte et al., eds. *Global Warming of 1.5°C. An IPCC Special Report.* In press. p. 542.

[21] ADB. 2012. Upholding Environmental Laws in Asia and the Pacific: 12 Things to Know. Article. 15 November.

cases. It also misses a valuable opportunity to highlight the connections between environmental protection and climate resilience in Asia and the Pacific. Thus, the authors of this report believe climate change outcomes in Asia and the Pacific would benefit from an expanded definition of climate change litigation.

Consideration 2: Adaptation Is Central to Climate Justice, and Spotting It Requires Vigilance

Lawyers and judges in Asia and the Pacific also grapple with climate change as an emerging area of law.[22] Limited awareness of local climate change impacts and effective responses mean that litigants might not raise climate change as an issue for adjudication. In this sense, climate change can slip into the courtroom unawares.

Spotting climate change as an issue for resolution requires judges to be mindful of the breadth of areas that climate change touches. The court described climate justice in *Leghari v. Federation of Pakistan*:

> So, *Climate Justice* goes beyond to providing adaptive strategies, to me it is a judicial mind-set. Climate Justice [*sic*] and its variant water justice require that we the judges be vigilant and apply climate-compatible and climate-resilient approach [*sic*] to matters that come before us. There is no such thing as a climate change case, in fact many cases that come before us dealing with urban development, licensing, land acquisition, project financing will invariably have a bearing on climate change—we just have to be vigilant to identify the issue and be always geared to do climate justice. Ladies and gentleman this is what Pakistan's judiciary has to offer the world of climate change (footnote 4).

Discussing a broader range of cases enables ADB to share judicial innovations and principles on issues that might seem unrelated to climate change but have benefits for climate action in Asia and the Pacific—a fundamental purpose of this report.

Narrow Definition of Climate Litigation for Non-Regional Cases

To prevent the scope of this report from becoming unwieldy, the authors apply a narrower definition of cases from countries outside Asia and the Pacific. Therefore, the discussion of non-regional cases focuses on those lawsuits that "raise issues of law or fact regarding the science of climate change and climate change mitigation and adaptation efforts."[23]

---

[22]   For a discussion about the emergence of climate law, see J. Peel. 2012. Climate Change Law: The Emergence of a New Legal Discipline. *Melbourne University Law Review*. 32 (3). pp. 922–979. See also, J.B. Ruhl. 2015. What Is Climate Change Law? *Oxford University Press Blog*. 22 August.

[23]   United Nations Environment Programme. 2017. *The Status of Climate Change Litigation: A Global Review*. Nairobi. p. 10.

Legal Citations

Legal citations vary by jurisdiction. As this document is written for judges and legal practitioners in Asia and the Pacific, the authors preserve national case citation formats, wherever feasible.

Looking Forward

Global Action and the Impact of COVID-19

We—humanity—can no longer delay taking climate action or treat climate change as a future problem, better dealt with by our children. In 2020, Asia and the Pacific is already experiencing the impacts of climate change. People in Asia and the Pacific suffer severe weather, heat waves, flooding, droughts, and sea level rise.[24] (See Report One for a more in-depth discussion regarding climate change and its impacts.)

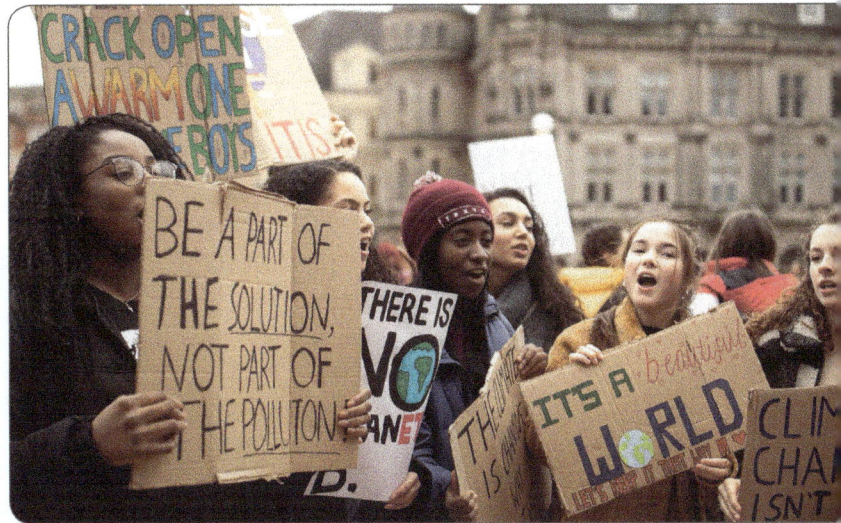

A demand for climate action in Birmingham. Globally, concerned citizens are demanding urgent climate action in coordinated climate marches (photo by Callum Shaw).

In 2019, nature sprouted a deadly new virus—severe acute respiratory syndrome coronavirus 2—causing the global coronavirus disease (COVID-19) pandemic. Global efforts to slow the spread of COVID-19 have seen governments use police powers to quarantine citizens. Traffic and passenger flights have decreased, and the chirping of birds has replaced the incessant din of traffic. During this extraordinary pause in daily life, skies cleared and the temporary drop in global GHG emissions was the biggest on record.[25] But, it is premature and mistaken to declare this pandemic-induced emissions drop "a climate triumph."[26] Emissions have dipped in previous global economic crises, only to sharply rebound as economies claw back growth, frequently astride fossil fuel-based industries.[27] Moreover, a global pandemic is not the way anyone wants to reduce emissions.

---

[24] Y. Hijioka et al. 2014. Asia. In V.R. Barros et al. *Climate Change 2014: Impacts, Adaptation, and Vulnerability*. Cambridge: Cambridge University Press. pp. 1327–1370; L.A. Nurse et al. 2014. Small Islands. In V.R. Barros et al. *AR5 Climate Change 2014: Impacts, Adaptation, and Vulnerability*. Cambridge: Cambridge University Press. pp. 1327–1370; and J. Aucan. 2018. Effects of Climate Change on Sea Levels and Inundation Relevant to the Pacific Islands. *Pacific Marine Climate Change Report Card: Science Review 2018*. pp. 43–49.

[25] International Energy Agency. 2020. *Global Energy Review 2020: The impacts of the COVID-19 crisis on global energy demand and CO_2 emissions*. Paris; S. Evans. 2020. Analysis: Coronavirus Set to Cause Largest Ever Annual Fall in CO_2 Emissions. *Carbon Brief*. 9 April; and J. Ambrose. Carbon Emissions from Fossil Fuels Could Fall by 2.5bn Tonnes in 2020. *The Guardian*. 12 April.

[26] J. Ambrose. Carbon Emissions from Fossil Fuels Could Fall by 2.5bn Tonnes in 2020. *The Guardian*. 12 April.

[27] Footnote 26; and *The Economist*. 2020. The Epidemic Provides a Chance to Do Good by the Climate. 26 March.

ADB estimates that growth in Asia will drop from 5.7% to 2.4% in 2020, excluding Asia's high-income newly industrialized economies.[28] The recession will hit the Pacific hardest, with the combined output in the subregion set to decline by 0.3% in 2020 as five of its 14 economies contract.[29]

The COVID-19 pandemic is also hindering climate negotiations. Parties to the Paris Agreement met in late 2019 for the 25th Conference of the Parties (COP 25) in Madrid. Dubbed a "disappointment" by the United Nations secretary-general, the forum did not produce the needed outcomes, especially on the Paris rulebook.[30] Countries deferred reaching agreement until 2020 on items like carbon markets, cooperation on loss and damage, transparency in reporting, and common time frames for climate pledges.[31] Even before the emergence of COVID-19, the stalled negotiations were unfortunate. Countries are supposed to file their second climate pledges before the end of 2020. But COVID-19 canceled important intercessional climate negotiations and the 2020 Conference of Parties (COP 26). The delay means that countries must start implementing the Paris Agreement without accord on important aspects of execution.

Business Responses to Climate Change

Outside of the political negotiations occurring in the context of the Paris Agreement, the business world is more forthright about the impacts of climate change on doing business. The former governor of the Bank of England recently acknowledged the changed risk profile of doing business in the 21st century due to climate change (footnote 7). Investor initiatives are pressuring the world's largest corporate GHG emitters to "curb emissions, improve governance, and strengthen climate-related financial disclosures."[32] The World Economic Forum adopted climate change as a key issue at its "better capitalism" themed 2020 meeting in Davos, underscoring the importance of building a low-emissions future.[33] In June 2020, the World Economic Forum announced the Great Reset initiative, which focuses on reshaping the global economy so that it functions in harmony with nature and respects human dignity.[34]

---

[28] ADB. 2020. *Asian Development Outlook 2020: What Drives Innovation in Asia? Special Topic: The Impact of the Coronavirus Outbreak—An Update.* Manila. p. xii.

[29] Footnote 28, p. xvi.

[30] *CarbonBrief.* 2019. COP25: Key Outcomes Agreed at the UN Climate Talks in Madrid. 15 December.

[31] Footnote 30; and KPMG International. 2019. COP25: Key Outcomes of the 25th UN Climate Conference. News release. Zug, Switzerland.

[32] Climate Action 100+. About Us. BlackRock (the world's largest asset manager) has also announced plans to sell $500 million of coal-related investments in line with its decision to adopt environmental sustainability a core goal. See S. Gandel. 2020. BlackRock to sell $500 Million in Coal Investments in Climate Change Push. *CBS News.* 14 January.

[33] R. Pomeroy. 2020. 5 Things We Learned about Climate Change at Davos 2020. *World Economic Forum.* 24 January; and J. Worland. 2020. How Davos Became a Climate Change Conference. *Time.* 27 January.

[34] C. Alessi. 2020. 'A golden opportunity'—HRH The Prince of Wales and Other Leaders on the Forum's Great Reset. World Economic Forum news release. 3 June.

Limiting global warming to 1.5°C above preindustrial temperatures requires urgent and unprecedented cooperation and collective action.[35] Recognizing the urgency of taking action, the Bill & Melinda Gates Foundation, one of the world's largest philanthropic foundations, has expanded its core work to include climate change. In explaining their decision, Bill and Melinda Gates said, "Tackling climate change is going to demand historic levels of global cooperation, unprecedented amounts of innovation in nearly every sector of the economy. . ."[36] Given the foundation's reputation for applying business techniques to social investments, its move into climate work reflects the business world's growing focus on the pursuit of collaborative action.

Sound judicial decisions can enhance global cooperation and innovation on climate change. They can also protect people's rights and referee government action on climate change.

Judicial Responses to Climate Change in 2020 and Beyond

ADB has worked with environmental judges in Asia and the Pacific under the Law, Policy, and Reform Program within the Office of the General Counsel for 10 years. The series of reports was born out of a desire to support judges in responding to climate action. In September 2016, ADB cohosted the Third Asian Judges Symposium on Law, Policy and Climate Change with the Supreme Court of the Philippines and the United Nations Environment Programme. Environmental judges made three clear points:

(i)   They acknowledged the threat of climate change, but they wanted to better understand the nature of the issue.
(ii) To write better judgments about climate change, they need access to information about climate law and litigation outcomes.
(iii) Working as an environmental judge is isolating, with strong judgments being frowned on for being an activist or interfering with government policy.

Judges in Asia and the Pacific have a vital role in guarding the rule of law and helping their nations achieve climate resilience and protect human and constitutional rights. However, each judge must determine how to contribute best to climate governance within their respective jurisdiction.

Knowledge about global comparative jurisprudence and international and national legal frameworks are important for helping judges do their job, making this information a fundamental component of the judicial tool kit on climate change. Report One of this series provides more information about climate change. Sharing information about global climate jurisprudence is the central

---

[35] Preindustrial refers to the era before the commencement of the industrial revolution, i.e., before the 1750s.
[36] B. Gates and M. Gates. 2020. *Why We Swing for the Fences.* Letter published on GatesNotes. 10 February.

focus of Report Two. Reports Three and Four provide more information on national legal frameworks in Asia and the Pacific and the global climate change legal framework.

Responding to the challenge of climate change does not make a judge an activist. All of ADB's member countries in Asia and the Pacific have committed to the Paris Agreement. Beyond national commitments to the Paris Agreement and the United Nations Framework Convention on Climate Change (UNFCCC), there are regional commitments to tackling climate change. In late 2019, the Association of Southeast Asian Nations affirmed their commitment to the Paris Agreement goals.[37] Determining rights and balancing outcomes in emerging fields of law are nothing new for courts. Superior courts are practiced at applying well-established legal principles to shape responses to new legal challenges. Although climate change presents us with a new and dangerous problem, judges can apply existing principles to resolve climate-related disputes.

Beyond legal principles, climate science is central to pursuing sustainable and resilient growth, promoting protection of rights, and achieving climate justice.

> Climate justice links human rights and development to achieve a human-centered approach, safeguarding the rights of the most vulnerable people and sharing the burdens and benefits of climate change and its impacts equitably and fairly. Climate justice is informed by science, responds to science and acknowledges the need for equitable stewardship of the world's resources.[38]

A strong rule of law relies on well-trained and resourced judges. Access to information about climate law and litigation is an essential judicial tool that enhances the judicial capacity for climate decision-making. This report serves as a starting point for judges. Online databases offer current information on climate and environmental law and litigation. Several online databases maintain current information about climate litigation. We encourage judges to use and share information with the following:

(i)   Sabin Center for Climate Change Law. https://climate.law.columbia.edu/;
(ii)   ECOLEX. https://www.ecolex.org/; and
(iii) Pacific Islands Legal Information Institute. http://www.paclii.org/.

ADB is proud of the progress made by the judiciaries across Asia and the Pacific. We look forward to working with the judiciaries on one of the greatest challenges of the 21st century.

---

[37] Association of Southeast Asian Nations (ASEAN). 2019. *ASEAN Joint Statement on Climate Change to the 25th Session of the Conference of the Parties to the United Nations Framework Convention on Climate Change (UNFCCC COP25).* 2 November.

[38] Mary Robinson Foundation—Climate Justice. 2020. *Principles of Climate Justice.* Cited in *Leghari v. Federation of Pakistan,* footnote 1, p. 22, para. 21.

Photo by Luis Ascui/ADB.

Marching for climate justice in Maastricht. Greta Thunberg's climate protest in Sweden galvanized people globally to march for climate justice. A growing number of lawsuits reference climate justice and argue that climate change threatens fundamental human rights (photo by Vincent M.A. Janssen).

PART ONE

RIGHTS-BASED LITIGATION AGAINST GOVERNMENTS

Governments are the most common defendants in climate change litigation. Litigants have increasingly relied on rights-based frameworks to compel governments to take climate action. In these rights-based suits, standing serves as a threshold issue. Plaintiffs must prove that they have a sufficient stake in the outcome of the case and that the judiciary can offer adequate redress. Once standing and procedural requirements are met, courts around the world deploy some legal tools to hold governments accountable.

Courts have used international human rights frameworks, constitutional rights, and domestic statutory requirements for governments to mitigate greenhouse gas (GHG) emissions. The Paris Agreement has served as a reference against which to measure the adequacy of emissions reduction targets.[1] In some cases, domestic courts have enforced national commitments made under the Paris Agreement. This section describes the range of judicial reasoning used to mandate governmental mitigation action.

I. Standing

A. Global Approaches

Standing doctrines (*locus standi*) address the question of who should have access to courts to adjudicate a particular claim. The criteria for establishing standing vary by jurisdiction but are generally aimed at ensuring that plaintiffs or petitioners have a sufficient stake in the outcome of the case. Their claims must also be capable of judicial resolution. Many jurisdictions have liberal standing requirements—e.g., a plaintiff must have a "sufficient" or "special" interest in the subject matter of the action.

In contrast, the United States (US) has significantly more restrictive requirements for federal cases, specifically that (i) the party has suffered an injury-in-fact or imminent risk of injury, (ii) the injury is fairly traceable to the defendant's allegedly unlawful conduct, and (iii) the injury can be redressed by a favorable court decision. Because of these more restrictive requirements, questions about standing have played a major role in cases brought against governmental actors in the US.

---

[1] *Paris Agreement*, Paris, 12 December 2015, *United Nations Treaty Series*, No. 54113.

1. Standing and Climate Change in the United States

The US Supreme Court first addressed the issue of standing for claims related to climate change in *Massachusetts v. US Environmental Protection Agency*.[2] A group of states, cities, and environmental organizations challenged the decision of the US Environmental Protection Agency (EPA) to not regulate GHG emissions (from motor vehicles) under federal air pollution law. The court held that the State of Massachusetts had standing to bring these claims as (i) the state had presented sufficient evidence of actual and imminent harms—sea level rise would likely swallow large amounts of coastal property, and (ii) these harms would be at least partially redressed if the EPA were to regulate emissions from motor vehicles.[3] The court noted that Massachusetts had a "special position and interest" in part because it "owns a great deal of the territory alleged to be affected" and in part because of its quasi-sovereign status.[4]

Subsequent US climate cases have raised questions about whether plaintiffs can also establish standing to sue where they are (i) private parties that do not have quasi-sovereign status, and/or (ii) seeking regulation of emission sources with a much smaller GHG footprint than the entire US motor vehicle fleet.

In *Washington Environmental Council v. Bellon*, a federal court of appeal held that two nongovernment organizations (NGOs) did not have standing to challenge Washington State's failure to regulate GHG emissions from five oil refineries. The plaintiffs did not show that the refineries' emissions meaningfully contributed to global GHG levels.[5] The court noted that the refineries were responsible for 101.1 million metric tons of carbon dioxide equivalent (CO_2e) annually (5.9% of total GHG emissions produced in the state of Washington), far less than the emissions in *Massachusetts v. EPA* (1.7 billion tons). As such, the court reasoned that the effect of those emissions on global climate change was "scientifically indiscernible, given the emission levels, the dispersal of greenhouse gases world-wide, and the absence of any meaningful nexus between Washington refinery emissions and global GHG concentrations now or as projected in the future."[6]

In *Juliana v. United States*, a federal appellate court in California held that plaintiffs do not have standing to sue the Government of the United States for affirmatively contributing to climate change and failing to adequately control emissions from fossil fuel development and use.[7] The appeals court found that the plaintiffs had alleged

---

[2]   *Massachusetts v. Environmental Protection Agency*, 549 U.S. 497 (2007).
[3]   Footnote 2, p. 1453.
[4]   Footnote 2, p. 523.
[5]   *Washington Environmental Council v. Bellon*, 732 F.3d 1131, 1135 (9th Cir. 2013), *reh'g en banc denied*, 741 F.3d 1075 (9th Cir. 2014).
[6]   Footnote 5, p. 1144. The court noted that the Bellon case also differed from *Massachusetts v. EPA* because no state plaintiff should be granted "special solicitude" in the standing analysis. However, the court also found that even if it "assume[d] that the Plaintiffs' members are entitled to a comparable relaxed standard, the extension of *Massachusetts* to the present circumstances would not be tenable." Footnote 5, p. 1145.
[7]   *Juliana v. United States*, No. 18-36082 (9th Cir. Jan. 17, 2020).

sufficiently personalized and concrete injuries—such as lost income for a ski resort employee and harmful impacts to a family farm—that were fairly traceable to the GHG emissions resulting from US fossil fuel production and use. However, the appeals court found that the remedy the plaintiffs requested—a court order to the federal government to develop and implement a comprehensive plan to draw down atmospheric concentrations of GHGs to 350 parts per million (ppm)—was beyond the court's authority. The plaintiffs have requested judicial review of this decision. (See Part One, Section II.A.5. Rights-Based Case in the United States for further discussion of this case.)

2. Standing and Climate Change in Australia and Europe

Outside of the US context, standing requirements tend to be more relaxed, and, in many cases, standing is never briefed or discussed.[8] But there are some cases in which non-US courts have also grappled with standing issues, including the question of what constitutes a "meaningful contribution" to climate change for standing purposes.[9]

Dual Gas Pty Ltd v Environment Protection Authority was a legal challenge to the Australian government's approval of a new power plant. The Victorian Civil and Administrative Tribunal (VCAT) in the state of Victoria found that the release of 4.2 million tons of CO_2e annually over a 30-year projected life span of the plant would contribute sufficiently to climate change to establish standing.[10]

In contrast, in *Friends of the Irish Environment CLG v Fingal County Council,* the High Court of Ireland found that an applicant lacked standing to challenge a county's decision to issue an airport authority a 5-year extension for planning permission to construct a new runway because there was no right of participation under the

---

[8]   See, e.g., *Leghari v. Federation of Pakistan,* PLD 2018 Lahore 364; *Court on its own Motion v. State of Himachal Pradesh and Others,* Application No. 237(THC)/2013 (CWPIL No. 15 of 2010), Application No. 238(THC)/2013 (CWP No. 5087 of 2011), and Application No. 239(THC)/2013 (CWP No. 5088 of 2011), (National Green Tribunal, 6 February 2014); and *Gbemre v. Shell Petroleum Development Company of Nigeria Ltd.,* FJC/B/CS/53/05 (2005). See also G.N. Gill. 2016. Environmental Justice in India: The National Green Tribunal and Expert Members. *Transnational Environmental Law.* 5 (1). pp. 175–205.

[9]   *Urgenda Foundation v The State of the Netherlands (Ministry of Infrastructure and the Environment),* HA ZA 13-1396, C/09/456689, ECLI:NL:RBDHA:2015:7145 found that an NGO had standing to sue the government for inadequate climate action. This was based on a Dutch law allowing NGOs to bring a court action to protect the public or collective interests of other people but denying separate standing for individual claimants "partly for practical reasons." The case was upheld on appeal. See also *Haughton v Minister for Planning and Macquarie Generation* [2011] NWSLEC 217, which found that an individual applicant had standing under both Australia's Environmental Protection Act, 1999 and the common law to sue the government for approval of coal-fired power plants without adequately considering the effect of the plants on climate change and sustainable development. Another relevant case is *PUSH Sweden, Nature and Youth Sweden and Others v. Government of Sweden* (Stockholm District Court, 2017). The court found that the NGOs lacked standing to sue the government for selling coal-fired power plants and associated mining assets because the NGOs had not experienced an injury from the governmental decisions at issue.

[10] *Dual Gas Pty Ltd v Environment Protection Authority* [2012] VCAT 308, para. 134.

planning law.[11] Further, the applicant could not demonstrate "any disproportionate interference" with the right to a clean environment.[12] (See Part Two, Section V.A.3.c. A Right to an Environment in Ireland for further discussion of this case.)

Similarly, in *Carvalho and Others v Parliament and Council*, the European Union (EU) General Court ruled that plaintiffs did not have standing to bring a case against the EU because they could not show particularized harm. Plaintiffs included 10 families from Fiji, France, Germany, Italy, Kenya, Portugal, and Romania, and the Swedish Sami Youth Association Sáminuorra, who sought to compel the EU to make more stringent GHG emissions reductions.[13] The plaintiffs claimed that the EU's emissions reduction target was insufficient to avoid dangerous climate change and threatened their fundamental rights. The EU General Court dismissed the case, reasoning that the plaintiffs did not have standing to bring the case under EU law because climate change affects every individual in one manner or another. EU case law on standing, however, requires that plaintiffs are affected in a way "peculiar to them or by reason of circumstances in which they are differentiated from all other persons, and by virtue of these factors distinguishes them individually."[14] This case is currently on appeal.

3. Private Citizens in Foreign Jurisdictions in Europe and New Zealand

There have also been private citizen suits brought in foreign jurisdictions where standing requirements have been impliedly met because the suit proceeded past the procedural stage. In *Lliuya v RWE AG*, for example, a Peruvian farmer sued a German electricity producer in a German court for climate damage in his hometown in Peru.[15] A German appeals court determined that the case should proceed. The case is now in the evidentiary phase. (See Part Three, Section II.A.3. Transboundary Nuisance Claims in Germany for a full case summary of *Lliuya v RWE AG*.)

In *Teitiota v Chief Executive of the Ministry of Business, Innovation and Employment*, an i-Kiribati sought refugee status in New Zealand in part because of climate effects on his home country Kiribati.[16] While the New Zealand Supreme Court did not grant refugee status to the plaintiff, the case was not dismissed on standing grounds. (See Part Five, Section I.A.1. Climate Migration in New Zealand for a full case summary of *Teitiota v Chief Executive of the Ministry of Business, Innovation and Employment* and discussion of other climate migration cases.)

---

[11] *Friends of the Irish Environment CLG v Fingal County Council* [2017] IEHC 695.

[12] Footnote 11, p. 293, para. 264.

[13] Judgment of 8 May 2019, *Carvalho and Others v Parliament and the Council*, T-330/18, not published, EU:T:2019:324.

[14] Judgment of 15 July 1963, *Plaumann & Co. v Commission of the European Economic Community*, C-25/62, EU:C:1963:17, p. 223.

[15] *Lliuya v RWE AG*, District Court of Essen, Dec. 15, 2016, Case No. 2 O 285/15, ECLI:DE:LGE:201 6:1215.2O285.15.00. For an unofficial English translation, see Sabin Center for Climate Change Law. Lliuya v. RWE AG (accessed 29 April 2020).

[16] *Teitiota v Chief Executive of the Ministry of Business, Innovation and Employment* [2014] NZCA 173.

Neither Lliuya nor Teitiota is against governments. However, these cases do demonstrate that private citizens can meet procedural and standing requirements when bringing a suit outside of their home country related to climate impacts experienced therein.

B.   Asia and the Pacific Approaches

This section explores how courts across South Asia, Southeast Asia, and the Pacific have ruled on standing in cases that address a range of environmental issues such as deforestation, air pollution, flood and disaster planning, water concession, and biodiversity protection. While many of these cases do not specifically refer to climate change, managing these issues can contribute to climate mitigation or adaptation efforts. Further, in 2019 and beyond, parties who litigate on these types of issues may be motivated by climate change. Judicial approaches to standing in environmental cases are thus relevant for climate litigation.

1.   Relaxed Standing in Southeast Asia

a)   *Class Actions and Future Generations in the Philippines*

Oposa v. Factoran relaxed standing for class actions and future generations in the Philippines.[17] The petitioners, who were minors, demanded that the Secretary of Environment and Natural Resources cancel all existing Philippine timber license agreements and stop approving new licenses. The petitioners argued that widespread deforestation had caused various environmental problems, including climate change. They asserted that 54% of the country's land area should be used for forest cover.

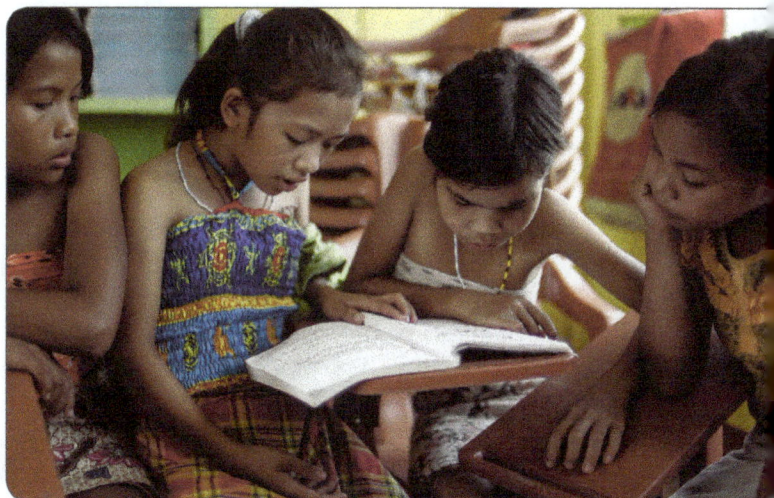

Girls from the Mangyan tribe from Mindoro, Philippines. In the 1990s, the Philippine Supreme Court broke new ground, confirming that children and future generations have standing to sue for environmental damage to forests on the principle of intergenerational equity (photo by Eric Sales/ADB).

The Philippine Supreme Court recognized the petitioners' standing to file a class suit for themselves, for others of their generation, and for succeeding generations. Such standing stemmed from the petitioners' right to a balanced and healthful ecology.[18] It was also a result of their intergenerational responsibility to preserve the "rhythm and harmony of nature" for the full enjoyment of a balanced and healthful ecology (footnotes 17 and 18).

The court held that the right to a balanced and healthful ecology concerned nothing less than self-preservation and self-perpetuation. As such, it need not even be written in the constitution, for it is presumed to exist from the start of the human race. The Department of Environment and Natural Resources, therefore, had a duty to protect and advance this right. (See Part One, Section II.B.1.b.

---

17   *Oposa v. Factoran*, G.R. No. 101083, 30 July 1993.
18   Section 16, Article II, Constitution of the Republic of the Philippines, 1987.

Quality of Life in Southeast Asia; Part One, Section II.B.2.a. Climate Justice in the Philippines and Pakistan; Part Two, Section VIII.B.1. Timber Licenses in the Philippines; and Part Five, Section VI.A. Children and Deforestation for further discussion of this case.)

b) Transcendental Importance and Standing of Mammals in the Philippines

Philippine courts treat standing as a procedural issue. They may relax the rule of standing when a plaintiff raises issues that are of transcendental importance, overreaching significance to society, or paramount public interest.[19]

Henares v. Land Transportation Franchising and Regulatory Board provided the Philippine Supreme Court with another opportunity to apply the twin concepts of intergenerational responsibility and justice.[20] Petitioners sought the issuance of a writ of mandamus commanding government agencies to require public utility vehicles to use compressed natural gas as an alternative fuel.

The court said that the petitioners' standing stemmed from their fundamental right to clean air. It affirmed previous rulings finding that a party's standing was a procedural technicality. Necessarily, the right to clean air was not only an issue of paramount importance to the petitioners because it concerned the very air they breathe, but it was also an issue imbued with public interest. This decision clarified that when a matter is of transcendental importance to the public and demands a prompt and definite resolution, the court may set aside the procedural technicality. (See Part One, Section II.B.3.b. The Transport Sector in the Philippines for a full case summary of *Henares v. Land Transportation Franchising and Regulatory Board.*)

Resident Marine Mammals of the Protected Seascape Tañon Strait et al. v. Secretary Angelo Reyes discussed the standing of marine mammals.[21] The case involved two consolidated petitions challenging the validity of the environmental compliance certificate and service contract granted to Japan Petroleum Exploration Co., Ltd. The certificate and contract were for the exploration, development, and exploitation of petroleum resources within a protected seascape. The petitioners comprised (i) the resident marine mammals of the Tañon Strait, such as toothed whales, dolphins, porpoises, and two natural persons called "the Stewards"; and (ii) the Central Visayas Fisherfolk Development Center. The petitioners protested the adverse ecological impact of the oil exploration activities, including a 50%–70% reduction in fish catch. They argued that the environmental compliance certificate was invalid because Japan Petroleum Exploration did not comply with Philippine EIA system requirements.

---

[19] *Biraogo v. The Philippine Truth Commission of 2010*, G.R. No. 192935, 7 December 2010.
[20] *Henares v. Land Transportation Franchising and Regulatory Board*, G.R. No. 158290, 23 October 2006.
[21] *Resident Marine Mammals of the Protected Seascape Tañon Strait et al. v. Secretary Angelo Reyes*, G.R. Nos. 180771 and 181527, 21 April 2015.

The court discussed the challenges that animal rights advocates and environmentalists face in protecting animals and inanimate objects. Traditional rules of standing require advocates to show that they are real parties in interest, which is challenging when the advocates suffer no direct harm or injury. Nevertheless, procedural rules only allow natural and juridical persons to bring lawsuits. However, the court noted that the landmark 2010 Philippine Rules of Procedure for Environmental Cases allow for citizen suits on the principle that humans are stewards of nature. As the rules recognize legal standing for stewards of nature, the court reasoned there was no need to grant standing to the resident marine mammals. (See Part, Two Section I.B.2. Oil Exploration in Protected Marine Areas in the Philippines for further discussion of this case.)

c) Standing for Environmental Organizations in Indonesia

A case against PT Inti Indorayon Utama, a paper milling company in Sumatra, paved the way for standing in environmental cases in Indonesia.[22] The company caused significant environmental damage to the surrounding countryside. Damage peaked when the company's artificial lagoon burst, releasing about 400,000 cubic meters of toxic waste into the Asahan River. Wahana Lingkungan Hidup Indonesia (WALHI), a national environmental NGO, sued the company and five government agencies before the Central Jakarta district court, arguing that it should be allowed to represent the public "environmental interest."[23]

The court recognized WALHI's standing to file the case based on two grounds. First, the court regarded the environment as "common property," stressing that there is a public interest in environmental preservation. Second, the environment itself is a legal subject with an intrinsic right to be sustained. WALHI could legitimately represent that environmental interest. Further, the court held that every person had the right and obligation to take part in environmental management.

The legal standing of environmental organizations to file lawsuits has now been cemented in article 38 of Indonesia's Environmental Management Act, 1997. In addition, the law recognizes the right of communities to bring class actions to court and report environmental problems that adversely affect them to law enforcers. It also recognizes the right of concerned government agencies to act in the communities' interest.

d) Adversely Affected Test in Malaysia

Malaysian Trade Union Congress & Ors v Menteri Tenaga, Air Dan Komunikasi & Anor laid down the standing requirements in applications for judicial review in Malaysia.[24]

---

22 District Court of Central Jakarta, Decision No. 820/Pdt./G/1988/PN, *PT Inti Indorayon Utama (PT IIU)* (1988).
23 D. Nicholson. 2009. Environmental Litigation in Indonesia: Legal Framework and Overview of Cases. In *Environmental Dispute Resolution in Indonesia*. Leiden: KITLV Press. pp. 51–52.
24 *Malaysian Trade Union Congress & Ors v Menteri Tenaga, Air Dan Komunikasi & Anor* [2014] 2 CLJ 525.

Malaysian Trades Union Congress (MTUC) and others disputed a 15% water tariff increase. The respondent, a water distribution concessionaire, had obtained ministerial approval for the increase. MTUC requested a copy of the concession agreement as well as the audit report justifying the increase. The minister refused access to the documents. MTUC and 13 other parties then sought judicial review of the minister's decision.

The Federal Court of Malaysia held that the "adversely affected test" governs applications for judicial review. This test only requires that an applicant demonstrates a real and genuine interest in the subject matter and not necessarily an infringement of a private right or the suffering of special damage. Given the facts, the court concluded that MTUC had shown a real and genuine interest in seeking the two documents. MTUC was, therefore, adversely affected and had standing to seek judicial review. However, the court did not grant MTUC access to the documents as the agreement was confidential and the audit report was an official secret. (See Part Two, Section VII.B.2.b. Water as a Human Right in Southeast Asia for further discussion of this case.)

2. Relaxed Standing in South Asia and Violations of Public Trust

Courts in Bangladesh, India, Pakistan, and Sri Lanka have relaxed rules of standing for litigants asserting violations of the public trust as well as those seeking to enforce constitutional or fundamental environmental rights.

a) "Any Person Aggrieved" Test in Bangladesh

In *M. Farooque Vs. Government of Bangladesh*, the Supreme Court of Bangladesh considered the standing of the Bangladesh Environmental Lawyers Association (BELA).[25] BELA sued the government over a flood action plan. BELA alleged that the plan violated laws and would endanger millions of human lives while also degrading natural resources and habitats.

Article 102(1) of the Bangladesh constitution enables "any person aggrieved" to sue for enforcement of a fundamental right. The court noted its duty to enforce fundamental rights, stating that "Any law, action and order made and passed in violation of fundamental rights is void. It is the duty of the Court to so declare."[26] Given the importance of protecting fundamental rights, the court held that any citizen seeking redress of a public wrong or injury or breach of fundamental rights had sufficient interest in a matter and was, therefore, a "person aggrieved" (footnote 26). However, the petitioner must be acting bona fide, meaning not for personal gain, and without political motivation or other underhanded purposes. The court reasoned that the government's flood action plan was a public sector subject and a matter of public concern. As such, BELA was aggrieved because

---

[25] *M. Farooque Vs. Government of Bangladesh* 17 BLD (AD) 1 (1997).
[26] Footnote 25, p. 26.

(i)   its case concerned the fundamental rights and constitutional remedies of an indeterminate number of people and is a matter of public concern; and

(ii) it had devoted considerable resources to mitigating the flood plan's ill effects and was acting in good faith and with a clear purpose.

The court, however, rejected the petitioner's argument that it could represent future generations. The court distinguished the petitioner's case from the Philippine case of *Oposa v. Factoran* because the Bangladesh constitution did not contain the right to a balanced and healthful ecology for present and future generations.

(See Part One, Section II.B.1.a. Life, Dignity, and Equality in South Asia for a full case summary of *M. Farooque Vs. Government of Bangladesh*. See Part One, Section I.B.1.a. Class Actions and Future Generations in the Philippines for a full case summary of *Oposa v. Factoran*. *Oposa* is also discussed in Part One, Section II.B.1.b. Quality of Life in Southeast Asia; Part One, Section II.B.2.a. Climate Justice in the Philippines and Pakistan; Part Two, Section VIII.B.1. Timber Licenses in the Philippines; and Part Five, Section VI.A. Children and Deforestation.)

b) Environmental Damage and Future Generations in South Asia

Food, water, energy, and health insecurities have the greatest adverse impact on local communities. Along with environmental sustainability, these considerations also influence town planning policies and decisions. In *Virender Gaur and Ors. v. State of Haryana and Ors.*, the Supreme Court of India considered the standing of residents challenging their government's decision to lease public land for the construction of a dharmsala.[27] The land was reserved for sanitation, recreation, playgrounds, and maintaining ecology.

The court held that the government's action "intimately, vitally and adversely affected" the residents. It said the decision was "destructive of the environment" and deprived residents "of facilities reserved for the enjoyment and protection of the health of the public at large."[28] It thus allowed the residents to proceed with their case. (See Part One, Section II.B.1.a. Life, Dignity, and Equality in South Asia; Part Three, Section I.B. Asia and the Pacific Approaches; and Part Three, Section I.B.1. Human Rights and Climate in the Philippines for further discussion of this case.)

Children playing in an urban park in Kolkata, India. Courts in South Asia have protected the right of citizens to urban natural and recreational parks because safeguarding the natural environment is essential to the enjoyment of basic human rights (photo by Amit Verma/ADB).

In *Shehla Zia and Others v. WAPDA*, the Supreme Court of Pakistan broadly defined standing in public interest litigation concerning environmental

---

27   *Virender Gaur and Ors. v. State of Haryana and Ors.,* (1995) 2 SCC 577

28   Footnote 27, p. 582.

protection.[29] Islamabad residents objected to the construction of an electrical grid station adjacent to their neighborhood. They argued that the grid station's electromagnetic field and high voltage transmission lines would negatively impact their health and the local environment.

The court recognized that citizens' right to a healthy environment was integral to their constitutional rights to life and dignity. One was deprived of life and dignity, said the court, if they lack food, clothing, shelter, education, health care, clean atmosphere, and unpolluted environment. The court also noted that a person was entitled to the protection of the law from being exposed to the hazards of electromagnetic fields—and any other hazards—which may be due to any grid station, factory, or similar installation. Such danger was bound to affect many people. Article 184 of the constitution on environmental protection may, therefore, be invoked because many citizens could not access representation in court due to a lack of awareness, information, or education. Poverty and disability may also impede access.

The Supreme Court noted that the technical evidence presented on the impact of electrical grids on human settlements was inconclusive and declined to issue a final order. Nonetheless, the court emphasized the need to balance the citizens' rights to life and safety with the government's plans for the welfare and economic progress of the country. Following the precautionary principle, effective controls should also be put in place to address possible threats. (See Part One, Section II.B.1.a. Life, Dignity, and Equality in South Asia for further discussion of this case.)

In 2016, a 7-year-old girl filed a public interest petition in the Supreme Court of Pakistan in *Ali v. Federation of Pakistan & Another*, a landmark case that impacts other facets of climate change litigation.[30] In this case, Ali disputes the government's plan to exploit untapped coal reserves in the Thar Desert that will increase Pakistan's GHG emissions. The petitioner claims that increasing Pakistan's emissions will further destabilize the climate, undermine Pakistan's international climate commitments, violate the public trust doctrine, and infringe the petitioner's constitutional right to life. This is Pakistan's first constitutional law petition by a minor on behalf of the public and future generations. While a court registrar initially rejected the case, the Supreme Court overruled that decision.[31] The case continues.

(See Part One, Section II.B.3.a. The Energy Sector in Pakistan for a full case summary of *Ali v. Federation of Pakistan and Another* as well as Part One, Section IV.B.2. International Commitments in Pending Cases in South Asia; Part Two, Section I.B.1.b. Constitutional Rights in Pakistan; and Part Three, Section III.B.2. Coal-Fired Electricity in Pakistan for further discussion of this case.)

---

[29] *Shehla Zia and Others v. WAPDA*, PLD 1994 SC 693.
[30] *Ali v. Federation of Pakistan & Another*, Constitution Petition in the Supreme Court of Pakistan, 2016.
[31] M.L. Banda and S. Fulton. 2017. Litigating Climate Change in National Courts: Recent Trends and Developments in Global Climate Law. *Environmental Law Reporter*. 47 (2). pp. 10121–10134.

c) Violations of Public Trust in Sri Lanka

In *Sugathapala Mendis v Chandrika Kumaratunga and Others*, the Supreme Court of Sri Lanka upheld the right of any citizen to seek redress for a violation of the public trust.[32] The petitioners challenged the government's decision to transfer an urban marsh to a private company, which intended to convert the land into a private golf resort. The government had acquired the land 9 years before for the public purpose of urban development and to protect surrounding suburban areas from flooding.

The court ruled that the petitioners could sue the public officials involved in approving the transfer for violating the public trust and the fundamental right to equality before the law, guaranteed under article 12(1) of the constitution. It reasoned that the petitioners could not be disqualified from having standing because their rights were the same as any other citizen. The court held that the government should act in accordance with the people's best interests. Such interest demanded that the government manage all facets of the country under the stringent limitations of public trusteeship imposed by the public trust doctrine. In short, the government must only use public power for the larger benefit of the people and the country's long-term sustainable development, and in accordance with the rule of law. (See Part Four, Section I.B.2.c. Protecting Adaptive Capacity of Inland Water Bodies for further discussion of this case.)

II. Constitutional and Rights-Based Cases

Courts are increasingly relying on the rights outlined in domestic constitutions and international human rights law to require governments to take climate change action. Thus rights-based analysis provides another tool, in addition to statutory requirements, to hold governments accountable. In deploying rights-based analysis, courts around the world have looked to international and regional frameworks for guidance. Courts have also linked constitutional provisions to particular government-backed industrial activities, e.g., enforcing constitutional rights in the context of fossil fuel extraction.

A. Global Approaches

This section describes the rights-based reasoning that courts outside the Asia and Pacific region have deployed in climate change litigation.

1. The Right to a Healthy Environment in Colombia

Enforcing the right to a healthy environment may become a new way to address climate-related harms. In *Advisory Opinion OC-23/17 of November 15, 2017*

---

[32] *Sugathapala Mendis v Chandrika Kumaratunga and Others* 2008 Sri LR 339.

Requested by the Republic of Colombia, the Inter-American Court of Human Rights recognized a healthy environment as a human right.

This was a landmark decision with clear implications for climate change.[33] The court reasoned that the adverse effects of environmental degradation and climate change affected the enjoyment of other human rights.[34] The court noted that the human right to a healthy environment had both individual and collective implications.[35] As a collective right, it implied a duty owed to both present and future generations. As an individual right, its violation may directly or indirectly impact the individual through the relationship to other rights such as the right to health, life, or personal integrity. Thus, the court reasoned that the right to a healthy environment was fundamental to humankind (footnote 33).

The court's opinion opens the door to rights-based litigation to address climate-related harms. It grants states that recognize the jurisdiction of the court—and their citizens—the right to file claims based on environmental harms that affect human rights. The opinion also provides persuasive precedent for other jurisdictions. (See Part One, Section II.A.3. The Rights of Nature in Colombia; and Part Six, Section I. Global Approaches: Transboundary Harm in South America for further discussion of this case.)

2. The Right to Private and Family Life in the Netherlands

National courts have also begun to use rights-based analysis to mandate governmental climate change action. In 2018, the Hague Court of Appeal issued its decision in *The State of the Netherlands (Ministry of Infrastructure and the Environment) v Urgenda Foundation*.[36] *Urgenda* is the first case globally to order a state to limit emissions for reasons other than statutory mandates.

The Urgenda Foundation, a Dutch environmental group, and 900 Dutch citizens sued the Government of the Netherlands. The plaintiffs alleged that the government had violated its duty of care by revising its predecessor's GHG emissions reduction goals to make them less ambitious. The court found that the government's new goal to reduce emissions by 17% was insufficient to meet its fair contribution to the Paris Agreement temperature goal of limiting global temperature increases to 2°C above preindustrial conditions.[37]

The court also held that the Netherlands had a duty of care to reduce its emissions by at least 25% compared to 1990 by end-2020 under articles 2 and 8 of the European Convention on Human Rights (ECHR). Article 2 protects the right to life.

---

[33] Advisory Opinion OC-23/17, Inter-Am. Ct. H.R., (ser. A) No. 23 (Nov. 15, 2017).

[34] Footnote 33, pp. 21–22.

[35] Footnote 33, p. 27.

[36] *The State of the Netherlands (Ministry of Infrastructure and the Environment) v Urgenda Foundation*, HA ZA 13-1396, C/09/456689, ECLI:NL:GHDHA:2018:2591, Hague Court of Appeal, 9 October 2018 (translation).

[37] Footnote 1, art. 2.

Article 8 protects the right to private life, family life, home, and correspondence. In reaching its decision, the court noted that science demonstrated that climate change posed a real and dangerous threat, including increased flooding and infectious diseases. Thus the court determined that climate change resulted "in the serious risk that the current generation of citizens will be confronted with loss of life and/or a disruption of family life."[38] Therefore, "it follows from Articles 2 and 8 ECHR that the State has a duty to protect against this real threat" (footnote 36).

The court rejected all the government's defenses, including the argument that a court order to reduce emissions undermined the principle of separation of powers. The court affirmed the judiciary's obligation to apply the provisions of treaties to which the Netherlands is party, including articles 2 and 8 of the ECHR. Further, the court found nothing in the Treaty on the Functioning of the European Union that prohibited a member state from taking more ambitious climate action than the EU as a whole. Furthermore, the global nature of climate change did not excuse the Government of the Netherlands from taking action within its territory.

In reaching its decision, the court also stressed the importance of taking immediate response to address climate change. The court reasoned that delayed action would require more ambitious measures in the future. The court also clarified that a reduction of 25% of emissions should be considered a minimum, given the Paris Agreement target of limiting global average temperature rise to 1.5°C–2°C above preindustrial levels (footnote 37).

The Government of the Netherlands filed an appeal to the Supreme Court of the Netherlands in 2019. The Supreme Court affirmed the decision of the lower courts on 20 December 2019.[39] It concluded that the government was obliged to do its part to respond to climate change given its commitments under the United Nations Framework Convention on Climate Change (UNFCCC) and the ECHR. Doing its part meant acting consistently with broadly accepted scientific opinion and internationally recognized standards on climate change. Scientific opinion and international standards confirmed there is an urgent need to reduce carbon emissions by 25%–40% by 2020.[40] Failure or delays in meeting emissions reduction targets expose communities to the risk of abrupt climate change. Further, the government had not explained why it would be feasible to delay meeting internationally accepted emissions reduction targets.

The Supreme Court dismissed arguments that GHG reduction was within the political domain. It affirmed that the Dutch courts must apply the ECHR and

---

[38] Footnote 36, p. 13.
[39] *The State of the Netherlands (Ministry of Economic Affairs and Climate Policy) v Urgenda Foundation*, Case No. 19/00135, ECLI:NL:HR:2019:2007, Supreme Court of the Netherlands, 20 December 2019 (translation).
[40] The court specifically referenced IPCC. 2007. *Climate Change 2007: The Physical Science Basis. Contribution of Working Group I to the Fourth Assessment Report of the Intergovernmental Panel on Climate Change.* Cambridge, United Kingdom and New York, NY, United States: Cambridge University Press. See footnote 39, para. 71 of the unofficial translation.

ensure that the government is taking suitable measures to protect residents from dangerous climate change impacts. The order requiring the government to reduce emissions by 25% aligned with minimum targets under international standards. It also allowed the state to determine specific implementation measures. Therefore, the court ordered the government to cut GHG by at least 25% compared to 1990 by the end of 2020. (See also Part One, Section IV. The Role of the Paris Agreement for a discussion of Paris-related cases.)

3. The Rights of Nature in Colombia

Future Generations v. Ministry of the Environment and Others is another leading case on rights and climate change.[41] In this case, 25 youth plaintiffs between the ages of 7 and 25 sued several bodies within the Government of Colombia, Colombian municipalities, and some corporations. The purpose of the case was to enforce their rights to a healthy environment, life, health, food, and water.[42] The plaintiffs alleged that their fundamental rights were threatened by climate change, along with the government's failure to reduce deforestation and comply with the zero-net deforestation target in the Colombia Amazon region by 2020 (as agreed under the Paris Agreement and the National Development Plan 2014–2018).[43] They filed a *tutela* (a special constitutional claim) to enforce their fundamental rights.

The Supreme Court of Colombia recognized that the fundamental constitutional rights of life, health, minimum subsistence, freedom, and human dignity were substantially linked to the environment and the ecosystem. It reasoned that without a healthy environment, subjects of law and sentient beings generally would not be able to survive, much less protect the fundamental rights of children or future generations.[44] Furthermore, the existence of the family, society, or the state could not be guaranteed without a healthy environment (footnote 44). The Supreme Court's logic was similar to the reasoning the Inter-American Court of Human Rights employed in its *Advisory Opinion OC-23/17 of November 15, 2017 Requested by the Republic of Colombia*. (See also Part One, Section II.A.1 The Right to a Healthy Environment in Colombia; and Part Six, Section I. Global Approaches: Transboundary Harm in South America for further discussion of *Advisory Opinion OC-23/17*.)

Future Generations v. Ministry of the Environment and Others is also important for "rights of nature" jurisprudence, which affords rights to Earth and all living beings. The Supreme Court recognized the Colombian Amazon region as a subject of rights, just as the Constitutional Court recognized the Atrato River as a subject of rights in *Center for Social Justice Studies et al. v. Presidency of the Republic et al.*[45] The Supreme Court decided that, like the Atrato River, the Colombian Amazon

---

41 Corte Suprema de Justicia [C.S.J.] [Supreme Court], Abril 5, 2018, M.P: L. Villabona, Expediente: 11001-22-03-000-2018-00319-01 (Colomb.).

42 Footnote 41, p. 2.

43 Footnote 41, pp. 1–4.

44 Footnote 41, p. 13.

45 Judgment T-622/16 (The Atrato River Case), Constitutional Court of Colombia (2016), translated by the Dignity Rights Project.

region was entitled to protection, conservation, maintenance, and restoration to protect the ecosystem for the global future.[46] In its final ruling, the Supreme Court ordered the government to formulate and implement action plans to address deforestation in the Amazon region.[47] (See Part One, Section IV.A.1. Reducing Deforestation in Colombia; and Part Two, Section VIII.A.1.c National Obligation under the Paris Agreement in Colombia for further discussion of *Future Generations v. Ministry of the Environment and Others*.)

4. The Right to a Healthy Environment in Nigeria and Norway

Litigants have also levied rights-based claims in the context of fossil fuel development. In *Gbemre v. Shell Petroleum Development Company of Nigeria Ltd. And Others*, a Nigerian federal court declared a private company's practice of gas flaring—and a law that permitted it—unconstitutional.[48] Jonah Gbemre, a representative of the Iwherekan community in the Niger Delta, filed suit against the Government of Nigeria and Shell. The suit alleged that Shell's flaring of methane from its gas production activities on the Niger Delta violated human rights to a clean and healthy environment.[49] The court recognized Gbemre's claim that gas flaring contributed to climate change by releasing CO_2 and methane.[50] It ruled that the practice of gas flaring was unconstitutional because it violated the fundamental rights of life and dignity of human persons guaranteed by the Constitution of the Federal Republic of Nigeria (which protects the right to a "pollution-free and healthy environment") and the African Charter on Human and People's Rights.[51] (See Part Three, Section I.A. Global Approaches: Human Rights in Nigeria and the Netherlands for further discussion of this case.)

In contrast, in *Greenpeace Nordic Association and Nature and Youth v. Ministry of Petroleum and Energy*, the Oslo District Court upheld the Norwegian government's decision to issue a block of oil and gas licenses to developers for deep-sea extraction in the Barents Sea.[52] Two environmental NGOs challenged the government's approval of the licenses as unconstitutional. The petition claimed that the issuance of the licenses violated article 112 of Norway's constitution, which stipulates that Norwegians have a "right to an environment that is conducive to health and to a natural environment whose productivity and diversity are maintained."[53] Such an environment, the plaintiffs argued, required staying within a global emission budget consistent with the 1.5°C–2°C temperature goal recognized by the Paris Agreement (footnote 37). The petition also cited other constitutional provisions that required government action to be

---

[46] Footnote 41, p. 45.
[47] Footnote 41, pp. 48–50.
[48] *Gbemre v. Shell Petroleum Development Company of Nigeria and Others*, FHC/B/CS/53/05 (Official Case No) ILDC 924 (NG 2005) (OUP reference).
[49] Footnote 48, pp. 1–3.
[50] Footnote 48, p. 5.
[51] Footnote 48, pp. 29–30.
[52] *Greenpeace Nordic Ass'n and Nature and Youth v. Ministry of Petroleum and Energy*, Case no. 16-166674TVI-OTIR/06 (Oslo District Court) (4 January 2018) (unofficial translation).
[53] Footnote 52, p. 14.

consistent with the precautionary principle and human rights protections. The District Court ruled in favor of the government. The court recognized that the Norwegian constitution conferred legal duties relevant to the case. However, the court reasoned that those legal duties would be fulfilled if the government complied with the Petroleum Act, which governs the procedure for production licenses. Because the government had assessed the environmental impact of the licenses, the government had fulfilled its legal duties. "The Court noted that the Storting, the Norwegian Parliament, had broadly agreed to open the southeast Barents Sea to licensing" (footnote 52). The Court decided that the involvement of the Storting sufficiently fulfilled the duty to take measures. Greenpeace Nordic and Nature and Youth have filed an appeal. (See Part One, Section IV. The Role of the Paris Agreement; and Part Two, Section I.A.2.c. Inadequate Justification in Europe and New Zealand for further discussion of this case.)

5. Rights-Based Case in the United States

Juliana v. United States is another case that advances rights-based arguments. In Juliana, 21 youth plaintiffs filed suit against the US government.[54] The plaintiffs wanted the government to develop a plan to phase out fossil fuel emissions and stabilize the climate system to protect vital resources upon which the plaintiffs depend.[55] The plaintiffs' key arguments were the following:

(i)   The nation's climate system is critical to their constitutional rights to life, liberty, and property.

(ii)   The government has violated substantive due process rights by allowing fossil fuel production, consumption, and combustion at dangerous levels.[56]

(iii) The government's failure to limit CO_2 emissions violates their constitutional right to equal protection before the law because plaintiffs are being denied fundamental rights afforded to prior and present generations.[57]

(iv)   The government has also violated the public trust doctrine and the common law duty on a sovereign to maintain the integrity of public trust resources within the sovereign's jurisdiction for present and future generations.[58]

A federal district court held that the plaintiffs had raised legitimate constitutional claims and found genuine issues of material fact that merited a trial.[59] The appellate court's reversal on standing grounds did not reach the merits of the claim. The plaintiffs have stated that they will seek further review. (See Part One, Section I.A.1. Standing and Climate Change in the United States for further discussion of this case.)

---

[54]   *Juliana v. United States*, 217 F. Supp. 3d 1224, 1248 (D. Or. 2016).

[55]   Footnote 54, p. 95.

[56]   Footnote 54, p. 85.

[57]   Footnote 54, p. 89.

[58]   Footnote 54, pp. 93–94.

[59]   *Juliana v. United States*, 339 F. Supp. 3d 1062 (D. Or., 2018).

B.   Asia and the Pacific Approaches

Asian courts have used constitutional rights to support environmental and, more recently, climate action.[60] This considerable volume of cases hinges on the premise that ecosystems and ecosystem services are the foundations for the full enjoyment of human rights.[61] Relevant rights include the rights to life, health, food, and safe drinking water. Environmental harm interferes with the enjoyment of these rights.[62] This is known as environmental constitutionalism, which traces its roots to international human rights instruments, and emerged in the legal lexicon at the 1972 Stockholm Convention on the Human Environment.[63]

1.   The Right to a Healthy Environment

a)   Life, Dignity, and Equality in South Asia

Asian courts have a wealth of jurisprudence that extends the right to life to a right to live with dignity in a healthy environment. Early cases in India included *Subhash Kumar v. State of Bihar and Ors.* and *Virender Gaur and Ors. v. State of Haryana and Ors.* Litigants have relied on this expanded right to life in a broad range of cases, including disputes challenging law and policy implementation, fossil fuel use and development, flood and disaster planning, and even town planning.

In *Subhash Kumar v. State of Bihar and Ors.* the Supreme Court of India held that the constitutional right to life included a right to pollution-free water and air, which was necessary for the full enjoyment of life.[64] (See Part Two, Section VII.B.2.a. Constitutional Rights in Fiji and South Asia for further discussion of this case.)

In *Virender Gaur and Ors. v. State of Haryana and Ors.*, the Supreme Court of India held that the constitutional rights to life and dignity included a right to a hygienic environment (footnote 27). It observed that the constitution commanded the state and citizens to maintain a hygienic environment for present and future generations. Further, human dignity relied on environmental protection and preservation to ensure a "hygienic atmosphere and ecological balance."[65]

---

[60] Climate action includes litigation raising an issue or fact about climate change causes or impacts. See J.B. Ruhl. 2015. What Is Climate Change Law? *OUPblog*. 22 August. Environmental action includes litigation seeking to protect the environment or restore impacts on the natural environment, including natural resources.

[61] A. Kreilhuber. 2017. New Frontiers in Global Environmental Constitutionalism. In E. Daly et al., eds. *New Frontiers in Environmental Constitutionalism*. Nairobi, Kenya: United Nations Environment Programme. p. 25.

[62] J. Knox. 2017. The United Nations Mandate on Human Rights and the Environment. In E. Daly et al., eds. *New Frontiers in Environmental Constitutionalism*. Nairobi, Kenya: United Nations Environment Programme. p. 17.

[63] E. Daly et al. 2017. Introduction to Environmental Constitutionalism. In E. Daly et al., eds. *New Frontiers in Environmental Constitutionalism*. Nairobi, Kenya: United Nations Environment Programme. p. 30. Courts have also cited the 1948 Universal Declaration of Human Rights.

[64] *Subhash Kumar v. State of Bihar and Ors.*, (1991) 1 SCC 598.

[65] Footnote 27, p. 580.

Citing Principle 1 of the Stockholm Declaration, the court held that environmental protection was a matter of grave concern. It was essential to humankind's well-being and the enjoyment of basic human rights.

(See Part One, Section I.B.2.b. Environmental Damage and Future Generations in South Asia for a full case summary of *Virender Gaur and Ors. v. State of Haryana and Ors.*; Part Three, Section I.B. Asia and the Pacific Approaches; and Part Three, Section I.B.1. Human Rights and Climate in the Philippines for further discussion of this case.)

Other courts in South Asia have adopted similar approaches. The Supreme Court of Bangladesh extended the right to life to a right to environmental protection and preservation in *M. Farooque Vs. Government of Bangladesh* (footnote 25). Public interest litigants argued that a government flood action plan would adversely affect more than 1 million people in the Tangail district. The court upheld the plan, but it also held that the constitutional right to life in Bangladesh encompassed "protection and preservation of environment, ecological balance free from pollution of air and water, [and] sanitation without which life can hardly be enjoyed."[66] (See Part One, Section I.B.2.a. Any-Person-Aggrieved Test in Bangladesh for a full case summary of *M. Farooque Vs. Government of Bangladesh.*)

The Supreme Court of Nepal tied environmental justice to the constitutional right to social justice in *Advocate Raju Prasad Chapagain vs Government of Nepal, Ministry of Agriculture and Cooperatives and Others*.[67] In that decision, the court confirmed there was a constitutional right to live in a clean environment, with a corresponding state responsibility to restrict adverse effects on the environment.

In 2015, the Supreme Court held that Nepal's constitutional right to life included all rights necessary for living a dignified life in *Advocate Prakash Mani Sharma vs Godavari Marble Industries Pvt. Ltd. and Others*.[68] It also clarified that a clean environment was essential to protecting the capacity of people to live with dignity. In 1994, the Supreme Court of Pakistan affirmed that the constitutional right to life included a right to a clean environment in *Shehla Zia v. WAPDA* (footnote 29). In that case, residents successfully challenged the development of an electricity substation. (See Part One, Section I.B.2.b. Environmental Damage and Future Generations in South Asia for a full case summary of *Shehla Zia v. WAPDA*.)

Sri Lanka's constitution does not explicitly include a right to life or environmental rights. However, article 12(1) grants citizens the right to equality before the law. In *Watte Gedara Wijebandara v Conservator General of Forests*, a petitioner disputed the government's decision to refuse his mining permit application.

---

[66] Footnote 25, p. 33, para. 101.
[67] *Advocate Raju Prasad Chapagain vs Government of Nepal, Ministry of Agriculture and Cooperatives and Others*, Nepal Kanoon Patrika (NPK) 2066 (2009), Part 10, Decision No. 8239.
[68] *Advocate Prakash Mani Sharma vs Godavari Marble Industries Pvt. Ltd. and Others*, Writ Petition 068-WO-0082 (Supreme Court of Nepal, 16 April 2015).

The Supreme Court held that the right to a clean environment and the principle of intergenerational equity were intrinsic to the right to equality before the law.[69]

b) Quality of Life in Southeast Asia

Southeast Asian courts have also contributed to the region's rich jurisprudence on environmental constitutionalism. The Court of Appeal of Malaysia determined that the constitutional right to life must incorporate all facets that are integral to life and quality of life. In *Tan Tek Seng v Suruhanjaya Perkhidmatan Pendidikan & Anor.*, the court said that citizens had a right to live in a reasonably healthy and pollution-free environment.[70]

The Philippine constitution contains the right to life. It also directs the state to "protect and advance the right of the people to a balanced and healthful ecology."[71] But that requirement to protect ecology falls within the state directive principles and not within the bill of rights. Nevertheless, the Supreme Court of the Philippines held that the right to a healthy environment was fundamental in *Oposa v. Factoran* (footnote 17). Such a right "belongs to a different category of rights altogether for it concerns nothing less than self-preservation and self-perpetuation" and need not be written in a constitution because it is "assumed to exist from the inception of humankind" (footnote 17).

(See Part One, Section I.A.1. Standing and Climate Change in the United States for a full case summary of *Oposa v. Factoran*. *Oposa* is also discussed in Part One, Section II.B.2.a. Climate Justice in the Philippines and Pakistan; Part Two, Section VIII.B.1. Timber Licenses in the Philippines; and Part Five, Section VI.A. Children and Deforestation.)

Asian courts place a clear emphasis on the fundamental right to live in an environment that supports present and future generations' life with dignity. This approach has clear implications for climate justice.

2. Mandating Government Climate Change Action

a) Climate Justice in the Philippines and Pakistan

If looked at through a climate lens, *Oposa v. Factoran* can be seen as an early Asian climate change case (footnote 17). The petitioners requested cancellation of all government-issued timber licenses because they were causing mass deforestation and irreparable environmental damage. The complaint argued that deforestation impaired Earth's capacity to absorb CO_2, leading to global warming. Deforestation also caused impacts like water shortages, droughts, and increased vulnerability to typhoons.

---

[69] *Watte Gedara Wijebandara v Conservator General of Forests* 2009 1 Sri LR 337, p. 356.
[70] *Tan Tek Seng v Suruhanjaya Perkhidmatan Pendidikan & Anor.* [1996] 1 MLJ 261.
[71] The Constitution of the Republic of the Philippines, 1987, art. II, sec. 16.

In granting the petition, the Supreme Court of the Philippines accepted the petitioners' fundamental right to protect the environment, founded on the twin concepts of intergenerational responsibility and intergenerational justice. It held that each generation has a duty to "preserve the rhythm and harmony of nature," including by conserving forests.[72] Without forests, "environmental balance would be [irreversibly] disrupted" (footnote 17).

(See Part One, Section I.A.1. Standing and Climate Change in the United States for a full case summary of *Oposa v. Factoran*. *Oposa* is also discussed in Part One, Section II.B.1.b. Quality of Life in Southeast Asia; Part One, Section II.B.2.a. Climate Justice in the Philippines and Pakistan; Part Two, Section VIII.B.1. Timber Licenses in the Philippines; and Part Five, Section VI.A. Children and Deforestation.)

One of Asia's most prominent climate change cases builds on environmental constitutionalism and the right to life. In *Leghari v. Federation of Pakistan*, a farmer sued his government because it implemented neither its National Climate Change Policy 2012 nor its Framework for Implementation of Climate Change Policy 2013.[73] Leghari argued that the government should pursue climate mitigation or adaptation efforts, and that the government's failure to meet its climate change adaptation targets had resulted in immediate impacts on Pakistan's water, food, and energy security. Such impacts offended his fundamental right to life.

The court agreed, describing climate change as a defining challenge of our time. The court reasoned that the constitutional rights to life and human dignity (under articles 9 and 14 of the constitution) included the right to a healthy and clean environment. Further, interpretation of these fundamental rights must be guided by (i) the constitutional values of democracy, equality, and social, economic, and political justice; and (ii) international environmental principles of sustainable development, precautionary principle, intergenerational and intragenerational equity, and the doctrine of public trust.[74]

Although the government had formulated a climate change policy and implementation framework, the court concluded there had been no real progress with implementation. To oversee the execution of the policy, the court constituted the Climate Change Commission and required it to submit regular progress reports.[75] The commission's final report in 2018 stated that 66% of the priority items within the implementation framework were complete.[76] After dissolving the commission, the court constituted a standing committee, creating an ongoing link between the court and the executive.

---

[72] Footnote 17; Constitution of the Republic of the Philippines, 1987, art. II, sec. 16.
[73] *Leghari v. Federation of Pakistan*, PLD 2018 Lahore 364.
[74] Footnote 73, para. 12.
[75] Footnote 73, para. 13.
[76] Footnote 73, para. 19.

In its final order, the court nominated climate justice as the successor to environmental justice.[77]

Environmental justice—said the court—revolved around enforcing national laws, with decisions informed by international legal principles. It focused on shifting or stopping pollutive industries.[78] Climate justice, as the court envisioned it, adopted a human-centered approach. It linked human rights with development. It sought to safeguard the rights of vulnerable peoples and share "the burdens and benefits of climate change and its impacts equitably and fairly."[79] Climate justice was "informed by science, responds to science and acknowledges the need for equitable stewardship of the world's resources" (footnote 79). However, realizing that climate justice was challenging, the court acknowledged that polluters often fell beyond national borders and were difficult to identify. Finally, the court outlined its vision for water justice as a human right to access clean water and a sub-concept of climate justice.

(Water justice is discussed further in Part Two, Section VII.B.3. Water Justice is Climate Justice in Pakistan; and Part Four, Section I.B.1.a. Climate and Water Justice in Pakistan.)

Leghari v. Federation of Pakistan is significant, not just for being Pakistan's first climate change case, but also because the court emphasized how climate change strategies involve many stakeholders. For example, the court-constituted Climate Change Commission included members from key institutions.

> " Enter Climate Change. With this the construct of Environmental Justice requires reconsideration. Climate Justice links human rights and development to achieve a human-centered approach, safeguarding the rights of the most vulnerable people and sharing the burdens and benefits of climate change and its impacts equitably and fairly. Climate justice is informed by science, responds to science and acknowledges the need for equitable stewardship of the world's resources. The instant case adds a new dimension to the rich jurisprudence on environmental Justice in our country. Climate Change has moved the debate from a linear local environmental issue to a more complex global problem. In this context of climate change, the identity of the polluter is not clearly ascertainable and by and large falls outside the national jurisdiction.
>
> Source: *Leghari v. Federation of Pakistan*, PLD 2018 Lahore 364, para. 21.

---

[77] Footnote 73, paras. 20–22.
[78] Footnote 73, para. 20.
[79] Footnote 73, para. 21.

Similarly, by regularly reviewing the commission's progress, the court helped ensure the effective and timely implementation of its judgment. (See Part Two, Section VII.B.3. Water Justice is Climate Justice in Pakistan; and Part Four Section I.B.1.a. Climate and Water Justice in Pakistan for further discussion of this case.)

b) Existential Threat and Intergenerational Equity in South Asia

In Nepal, Padam Bahadur Shrestha sought greater government climate change action in *Advocate Padam Bahadur Shrestha vs Prime Minister and Office of Council of Ministers and Others*.[80] His petition argued that climate change was an existential threat, endangering all humankind, animals, flora, and ecology. The government's failure to enact climate legislation and effectively implement its Climate Change Policy of 2011 was amplifying this existential threat. The existential threat created by climate change impaired his constitutional rights to (i) live with dignity, (ii) live in a healthy and clean environment, (iii) access basic healthcare services, and (iv) food and protection from starvation.[81] The petitioner further argued that a specific climate change law was needed as the Environment Protection Act made no provision for climate change mitigation and adaptation. He contended that the gap must be rectified immediately.

Gosainkunda Lake in Nepal's Langtang National Park. The Supreme Court of Nepal concluded that climate change is an existential threat endangering all humankind, animals, flora, and ecology (photo by Sergey Pesterev).

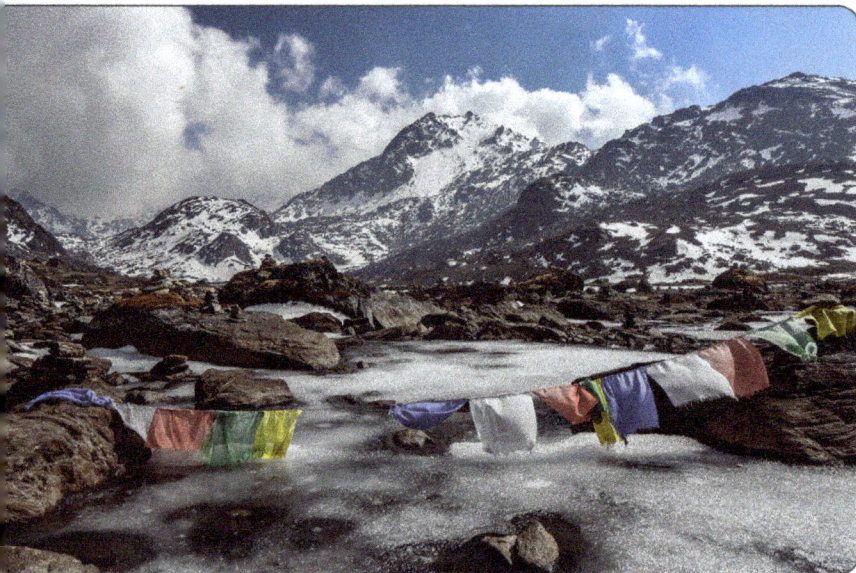

Ruling in favor of the petitioner, the Supreme Court of Nepal concluded that action was needed to ensure climate justice, sustainable development, and intrageneration and intergeneration justice. Nepal's commitments under multilateral climate change treaties and the operation of the 2015 constitution required action. Article 51(g) of the Constitution of Nepal obligated the government to protect the environment. The court concluded that climate change impaired the petitioner's constitutional right to a dignified life and a clean and healthy environment.[82]

The court issued a writ of mandamus, ordering the government to pass and implement a climate change law immediately. Further, pending passage of the climate change law, the court directed the government to implement its climate change policy, National Adaptation Programme of Action 2010, and National Framework on Local Adaptation Plans for Action 2011.

In *Ridhima Pandey v. Union of India and Another*, a 9-year-old petitioner pushed

---

[80] *Advocate Padam Bahadur Shrestha vs Prime Minister and Office of Council of Ministers and Others*, Case No. 074-WO-0283, Supreme Court of Nepal, 25 December 2018 (2075/09/10 BS).
[81] Constitution of Nepal of 2015, articles 16, 30, 35, and 36.
[82] Constitution of Nepal of 2015, article 16 grants people the right to live with dignity, and article 30 grants people the right to a healthy and clean environment.

for climate action based on her constitutional rights in the National Green Tribunal (NGT) of India.[83] Pandey argued that she, along with all children and future generations, had the right to a healthy environment under the principle of intergenerational equity (footnote 83). She asserted that the public trust doctrine, as well as India's laws and policies, obliged the government to take effective and science-based measures to mitigate and adapt to climate change. While the government had issued many pronouncements, policies, and plans, it had implemented none adequately. Consequently, India was experiencing rising sea levels, climate-induced migration, changed precipitation patterns, melting glaciers, as well as negative impacts on mangroves and agriculture.

Pandey also argued that climate change affects children disproportionately.[84] Children were more vulnerable to impacts like heat waves, displacement, diseases, and malnutrition. As climate was an inherent part of the environment, she asserted that safeguarding the environment and protecting forests was critical to addressing climate change.

Pandey requested orders that required (i) the inclusion of climate change assessments in environmental impact assessments (EIAs), (ii) holistic assessments of requests to convert forests, and (iii) the creation of a national GHG emissions inventory and carbon budget up to 2050. A carbon budget would ensure India's contribution to reducing atmospheric CO_2 to 350 parts per million (ppm) by 2100, a threshold prescribed by the "best available climate science."[85] The 350-ppm threshold emerged in 2008. Ten climate scientists published a study asserting that the "preservation of a climate resembling that to which humanity is accustomed, the climate of the Holocene," required a reduction of global atmospheric CO_2 levels to 350 ppm.[86]

In January 2019, the NGT dismissed the claim with a two-page decision.[87] It held that government authorities were obligated to conduct EIAs in accordance with the Environment (Protection) Act, 1986. Climate change must be considered under the statutory scheme. As the petitioner was not challenging the EIA scheme itself, the NGT did not issue any of the requested directions. It did not otherwise address Pandey's arguments.

(See Part One, Section III.B.1. Climate Change Commitments in South Asia; Part One, Section IV.B.1. International Commitments in Settled Cases in South Asia; and Part Five, Section VI.B. Children and Disproportionate Impacts of Climate on Their Future for further discussion of this case.)

---

[83] *Ridhima Pandey v. Union of India & Another*, Original Application No. 187 of 2017 (National Green Tribunal, 15 January 2019). Paragraphs 7–12 of the petition dated 25 March 2017 identify the obligations under the Paris Agreement.

[84] Footnote 83, p. 25, ground (C).

[85] Footnote 83, pp. 3 and 49–50.

[86] J. Hansen et al. 2008. Target Atmospheric CO_2: Where Should Humanity Aim? *The Open Atmospheric Science Journal*. 2. p. 226.

[87] Footnote 83.

3. Pending Constitutional and Rights-Based Cases

a) The Energy Sector in Pakistan

A young girl in Pakistan challenged the government's plan to exploit untapped coal reserves in the Thar Desert in *Ali v. Federation of Pakistan & Another* (footnote 30). She argued that exploitation of the Thar coalfields would release approximately 327 billion tons of CO_2, more than 1,000 times Pakistan's previous estimate for annual GHG emissions. Coal mining in the Thar Desert would also worsen air pollution, impact water quality, and displace residents. She claimed that thousands of Thari people were driven from their land in violation of their right to property, dignity, and equal protection before the law. The petition argued that Pakistan could potentially use renewable energy to power all of its energy needs, including in the transport, industrial, and agriculture sectors. Ali also sought protection for mangroves for sequestering carbon and protecting against sea level rise.

Ali maintained that exploiting the coalfields would further destabilize the climate system and infringe citizens' constitutional rights to life, liberty, dignity, information, equal protection before the law, among others. The right to life, she argued, included an "inalienable right to a stable climate system" void of dangerous levels of CO_2.[88]

The petitioner also asserted that increasing Pakistan's GHG emissions was criminally negligent and would violate the doctrine of public trust. The doctrine of public trust meant the respondents had a "non-discretionary, fiduciary duty to help reduce atmospheric CO_2 levels in order to conserve and protect the atmosphere, restore the stability of the Climate [*sic*] system and restore the energy balance of mother Earth at large."[89] Ali noted that Pakistan committed to and was bound by the UN Framework Convention on Climate Change (UNFCCC) and the Paris Agreement. While she acknowledged that Pakistan could not solve climate change alone, she said that it must do its fair share to keep atmospheric CO_2 concentrations within the safe level. This case remains sub judice.

(See Part One, Section I.B.2.b. Environmental Damage and Future Generations in South Asia; Part One, Section IV.B.2. International Commitments in Pending Cases in South Asia; Part Two, Section I.B.1.b. Constitutional Rights in Pakistan; and Part Three, Section III.B.2. Coal-Fired Electricity in Pakistan for further discussion of this case.)

In *Maria Khan et al. v. Federation of Pakistan et al.*, five women argued that the national government's failure to reduce emissions in the energy sector violated their constitutional rights.[90] Further, as climate change would disproportionately

---

[88] Footnote 30, p. 37, ground (a).
[89] Footnote 30, p. 31, ground (v).
[90] *Maria Khan et al. v. Pakistan et al.*, Writ Petition No. 8960 of 2019, High Court of Lahore.

affect women, the government's climate inaction offended the constitutional right of women to equal protection before the law. The petitioners specifically targeted the need for mitigation action.[91] They contended that (i) reducing fossil fuel combustion and switching to green energy sources, and (ii) developing carbon sinks to sequester carbon were the two main climate mitigation measures.

Emissions reductions in the energy sector were critical, according to the petitioners, as the sector was responsible for 47% of Pakistan's total emissions. In Pakistan's 2016 NDC, the government committed to a 20% reduction of its 2030 projected GHG emissions. Despite this, petitioners maintained that respondents had neither prioritized clean energy projects nor approved a renewable energy project since December 2017. The petitioners alleged that this failure betrayed the government's "stated commitment under the Paris Agreement to encourage and foster the development of renewable energy sources" (footnote 91).

Khan et al. also argued that the respondents violated the public trust doctrine and principle of intergenerational equity, as well as the concept of climate justice developed in *Leghari v. Federation of Pakistan*. The petitioners sought orders declaring that the government must support renewable energy projects and enforce the Paris Agreement in letter and spirit. This case is sub judice.

(See Part One, Section III.B.1. Climate Change Commitments in South Asia; Part One, Section IV.B.2. International Commitments in Pending Cases in South Asia; and Part Five, Section V.A. Impacts on Women from Alleged Climate Inaction for further discussion of this case.)

b) The Transport Sector in the Philippines

Most countries in Asia and the Pacific rely on fossil fuels for energy and transport. Despite the increasing availability, falling cost, and lower emissions of renewable energies, fossil fuels still dominate energy production.[92] In 2010, the transport sector produced 23% of total energy-related CO_2 emissions, with road transport contributing 72% of those emissions.[93] Oil dominated the transport sector. In 2010, 94% of the world's transport consumed over 53% of primary oil.[94]

Litigants in the Philippines challenged fossil fuel use in cars based on the legal principles of the right to life and the right to a clean and healthy environment. In *Henares v. Land Transportation Franchising and Regulatory Board*, petitioners requested mandamus orders compelling the government to require all public road

---

[91]   Footnote 90, para. 2.
[92]   J.L. Sawin et al. 2017. *Renewables 2017 Global Status Report*. Paris: Renewable Energy Policy Network for the 21st Century.
[93]   R. Sims et al. 2014. Transport. In O. Edenhofer et al., eds. *Climate Change 2014: Mitigation of Climate Change. Contribution of Working Group III to the Fifth Assessment Report of the Intergovernmental Panel on Climate Change*. Cambridge, United Kingdom and New York, US: Cambridge University Press. p. 603 and Figure 8.1 on p. 606.
[94]   Footnote 93, p. 608.

transport to use compressed natural gas (footnote 20). Fossil fuels increased air pollution and led to detrimental health effects for the public. The petitioners contended they had a constitutional right to breathe clean air, which the government had failed to protect.

The court agreed that the right to clean air was not only "an issue of paramount importance to petitioners for it concerns the air they breathe, but it is also impressed with public interest."[95] However, the court dismissed the petition for lack of available remedies. It concluded that courts were constrained to issuing mandamus orders to compel a duty specifically ordered by law. In this case, there was no law mandating government authorities to require motor vehicle owners to use compressed natural gas.

(See Part One, Section I.B.1.b. Transcendental Importance and the Standing of Mammals in the Philippines for further discussion of this case.)

In 2017, a decade later, petitioners again sued the Government of the Philippines, seeking to reduce air pollution from vehicular emissions in *Segovia et al. v. Climate Change Commission et al.*[96] They argued that the government's failure to address air pollution was prejudicing life, health, and the property of all Filipinos. Petitioners alleged that the government should reduce "personal and official consumption of fossil fuels" by at least 50%.[97] They asserted that the government should (i) reduce vehicular traffic by implementing road sharing with pedestrians and cyclists, (ii) devote public open spaces to sustainable urban farming, and (iii) allocate more budget to mitigating environmental pollution.

The petition failed. The court accepted the government's evidence that it was implementing environmental laws and prioritizing programs aimed at addressing and mitigating climate change. (See Part One, Section III.B.3. Transport Emissions Reduction Commitments in the Philippines; and Part Two, Section V.B.2.b. Road Sharing in the Philippines for further discussion of this case.)

c) Glacier Protection in South Asia

Courts have also expressed their concern regarding climate impacts to glaciers, especially their retreat and role in water security. See Box 1 for a discussion of climate impacts to Asia's glaciers, their role in providing fresh water, and the rate at which Asian mountain glaciers would melt by 2100 under different warming scenarios.

---

95 Footnote 20, per Quisumbing J.
96 *Segovia et al. v. Climate Change Commission et al.*, G.R. No. 211010, 7 March 2017.
97 Footnote 96, p. 5.

Box 1: Shrinking Asian Glaciers

Earth's glaciers store around 69% of its fresh water.[a] Asia's glaciers store the largest quantities of frozen water outside the poles.[b] Across Asia, up to 800 million people rely on glacier meltwater for drinking water, irrigation, industry, navigation, and hydroelectric power.[c] Up to 221 million people rely on seasonal meltwater for their basic needs (footnote c). During droughts, glacial meltwater is a major source of water for the upper Indus, Aral, and Chu/Issyk-Kul river basins (footnote c). But, warming in the Asian mountains is higher than the global average (footnote b).

Glaciers are melting faster than previously projected, including by the IPCC.[d] A recent study estimates that glaciers are melting at 1.6 times the balance rate—the melting is outpacing snowfall (footnote c). If the world limits warming to 1.5°C, Asian mountain glaciers will lose around one-third of their mass by 2100.[e] They could lose almost half of their mass if warming reaches 3.5°C and two-thirds of their mass if the world does not curb warming.[f]

Everest Base Camp and the Khumbu Icefall, Nepal
(photo by v2osk).

IPCC = Intergovernmental Panel on Climate Change.

[a] National Snow and Ice Data Center. All About Glaciers; and United States Geological Survey. The Distribution of Water On, In, and Above the Earth.

[b] Agence France-Presse. 2017. Asia's Glaciers to Shrink by a Third by 2100, Threatening Water Supply of Millions. *The Guardian*. 14 September.

[c] H. Pritchard. 2019. Asia's Shrinking Glaciers Protect Large Populations from Drought Stress. *Nature: International Journal of Science*. 569 (7758). pp. 649–654; C. Gramling. 2019. Himalayan Glacier Melting Threatens Water Security for Millions of People. *ScienceNews*. 29 May.

[d] M. Zemp et al. 2019. Global Glacier Mass Changes and Their Contributions to Sea-Level Rise from 1961 to 2016. *Nature: International Journal of Science*. 568 (7752). pp. 382–386. Authors referred to key reports cited by the IPCC in its report *Global Warming of 1.5°C. An IPCC Special Report*; P. Deneen. 2019. Glaciers Account for More Sea Level Rise Than Previously Thought. *GlacierHub*. 24 April.

[e] J.G. Cogley. 2017. The Future of Asia's Glaciers. Nature: International Journal of Science. 549 (7671). pp. 166–167.

[f] Climate Action Tracker. 2018. Some Progress since Paris, But Not Enough, as Governments Amble towards 3°C of Warming.

Source: Authors.

In India, in *Court on its own Motion v. State of Himachal Pradesh and Others*, the NGT issued directions to protect the glaciers of Himachal Pradesh.[98] Tourism-related traffic pollution was causing air pollution, affecting glaciers in Manali, Himachal Pradesh. Increased traffic emitted unburned hydrocarbon and carbon soot, blackening snow cover in the mountains.[99] Citing various studies, the NGT reported that 40% of glacial retreat could be attributed to black carbon—soot, a by-product of agricultural waste and vehicles.[100] Another study from 1990–2001 showed that the Parbati Glacier in Himachal Pradesh had receded at the rate of 52 meters per year.[101]

The NGT observed that excess atmospheric CO_2 was causing global warming, with emissions stemming from industries, power stations, and motor vehicles. In India, global warming would cause early ice melt. The court considered there was a need for mechanisms to protect glaciers "in the interest of environmental and ecological balance."[102]

Reasoning that the "citizens of the country have a fundamental right to a wholesome, clean and decent environment," the NGT passed directives to protect the eco-sensitive glacial region.[103] The directives included ways to address vehicular pollution, deforestation, cleanliness and hygiene of the environment, as well as general directions to prevent and control environmental degradation and damage in the glacial region.[104]

The High Court of Uttarakhand acted to protect Himalayan glaciers from fossil fuel pollution and environmental degradation in *Tara Singh Rajput v. State of Uttarakhand*.[105] The petitioners argued that indiscriminate tree cutting and unauthorized constructions were damaging the fragile Bhimtal Lake area. Concerned about glaciers, the court also discussed the impacts of climate change and fossil fuel pollution. Declining snowfall and ice melt due to climate change meant that that glaciers were rapidly retreating. Shrinking glaciers would mean reduced river flows in the future, causing immense hardship to communities that rely on rivers for water.

In the face of such dire consequences, the court reasoned that everyone had a duty to protect the glaciers and restore them to their pristine glory. It issued orders regulating construction and sewerage treatment. The orders also banned plastic use, fossil fuel use, logging, and the open burning of garbage near glaciers. Noting that it had taken nature millions of years to form the glaciers, society could not permit glaciers to be "lost forever by one or two reckless/irresponsible generations."[106]

---

[98] *Court on its own Motion v. State of Himachal Pradesh and Others*, Application No. 237(THC)/2013 (CWPIL No. 15 of 2010), Application No. 238(THC)/2013 (CWP No. 5087 of 2011), and Application No. 239(THC)/2013 (CWP No. 5088 of 2011), (National Green Tribunal, 6 February 2014).

[99] Footnote 98, para. 7.

[100] Footnote 98, paras. 4–5.

[101] Footnote 98, para. 4.

[102] Footnote 98, para. 34.

[103] Footnote 98, paras. 11–12.

[104] Footnote 98, paras. 23–24, 30, and 38.

[105] *Tara Singh Rajput v. State of Uttarakhand*, (2016) SCC OnLine Utt 1730.

[106] Footnote 105, para 23.

(See Part Four, Section I.B.2.c. Protecting Adaptive Capacity of Inland Water Bodies for further discussion of this case.)

4. Rights of Nature and Climate Change Litigation

Nature often takes the back seat in an ever-increasing anthropocentric world. In a 2018 report, the IPCC projected the impact on habitats for 105,000 species of a global average warming of 1.5°C.[107] Species that will lose more than half of their habitat—their "climatically determined geographic range"—include 6% of insects, 8% of plants, and 4% of vertebrates (footnote 107). With a 2°C warming, the percentage of species that will lose over half of their habitats will at least double.

Extending the constitutional protection on the right to life to animals could be an effective tool in protecting diversity and boosting ecosystem resilience to climate change. By linking constitutional rights with animal rights, Asian jurisprudence has value for all jurisdictions in this era of climate change.

a) Animals in South Asia

In *Animal Welfare Board of India v. A. Nagaraja and Ors.*, the Supreme Court of India held that every species has a constitutional right to life and security, subject to laws permitting the deprivation of an animal's life for human necessity.[108] The court reasoned that an animal's right to life meant "something more than mere survival," existence, or being of instrumental value for human beings (footnote 108). Animals had a right to lead a life of some intrinsic worth, with honor and dignity, and with fair treatment.[109] When considering the combined rights granted by the constitution and the Prevention of Cruelty to Animals Act, 1960, the court held that animals had a right to live in a healthy and clean atmosphere.

In *Centre for Environment Law, WWF-I v. Union of India and Others*, the Supreme Court of India weighed the rights of the endangered Asiatic lions to a second habitat.[110] The court considered that conserving and protecting the environment "is an inseparable part of [the] right to life."[111] Human beings thus have a constitutional obligation to protect a species from extinction. The court reasoned that the "species best interest standard" (an eco-centric approach) should drive habitat selection for the Asiatic lion.[112]

These decisions provide useful examples of the scope for climate cases hinged on animal rights. While few jurisdictions in Asia and the Pacific have expanded

---

[107] IPCC. 2018. Summary for Policymakers. In V. Masson-Delmotte et al., eds. *Global Warming of 1.5°C. An IPCC Special Report*. In press. para. B3.1, p. SPM–10.

[108] *Animal Welfare Board of India v. A. Nagaraja and Ors.*, (2014) 7 SCC 547. The case concerned the use of bulls in the Jallikattu festival and bullock cart races.

[109] Footnote 108, para. 72.

[110] *Centre for Environment Law, WWF-I v. Union of India (UOI) and Ors.*, (2013) 8 SCC 234.

[111] Footnote 110, para. 48.

[112] Footnote 110, para. 49.

the right to life to cover animals, these decisions provide judicial guidance on making such a finding. Further, where a jurisdiction recognizes that environmental protection is integral to a human's constitutional right to life, courts might acknowledge the importance of protecting other species and their habitats from climate change because ecosystems rely on collaboration between species. Failing ecosystems will undermine the capacity of nearby life to flourish.

b) Water Bodies in South Asia

Recognizing the need to protect biodiversity, Indian courts have granted legal rights and status to rivers.

Mohd. Salim v. State of Uttarakhand and Ors. concerned the legal status of the rivers Ganga and Yamuna.[113] The High Court of Uttarakhand declared that the rivers—including their tributaries and streams—were juristic entities, "with all corresponding rights, duties and liabilities of a living person in order to preserve and conserve river Ganga and Yamuna."[114] The court directed the state government to establish the Ganga Management Board in cooperation with the central government.[115] Failure to act at the state level would entitle the central government to step in. The court considered such steps necessary as the rivers "are losing their very existence."[116] The state government appealed this decision to the Supreme Court of India, which has issued interim orders staying the high court's decision.[117]

The High Court of Uttarakhand again granted legal status to water bodies and terrestrial ecosystems in *Lalit Miglani v. State of Uttarakhand*.[118] It held that glaciers, rivers, lakes, other water bodies, forests, meadows, valleys, jungles, wetlands, grasslands, and air were legal entities. They had, said the court, "a right to exist, persist, maintain, sustain and regenerate their own vital ecology system. The rivers are not just water bodies. These are scientifically and biologically living" (footnote 118). Hence, the court considered that humans had a constitutional, legal, and moral duty to protect the environment and ecology.[119]

The court declared high-ranking government officials as guardians responsible for protecting, conserving, and preserving glaciers, rivers, lakes, other water bodies, forests, meadows, valleys, jungles, wetlands, grasslands, and air within Uttarakhand. The court also directed the officials to uphold the status of these biological systems and promote their health and well-being.

---

[113] *Mohd. Salim v. State of Uttarakhand and Ors.*, W.P. (PIL), 126/2014 (Uttarakhand High Court, 20 March 2017).

[114] Footnote 113, para. 19.

[115] Footnote 113, paras. 19–20.

[116] Footnote 113, para. 10.

[117] *The State of Uttarakhand v. Mohd. Salim*, I.A., No. 125697/2017 (Supreme Court of India, 8 January 2018); Environmental Law Alliance Worldwide. 2017. Case Summary: Salim v. State of Uttarakhand.

[118] *Lalit Miglani v. State of Uttarakhand*, (2017) SCC Online UTT 392. para. 63.

[119] Footnote 118, paras. 39, 47, and 59.

III. Statutory and Policy Commitments

As national governments increase their commitment to climate change through legislation, regulation, and policy, governments are increasingly being taken to court for failing to enforce climate-related domestic law and executive decisions. As the High Court of New Zealand noted in *Thomson v Minister for Climate Change Issues*, "it may be appropriate for domestic courts to play a role in government decision making about climate change policy."[120] This section describes legal attempts to hold governments accountable for failing to comply with domestic law or executive decisions.

A. Global Approaches

1. Violating the Law in Europe

In *Notre Affaire à Tous and Others v. France*, four NGOs sent a letter of formal notice to the Government of France. The letter initiated the first stage in a legal proceeding against the French government for inadequate action on climate change.[121] The plaintiffs alleged that the government's failure to implement proper measures to effectively address climate change violated its statutory duty to act.[122] The plaintiffs argued that the state has "specific" obligations to mitigate GHG emissions under EU and national law as well as specific obligations to prepare for the impacts of climate change in France.[123]

Following principles established in the *Urgenda* case—the first case to order a state to limit emissions for reasons other than statutory mandates—the plaintiffs pointed to further obligations of the state to act on climate change to uphold the rights to life, privacy, and family under the European Convention on Human Rights (ECHR).[124] The plaintiffs sought to enjoin the government to remedy its inadequate action on climate change.[125] The case is pending.

(See Part One, Section IV.A.2. Reducing Emissions in Canada and France; and Part Four, Section I.A.1. A Violation of Human Rights in Australia and France for further discussion of *Notre Affaire à Tous and Others v. France*. See also Part One, Section II.A.2. The Right to Private and Family Life in the Netherlands for a full case summary of *Urgenda*. *Urgenda* is also discussed in Part Three, Section III.A. Global Approaches: A Duty of Care in the Netherlands.)

In *R (Friends of the Earth) v Secretary of State for Transport & Others*, an environmental charity and 11 citizen claimants alleged that the Government of the United Kingdom (UK) violated the Climate Change Act 2008, as well as other domestic law, by

---

[120] *Thomson v Minister for Climate Change Issues* [2017] NZHC 733 para 133.
[121] Letter of Formal Notice to Officials, *Notre Affaire à Tous and Others v. France* (filed Dec. 17, 2018).
[122] Footnote 121, p. 1.
[123] Footnote 121, p. 15.
[124] Footnote 121, pp. 18–19.
[125] Footnote 121, pp. 40–41.

failing to revise its 2050 carbon emissions reduction target in keeping with the Paris Agreement and the latest climate science.[126] The High Court decided that the claims were not legitimate and denied permission for the case to proceed.[127]

The Court of Appeal reversed the High Court's decision. It held that the secretary failed to consider the Paris Agreement goals as part of the government's policy on climate change when preparing the airport national policy statement. This omission violated the Planning Act, 2008 and the requirement to prepare a strategic environmental impact assessment under EC Council Directive 2001/42/EC. The decision approving the third runway at Heathrow was, therefore, without legal effect. (See also Part One, Section IV. The Role of the Paris Agreement.)

In *Friends of the Irish Environment CLG v Government of Ireland & Ors*, an environmental advocacy group filed suit in the High Court of Ireland, alleging that the Irish government's approval of the 2017 National Mitigation Plan violated Ireland's Climate Action and Low Carbon Development Act 2015, the Constitution of Ireland, and the right to life and the right to private and family life guaranteed under the ECHR.[128] The plaintiffs argued that the National Mitigation Plan, which aimed to cut GHG emissions by 80% by 2050 compared to 1990 levels, would not achieve substantial emissions reduction within the next few decades, and requested that the High Court order the government to write a new plan (footnote 128). The court ruled for the government, and the case is now on appeal.

In *Family Farmers and Greenpeace Germany v Germany*, three German families and Greenpeace Germany filed suit in the Administrative Court of Berlin. They argued that the Government of Germany had violated their constitutional rights and EU law by failing to take sufficient action to meet its 2020 GHG emissions reduction target set by the Climate Protection Program 2020.[129]

The German government had calculated that it would miss its goal to reduce emissions by 0% by 2020, compared to 1990 levels, according to the pleadings.[130] The plaintiffs argued that this failure undermined their human rights under article 2(2) (right to life and health), article 12(1) (occupational freedom), and article 14(1) (right to property) of the German constitution,[131] and violated Germany's minimum obligations under the EU Effort Sharing Decision (406/2009/EC).[132] The plaintiffs sought government enforcement of the national climate protection target to reduce GHG emissions in Germany up to the year 2020 by 40%, relative to 1990 levels.[133]

---

[126] *R (Friends of the Earth) v Secretary of State for Transport & Others* [2020] EWCA Civ 214.

[127] *Plan B Earth and Others v Secretary of State for Transport* [2019] EWHC 1070 (Admin).

[128] *Friends of the Irish Environment CLG v Government of Ireland & Ors* 2018/291 JR.

[129] *Family Farmers and Greenpeace Germany v Germany*, Administrative Court of Berlin, Oct. 25, 2018, Case No. 00271/17/R /SP. For an English translation, please see Sabin Center for Climate Change. Family Farmers and Greenpeace Germany v. Germany.

[130] Footnote 129, pp. 4–5.

[131] Footnote 129, pp. 8–9.

[132] Footnote 129, pp. 5–6.

[133] Footnote 129, p. 6.

Family Farmers was the first climate lawsuit to refer to the recent publication of the IPCC special report *Global Warming of 1.5°C* (footnote 133). (See also Part One, Section IV. The Role of the Paris Agreement.)

2. Urging Better Regulation to Protect Against Bushfires in Australia

In April 2020, Bushfire Survivors for Climate Action sued the New South Wales Environment Protection Authority under the New South Wales Protection of the Environment Operations Act, 1997.[134] The plaintiffs asserted that they were harmed by the 2019–2020 bushfires, which climate change intensified. The plaintiffs sought to compel the authority to "create environmental quality objectives with respect to greenhouse gas emissions, regulate the pollution and use their existing powers to do so."[135] In November 2020, the court ruled that it would hear climate change evidence from Australia's former chief scientist.

B. Asia and the Pacific Approaches

In Asia, fewer litigants have relied upon legal and policy commitments to push for climate change action. Litigants have focused on national action planning; environmental impact schemes; and forestry, renewable energy, and transportation policy commitments to compel more ambitious climate action. The authors found no evidence of litigation in the Pacific based on legal and policy commitments.

1. Climate Change Commitments in South Asia

Given the inevitable impacts of climate change, governments must ensure that adequate planning and preparations are made. Climate change action plans in India were the issue in *Gaurav Kumar Bansal v. Union of India & Ors.*[136] The petitioner sued the central government over its failure to implement the national action plan on climate change. He sought orders requiring the central government to disclose all steps taken to implement the national action plan on climate change. He also requested orders requiring state governments to act in accordance with the national action plan.

The Ministry of Environment and Forests responded that some state-level plans had been approved, while others had been submitted for approval. The ministry also requested different states to implement and act in accordance with the national plan.

---

[134] Sabin Center for Climate Change Law. Bushfire Survivors for Climate Action Incorporated v. Environment Protection Authority (accessed 14 November 2020).

[135] A. Reardon and J. Hunt. 2020. NSW Fire Survivors Take EPA to Court in Push to Force Action on Climate Change. *ABC News*. 20 April.

[136] *Gaurav Kumar Bansal v. Union of India & Ors.*, Original Application No. 498 of 2014 (National Green Tribunal, 23 July 2015).

The NGT directed the states to prepare their respective draft plans and have them approved expeditiously. The tribunal also invited the petitioner to file a specific case for violation of the national action plan, should the need arise. (See Part Four, Section I.B.1.b. Adaptation Plans in South Asia for further discussion of this case.)

Ridhima Pandey argued that the central government's climate change response was ineffective in *Ridhima Pandey v. Union of India & Another* (footnote 83). She contended that the definition of "environment" under the Environment (Protection) Act, 1986 included the climate within its ambit. Further, if the government implemented effective, science-based measures under India's existing environmental legal framework, it could mitigate climate impacts.[137] Pandey claimed that India's EIA scheme required project proponents to divulge information on how their project would impact the climate. However, she claimed that responsible government agencies had been lax when assessing this requirement.

The NGT did not grant Pandey's claim. It held that climate change was covered under the existing EIA scheme.[138] Further, as the petition did not challenge the scheme itself, the NGT considered it unnecessary to issue any directions.

(See Part One, Section II.B.2.b. Existential Threat and Intergenerational Equity in South Asia for a full case summary of *Ridhima Pandey v. Union of India & Another*; Part One, Section IV.B.1. International Commitments in Settled Cases in South Asia; and Part Five, Section VI.B. Children and Disproportionate Impacts of Climate on Their Future for further discussion of this case.)

In *Maria Khan et al. v. Federation of Pakistan et al.*, petitioners argued that the Government of Pakistan was failing to implement its Renewable Energy Policy, 2006 (footnote 90). They alleged that the government had not processed or approved any renewable energy projects since December 2017. This failure, they said, contradicted the clear policy and legal mandate to negotiate and execute renewable energy concession agreements.

The petitioners also argued that increasing the uptake of renewable energy was critical for reducing Pakistan's national GHG emissions. The energy sector was responsible for 47% of total national GHG emissions. Even though Pakistan was not a major GHG emitter, petitioners contended it was one of the world's most climate-vulnerable countries. Therefore, Pakistan should take the lead in climate action, which included updating its renewable energy policy. The failure to devise and promulgate a new policy constituted deliberate action, infringing petitioners' fundamental rights. This case is still pending.

---

[137] Pandey referred to the Forest (Conservation) Act, 1980; Air (Prevention and Control of Pollution) Act, 1981; Environmental (Protection) Act, 1986; Biological Diversity Act, 2002; and all relevant implementing rules.

[138] Footnote 83, para. 2.

(See Part One, Section II.B.3.a. The Energy Sector in Pakistan for a full case summary of *Maria Khan et al. v. Federation of Pakistan et al.*; Part One, Section IV.B.2. International Commitments in Pending Cases in South Asia; and Part Five, Section V.A. Impacts on Women from Alleged Climate Inaction for further discussion of this case.)

2. Forestry Commitments in South Asia

Protecting the world's natural carbon sinks[139] safeguards their capacity to absorb around 30% of anthropogenic CO_2 emissions.[140] It also protects against the release of GHG emissions from deforestation or forest fires.[141] In 2019, the IPCC reported that agriculture, forestry, and other land use made up 23% of total anthropogenic GHG emissions during 2007–2016.[142] Deforestation was chiefly responsible for these emissions (footnote 142).

In *Rajiv Dutta v. Union of India and Ors.*, the NGT considered the climate change implications of large-scale forest fires in the northern Indian states of Uttarakhand and Himachal Pradesh in 2016.[143] The applicant sued the central and state governments, arguing they were obliged to curb existing fires, prevent future fires, and restore forest ecology. The respondents asserted that they had taken sufficient action by implementing a range of policies and programs to tackle forest fires. Despite these efforts, evidence during the hearing established that human action had caused over 97% of India's forest fires and that large-scale forest fires persisted.

The decision explained the critical role of forests in absorbing and storing anthropogenic carbon emissions—carbon sequestration.[144] The NGT described the potential for climate change to increase wildfire frequency and for wildfires, in turn, to further climate change by releasing GHG, aerosols, and soot.[145]

---

[139] A sink is a "reservoir (natural or human, in soil, ocean, and plants) where a greenhouse gas, an aerosol or a precursor of a greenhouse gas is stored." J.B.R. Matthews, ed. 2018. Annex I: Glossary. In V. Masson-Delmotte et al., eds. *Special Report: Global Warming of 1.5°C.* In press.

[140] V.K. Arora and J.R. Melton. 2018. Reduction in Global Area Burned and Wildfire Emissions since 1930s Enhances Carbon Uptake by Land. *Nature Communications.* 9 (1). pp. 1–10; Article 5(1) of the Paris Agreement acknowledged the need to protect global carbon sinks.

[141] H. Tian et al. 2016. The Terrestrial Biosphere as a Net Source of Greenhouse Gases to the Atmosphere. *Nature.* 531 (7593). pp. 225–228.

[142] IPCC. 2019. Summary for Policymakers. In P.R. Shukla et al., eds. *Climate Change and Land: An IPCC Special Report on Climate Change, Desertification, Land Degradation, Sustainable Land Management, Food Security, and Greenhouse Gas Fluxes in Terrestrial Ecosystems.* In press. p. 7, para. A3.1.

[143] *Rajiv Dutta v. Union of India,* Original Application No. 216 of 2016 (M.A. No. 397 of 2017) (National Green Tribunal, 3 August 2017).

[144] The IPCC defines carbon sequestration as the "process of storing carbon in a carbon pool." IPCC. 2018. Annex I: Glossary. In V. Masson-Delmotte et al., eds. *Global Warming of 1.5°C. An IPCC Special Report.* In press.

[145] Soot is otherwise known as black carbon. IPCC. 2018. Annex I: Glossary. In V. Masson-Delmotte et al., eds. *Global Warming of 1.5°C. An IPCC Special Report.* In press. p. 543.

The NGT concluded that the government authorities had failed to prevent forest disasters in line with their constitutional mandate to safeguard forests and wildlife. They had also failed to implement the national forest policy and their forest fire management plans. These failures caused "loss of forest biodiversity, degradation of environment and air quality ... thereby affecting public health besides leading to a long-term effect of climate change."

> **Precautionary principle is one of the basic principles of environmental jurisprudence and is linked to article 21, which provides for the right to clean environment as a fundamental right.**
>
> Source: *Rajiv Dutta v. Union of India*, Original Application No. 216 of 2016 (M.A. No. 397 of 2017) (National Green Tribunal, 3 August 2017). para. 75.

Quoting from *Indian Enviro-Legal Action v. Union of India*, the NGT observed, "Enactment of a law but tolerating its infringement is worse than not enacting a law at all."[146] The NGT directed the central government to formulate—in consultation with state governments—a national policy for forest fire prevention and control. It also ordered state governments to create and enact forest fire management plans.

In Pakistan, the Lahore High Court stressed the importance of national and state governments meeting their statutory forestry commitments in *Ahmad Hassan and Others v. Ministry of Climate Change, Government of Pakistan and Others*. The petitioners argued that Pakistan's forests were on the verge of extinction because national and state government agencies had failed to implement climate change and forestry policies.[147] Further, failing to protect forests violated the petitioners' rights to life and dignity, and rights of access to public places of entertainment and leisure.

The court discussed the poor state of Pakistan's forests. Existing deforestation rates meant that Pakistan's forests would be "consumed within the next few years."[148] Citing research, the court discussed the critical role of forests in sequestering carbon, conserving biodiversity, protecting sources of water, and preventing soil erosion.

Granting the requested mandamus order, the court concluded that the government agencies were duty bound to adhere to their policies under the doctrine of sovereignty. Citizens, it said, were entitled to have faith and confidence in governmental authorities to implement laws and policies. Had the government agencies fulfilled their statutory obligations "in letter and spirit with proper mechanism and procedure, the forest of Pakistan could have been saved [from] further depletion and deforestation."[149] The court issued a range of directions to ensure the national and state government agencies to "safely manage, conserve, sustain, maintain, protect, and grow forests and plant trees in urban cities."[150]

---

[146] Footnote 143, para. 76, quoting *Indian Enviro-Legal Action v. Union of India*, (1996) 5 SCC 281.
[147] *Ahmad Hassan and Others v. Ministry of Climate Change, Government of Pakistan and Others*, Writ Petition No. 192069 of 2018 (High Court of Lahore, 30 August 2019).
[148] Footnote 147, pp. 11–12.
[149] Footnote 147, p. 71.
[150] Footnote 147, p. 73.

3. Transport Emissions Reduction Commitments in the Philippines

Petitioners in the Philippines argued that road sharing presented a sustainable response to climate change in *Segovia et al. v. Climate Change Commission et al.* (footnote 96).

The petitioners alleged that the government's failure to implement its climate change laws and policies had resulted in poor air quality, violating their constitutional right to a balanced and healthful ecology.[151] They argued that the government's failure to reduce its fossil fuel consumption violated atmospheric trust.[152] The petitioners proposed a range of options to reduce pollution, including road sharing, which entailed halving roads to create all-weather sidewalks and bicycling lanes. They also sought directives to compel the Office of the President, cabinet officials, and cabinet employees to take public transportation half the time and cut their fuel consumption by 50%.

Ultimately, this petition proved too novel and specific. The court was not convinced that the petitioners had proved a breach of law or a failure to act. While air quality still did not meet the national standards, the court was satisfied that the government had acted to reduce particulate matter.[153] Further, the court viewed the road sharing request as an attempt to control how the executive actualizes legislation or policy.

(See Part One, Section II.B.3.b. The Transport Sector in the Philippines; and Part Two, Section V.B.2.b. Road Sharing in the Philippines for further discussion of this case.)

IV. The Role of the Paris Agreement

In the landmark Paris Agreement, nearly 200 countries committed to limiting average global temperatures to well below 2°C above preindustrial levels, and pursuing efforts to limit the temperature increase even further to 1.5°C.

---

[151] The petitioners cited Republic Act No. (RA) 97291 (Climate Change Act), and RA 87492 (Clean Air Act); Executive Order No. 774; Administrative Order No. 254, s. 2009; and Administrative Order No. 171, s. 2007.

[152] The concept of atmospheric trust maintains that governments have a fiduciary duty to protect the atmosphere from dangerous global warming to ensure the survival and prosperity of future generations. See M.C. Wood. 2009. Atmospheric Trust Litigation. In W.H. Rodgers, Jr. and M. Robinson-Dorn, eds. *Climate Change: A Reader.* Durham: Carolina Academic Press; and R. Costanza. 2016. Correspondence: Hold Atmosphere in Trust for All. *Nature.* 529 (7587). p. 466.

[153] Particulate matter refers to the mixture of tiny particles and liquid droplets in the air, causing pollution. See US Environmental Protection Agency. What is Particulate Matter? The court cited projects and programs such as the priority tagging of expenditures for climate change adaptation and mitigation, the integrated transport system (aimed at decongesting major thoroughfares), the truck ban, the Anti-Smoke Belching Campaign, mobile bike service programs, and urban re-greening programs.

Since then, a growing number of plaintiffs have relied on the Paris Agreement's temperature goal to argue that national emissions reduction targets are inadequate. In considering lawsuits against government actors, courts have also used the Paris Agreement as part of the factual basis for mandating climate action. This section describes the role of the Paris Agreement in judicial reasoning in rights-based lawsuits against governments.

A. Global Approaches

1. Reducing Deforestation in Colombia

National commitments made under the Paris Agreement have been enforced in domestic courts in Colombia. In *Future Generations v. Ministry of the Environment and Others* (footnote 41), the Colombian Supreme Court noted that the government committed to reducing deforestation in the Amazon when it ratified the Paris Agreement. Accordingly, the court ordered the government to develop an action plan to reduce deforestation in the Amazon region and tackle climate change. Under the Paris Agreement and national law, the government had agreed to reduce deforestation in the Colombian Amazon region to zero by 2020. The Supreme Court called the Paris Agreement part of the "global ecological public order" and reasoned that the government's failure to take measures to reduce deforestation constituted "a serious ignorance of the obligations acquired by the State in the Framework Convention on Climate Change of Paris 2015."[154]

The court's framing of the government's Paris goals as a "commitment" signals that courts can enforce government obligations under the Paris Agreement domestically (footnote 41). (See also Part One, Section II.A.3. The Rights of Nature in Colombia for a full case summary of *Future Generations v. Ministry of the Environment and Others*; and Part Two, Section VIII.A.1.c. National Obligation under the Paris Agreement in Colombia for further discussion of this case.)

2. Reducing Emissions in Canada and France

In addition to seeking enforcement of national commitments under the Paris Agreement, plaintiffs used the Paris Agreement as a yardstick for measuring national emissions reduction targets.

In *ENvironnement JEUnesse v. Canada*, an environmental nonprofit organization argued that the Canadian government's emissions reduction target was insufficient in light of the Paris Agreement.[155] The plaintiffs argued to the Superior Court of Québec that Canada's emissions reduction targets violated four international commitments, including the one the government made by ratifying the Paris Agreement. The plaintiffs ultimately claimed that the government's insufficient

---

[154] Footnote 41, p. 8 (unofficial translation).
[155] *ENvironnement JEUnesse v. Attorney General of Canada*, Superior Court of Québec (unofficial translation).

climate action violated the fundamental rights of young people guaranteed by Canadian constitutional law through the Canadian Charter of Rights and Freedoms and Québec's Charter of Human Rights and Freedoms. The case—a class action suit on behalf of all Canadians under age 35—has not yet been decided.

The plaintiffs in *Notre Affaire à Tous and Others v. France* were more ambitious in their Paris Agreement-based litigation (footnote 121). They claimed they had a right to live in a sustainable climate system, which was a general principle of law supported by the Paris Agreement, along with other texts of international, national, and European law.[156] According to their logic, France was obligated to adopt public policies that would preserve a sustainable climate system.

The case is still pending in the Administrative Court of Paris. (See Part One, Section III.A. Global Approaches: Violating the Law in Europe for a full case summary of *Notre Affaire à Tous and Others v. France;* and Part Four, Section I.A.1. A Violation of Human Rights in Australia and France for further discussion of this case.)

B.   Asia and the Pacific Approaches

The Paris Agreement's ambition mechanism requires parties to communicate a new or updated nationally determined contribution (NDC) every 5 years.[157] Successive NDCs must be more ambitious than their predecessor and contribute to the agreement's long-term temperature goal (footnote 157). As governments made international pledges in their first NDCs, citizens in Asia and the Pacific came to the courts to hold governments accountable for these commitments.

1.   Seeking Climate Action in South Asia

Ridhima Pandey sued the Government of India, seeking more aggressive climate action in line with the goals of the Paris Agreement in *Ridhima Pandey v. Union of India & Another* (footnote 83). Pandey argued that her government was bound by its obligations under the Paris Agreement. It had committed to lower carbon. Although the Paris Agreement set targets limiting average warming to 2°C and 1.5°C, these targets were negotiated and not based on science.

Therefore, claimed the petitioner, the government should try to reduce CO_2 to less than 350 ppm by 2100. She argued that "climate recovery" relied upon the world to reduce atmospheric CO_2 to 350 ppm, a target consistent with "best available science."[158] Furthermore, more effective climate action—to conserve and enhance sinks, ensure public participation, and lower emissions—could set India on a path consistent with its Paris Agreement commitments.

---

[156]   Footnote 121, p. 19 (unofficial translation).
[157]   Footnote 1, art. 4.
[158]   Footnote 83, p. 3.

The National Green Tribunal (NGT) dismissed the case in January 2019. It concluded that Indian authorities must evaluate EIAs under the existing statutory scheme. As the petition did not challenge the scheme, the NGT found there was no need to make any directions.

This case demonstrates the hurdles which petitioners must overcome. Victory is not assured, even with credible scientific evidence to support the case. Under the Paris Agreement, countries committed to limiting global warming to "well below 2°C above pre-industrial levels."[159] The agreement does not refer to carbon budgets or require parties to seek to limit global CO_2 concentrations to 350 ppm. Courts may be reluctant to intervene where a national government's commitments are on track to limit global warming to 2°C, which is within the range of doing one's fair share. Nevertheless, a 2°C warming is not fully consistent with the Paris Agreement's long-term temperature goal.

(See Part One, Section II.B.2.b. Existential Threat and Intergenerational Equity in South Asia for a full case summary of *Pandey v. Union of India & Another* and information regarding the 350-ppm threshold. *Pandey* is also discussed in Part One, Section III.B.1. Climate Change Commitments in South Asia; and Part Five, Section VI.B. Children and Disproportionate Impacts of Climate on Their Future for further discussion of this case.)

2. Applying International Commitments to Protect Biodiversity

The Supreme Court of Nepal judged it relevant to consider international climate commitments when assessing the legality of a disputed road project in *Simkhada v. Office of the Prime Minister*.[160] The government approved a road construction project through Chitwan National Park, a United Nations Educational, Scientific and Cultural Organization (UNESCO) World Heritage Site with declared wetlands under the Ramsar Convention on Wetlands of International Importance Especially as Waterfowl Habitat.[161] The park is one of the last refuges for the single-horned Asiatic rhinoceros and the Bengal tiger.

The petitioners asserted that the road would fragment the park, gravely undermining its purpose—protecting unique and endangered biodiversity. Allowing road construction through Chitwan Park would, therefore, contravene constitutional rights to life and environmental protection and the Environment Protection Act, 1997 (2053 BS). Further, as the road would negatively impact a UNESCO World Heritage-listed park, the decision breached the Nepal Treaty Act, 1990 (2047 BS).

---

[159] Footnote 1, art. 2(1)(a).

[160] *Advocate Ramchandra Simkhada and Others vs Office of the Prime Minister and Council of Ministers, Government of Nepal and Others*, Writ Petition No. 068-WO-0597 (Supreme Court of Nepal, 13 February 2019).

[161] *Convention on Wetlands of International Importance Especially as Waterfowl Habitat*, Ramsar, Iran, 2 February 1971, *United Nations Treaty Series*, Vol. 996, No. 14583, p. 245.

The court observed that while the state must primarily comply with the constitution, it also has responsibilities under international treaties and as a conscientious member of the global community. The court reasoned that the UNESCO World Heritage listing implied that "the heritage is legated to us by our ancestors and we will . . . cause no harm—direct or indirect—to such heritage."[162] Further, Nepal had voluntarily pledged to pursue low-carbon economic and social development that safeguarded natural heritage under the Paris Agreement—an accord dedicated to the health of global ecosystems and Earth's well-being. As the treaty act incorporates provisions of international instruments into Nepal's law, the state could not avoid its international climate and environmental promises.

Given the park's rich biodiversity, importance to Nepal's ecotourism industry, and listing as a World Heritage Site, the court found that it was essential to preserve the park for the benefit of present and future generations. The court held that the decision to approve the road was defective.

(See Part Two, Section V.B.2.c Road Projects Impacting Biodiversity in Nepal for further discussion of this case.)

3. International Commitments in Pending Cases in South Asia

In 2016, a 7-year-old girl sued the Pakistan government, challenging its plan to develop coalfields in the Thar desert in *Ali v. Federation of Pakistan & Another* (footnote 30). She argued that burning coal would frustrate not only the government's policy but also its international commitments to climate change. The coalfields would increase Pakistan's coal production from "4.5 to 60 million" metric tons per year (footnote 30).

The petition further argued that Pakistan's NDCs lacked quantifiable information on national contributions to GHG emissions reduction. NDCs were rooted in Vision 2025 of Pakistan, 2014, which envisioned exploiting Pakistan's untapped coal reserves. The NDCs did not state when Pakistan's emissions would peak, nor did it set a carbon budget. These deficiencies, she said, meant that Pakistan was failing to meet its commitments under the UNFCCC and the Paris Agreement. It was also failing to do its "share as a responsible member of the global community in reducing atmospheric CO_2 and achieving global Climate [*sic*] stabilization."[163] *Ali v. Federation of Pakistan & Another* has not yet been decided.

(See Part One, Section II.B.3.a. The Energy Sector in Pakistan for a full case summary of *Ali v. Federation of Pakistan & Another* as well as Part One, Section I.B.2.b. Environmental Damage and Future Generations in South Asia; Part One, Section IV.B.2. International Commitments in Pending Cases in South Asia; Part Two, Section I.B.1.b. Constitutional Rights in Pakistan; and Part Three, Section III.B.2. Coal-Fired Electricity in Pakistan for further discussion of this case.)

---

[162] Footnote 160, p. 28.
[163] Footnote 30, p. 29.

The petitioners in *Maria Khan et al. v. Federation of Pakistan et al.* argued that the government had taken insufficient action to reduce carbon emissions (footnote 90). Pakistan's energy sector was responsible for 47% of its total GHG emissions, followed by the agriculture sector, with 45% of total emissions.

In 2016, Pakistan communicated its NDCs to the UNFCCC secretariat, which committed to a 20% reduction of its 2030 projected GHG emissions. Despite making this commitment, the petitioners argued that the respondents had not prioritized clean energy projects or approved a renewable energy project since December 2017. They alleged that this failure betrayed the government's "stated commitment under the Paris Agreement to encourage and foster the development of renewable energy sources" (footnote 91).

Khan et al. also argued that the Paris Agreement represented an "unequivocal acknowledgment by all state parties" that individual contributions to global GHG emissions were irrelevant.[164] Parties must collaboratively pursue their most ambitious emissions reductions to comply with the Paris Agreement. The respondents' failures to pursue emissions reductions via renewable energy violated the female petitioners' right to life and equal protection before the law. Women, they argued, were more vulnerable to climate change and therefore deserved greater protection.

The petitioners sought declarations that the state (i) must support renewable energy projects, and (ii) has failed to comply with its commitments under the Paris Agreement and must, therefore, comply in "letter and in spirit" with the climate agreement.[165] They also wanted a comprehensive strategy to enhance Pakistan's mitigation measures. The case is still pending.

(See Part One, Section II.B.3.a. The Energy Sector in Pakistan for a full case summary of *Maria Khan et al. v. Federation of Pakistan et al.*; Part One, Section III.B.1. Climate Change Commitments in South Asia; and Part Five, Section V.A. Impacts on Women from Alleged Climate Inaction for further discussion of this case.)

These cases represent judicial recognition of the need to act boldly and swiftly on climate change. Judges in Asia and the Pacific are aware of the Paris Agreement, the global consensus surrounding it, and the necessity for all governments to do what it can and keep its commitments. The further challenge will be to sustain the pressure on governments to follow the court's orders and meaningfully implement climate laws and policies.

---

[164] Footnote 90, para. 15.
[165] Footnote 90, pp. 18–19.

Photo by Deng Jia/ADB.

Coal-fired power plant in Ulaanbaatar, Mongolia. Citizens around the world have begun to sue governments over decisions to permit coal-fired power (photo by Ariel Javellana/ADB).

PART TWO

PERMITTING AND JUDICIAL REVIEW

Plaintiffs and other stakeholders who seek to limit GHG emissions have deployed a range of strategies to challenge natural resource extraction and development decisions at the permitting stage. Stakeholders have also sought judicial review of these decisions.

This section begins by describing legal attempts to stop the extraction of fossil fuels before development. Lawsuits challenging EIAs play a crucial role in halting resource extraction. At the very least, they require that developers consider climate change impacts in environmental review processes. Concerted campaigns by environmental actors—like the Sierra Club's Beyond Coal Campaign—step beyond climate arguments, using economic analysis to point to more cost-effective and environmentally friendly energy sources than fossil fuels.

This section also outlines a range of challenges to pipelines and other fossil fuel transportation projects. The majority of these cases rely on EIA law. This section discusses cases that hinge on EIA law in the context of pipelines and other fossil fuel transportation projects as well as resource extraction and focuses on mitigation considerations. (See Part Four, Section II. Reverse Environmental Impact Assessments for a discussion of environmental impact assessment-based cases from an adaptation perspective.)

In other cases, courts have heard challenges from landowners and environmental groups to property appropriation. Judicial review has also been critical in upholding renewable energy projects and governmental authority to implement renewable energy policies. Judiciaries around the world have also intervened in transportation-related cases where an increase in GHG emissions is at stake.

In cases where courts have reviewed local and national planning decisions that regulate water extraction, courts have stressed the impact of climate change on water levels. In these water-related cases, courts have also affirmed the right to clean water.

Similarly, judicial reasoning has served as a defense against deforestation—courts have upheld federal action that protects forests, enforced national commitments to reduce deforestation, and ordered governments and private companies who have destroyed forests to restore them. This section concludes with a discussion of other land use-related cases. The section uses the term judicial review broadly to include any case, where a court reviews government action.

I. Leave It in the Ground

A. Global Approaches

1. Challenges to Extraction Leases

Climate scientists advise that limiting the rise of average global temperatures requires leaving most fossil fuels undeveloped.[1] Studies have shown that trillions of dollars of extractable coal, oil, and gas must remain unexploited if global temperature rise is to stay under 2°C, the temperature goal countries committed to with the Paris Agreement (footnote 1).

"Leave it in the ground" refers to the principle of leaving fossil fuels untapped to safeguard the climate. Direct challenges to lease approvals for fossil fuel extraction provide one avenue for keeping fossil fuels in the ground. Suing governments and private actors for failure to adequately assess the environmental and climate impacts of extraction projects provides another avenue. This subsection focuses on challenges to extraction lease sales and planning approvals for fossil fuel development.

a) Coal Mines in the United Kingdom

Local-level planning decisions can implicate national climate policy. In *HJ Banks & Company Ltd v Secretary of State for Housing Communities and Local Government*, a specialist planning court within the High Court of Justice quashed a UK cabinet member's decision to refuse planning permission for an open-cut coal mine.[2] The secretary of state for Housing, Communities, and Local Government issued the refusal after considering the adverse effects of GHG emissions. The development company challenged the denial.

The court held that the secretary (i) provided insufficient reasoning to explain why preventing the project would reduce GHG emissions, and (ii) did not adequately explain how power generation would be replaced by less carbon-intensive sources than imported coal. The court ultimately found that the government official provided inadequate reasoning for how national climate change policy was inconsistent with granting permission for the mine.

(See Part Two, Section I.A.2.c. Inadequate Justification in Europe and New Zealand for further discussion of this case.)

---

[1] C. McGlade and P. Ekins. 2015. The Geographical Distribution of Fossil Fuels Unused when Limiting Global Warming to 2°C. *Nature.* 517 (7533). pp. 187–190.

[2] *HJ Banks & Company Ltd v Secretary of State for Housing Communities and Local Government* [2018] EWHC 3141 (Admin).

b) Fossil Fuel Lease Sales in the United States

The lease sale stage presents a critical opportunity to assess the cumulative effects of oil and gas development on the environment. In *Native Village of Point Hope v. Jewell*, a US federal appellate court held that an environmental impact statement (EIS) that supported a federal agency's approval of an oil and gas lease sale was inadequate.[3] The federal agency approved an oil and gas lease sale in the Chukchi Sea, off the northwest coast of Alaska, after relying on an EIS with incomplete information. The court noted that the federal agency, which manages offshore energy resources, had arbitrarily chosen a 1 billion barrel estimate for the amount of economically recoverable oil from the lease sale. Thus, the lease approval was based on inadequate information.

The court reversed the lower court's grant of summary judgment to the agency. The court reasoned that "it is only at the lease sale stage that the agency can adequately consider cumulative effects of the lease sale on the environment, including the overall risk of oil spills and the effects of the sale on climate change."[4] The court, therefore, held in relevant part that since oil production was reasonably foreseeable, the agency should have based its environmental impact analysis on the full range of likely production of oil.

The case affirmed that legal challenges at the permitting stage could be effective in efforts to leave fossil fuels in the ground. (See Part Two, Section I.A.2. Environmental Impact Assessment Cases for a discussion of other EIS cases.)

2. Environmental Impact Statement Cases

EIA laws provide a basis for suing governments—and, in some cases, project proponents—when proposals are approved without adequate assessment of environmental impacts, including contributions to climate change. Legal requirements about EIA arise from both domestic and international law.

a) Transboundary Litigation in South America

In *Argentina v. Uruguay* (often referred to as the "Pulp Mills on the River Uruguay" case), the International Court of Justice (ICJ) found that there was a "requirement under general international law to undertake EIA where there is a risk that a proposed industrial activity may have a significant adverse impact in a transboundary context, in particular, on a shared resource."[5] This decision was consistent with Principle 17 of the Rio Declaration on Environment and Development, the Convention on Environmental Impact Assessment

---

[3] *Native Village of Point Hope v. Jewell*, 740 F.3d 489, 493 (9th Cir. 2014).
[4] Footnote 3, p. 504.
[5] *Argentina v. Uruguay (Pulp Mills on the River Uruguay)*, Judgment on the Merits, ICGJ 425 (IJC 2010) at 83.

in a Transboundary Context (the Espoo Convention), and Article 7 of the International Law Commission Draft Articles on Prevention of Transboundary Harm.

Many countries, multilateral development banks, and international organizations have also enacted laws or policies requiring an EIA for projects with potentially significant environmental impacts.

(See Part Six, Section I. Global Approaches: Transboundary Harm in South America for a full case summary of *Argentina v. Uruguay*.)

b) Downstream Emissions in Australia and the United States

In the US and other jurisdictions, dozens of lawsuits have been filed, challenging fossil fuel production proposals on the grounds that the government or project proponent did not adequately consider climate change.[6] Numerous decisions hold that the effect of fossil fuel production on GHG emissions and climate change must be accounted for in EIAs. Furthermore, these analyses must encompass direct emissions from production activities and indirect emissions from the downstream combustion of the produced fossil fuels.

In *High Country Conservation Advocates v. US Forest Service*, a US district court held that downstream emissions from the combustion of coal were a reasonably foreseeable effect of coal production, which must be disclosed in federal reviews conducted under US environmental law.[7] The court also held that the reviewing agency must disclose the social costs of the emissions, just as it had disclosed economic benefits in the EIS for the proposed coal production.

Since that decision was issued, there have been numerous US cases reinforcing the principle that downstream emissions must be accounted for in coal, oil, and gas projects. These decisions have further required project proponents to disclose the social costs of emissions in the proposal's cost–benefit analyses. Courts have concluded that this information is needed to present a fair and balanced assessment for decision-makers and the public.[8]

For example, in *WildEarth Guardians v. BLM*, a US appellate court held that it was irrational for the government to assume that approving two coal leases would not affect downstream emissions because the same amount of coal would be sourced from elsewhere if it did not approve the two leases. The court found that

[6]   M. Burger and J. Wentz. 2017. Downstream and Upstream Greenhouse Gas Emissions: The Proper Scope of NEPA Review. *Harvard Environmental Law Review*. 41 (1). p. 109–187.

[7]   *High Country Conservation Advocates v. US Forest Serv.*, 52 F. Supp. 3d 1174, 1198 (D. Colo. 2014).

[8]   For a more in-depth review of the US case law, see footnote 6 and M. Burger and J. Wentz. 2019. Evaluating the Effect of Fossil Fuel Supply Projects on Greenhouse Gas Emissions and Climate Change Under NEPA. *Columbia Public Law Research Paper*. No. 14-634. New York: Sabin Center for Climate Change Law, Columbia Law School.

this "perfect substitution" argument was contradicted by the basic principles of supply and demand.[9]

Similarly, in *Gloucester Resources Limited v Minister for Planning*, an Australian court held that downstream emissions must be disclosed on the environmental review for a coal mining proposal. The court struck down the proposal for the new coal mine. It held that the reviewing agency could properly deny the permit for a new coal mine based on climate-related considerations.[10]

In reaching its decision, the court noted that "the exploitation and burning of a new fossil fuel reserve, which will increase GHG emissions, cannot assist in achieving the rapid and deep reductions in GHG emissions that are necessary in order to achieve 'a balance between anthropogenic emissions by sources and removals by sinks of GHGs in the second half of this century' (Article 4(1) of the Paris Agreement)."[11]

The court also noted that approving a new coal mine would not help achieve "the long term temperature goal of limiting the increase in global average temperature to between 1.5°C and 2°C above pre-industrial levels (Article 2 of the Paris Agreement)" (footnote 10). This decision was the most recent in a line of Australian cases that ruled that downstream emissions qualified as indirect effects of coal mining proposals.[12]

(See Part One, Section IV. The Role of the Paris Agreement for a discussion of how courts treat the agreement.)

In *Australian Coal Alliance Incorporated v Wyong Coal Pty Ltd*, however, the same court upheld the approval of a new coal mine, although the reviewing agency had not considered downstream GHG emissions.[13] The court distinguished its decision from *Gloucester* by noting that it only had jurisdiction to consider the reviewing agency's decision-making process. It could not assess the downstream GHG emissions of the proposed coal mine, but it could determine whether the reviewing agency's assessment was lawful.

Therefore, *Gloucester* was an important signal that downstream GHG emissions remained a critical part of the environmental assessments of any coal mine. The court also determined that environmental decisions could be controversial and that the reviewing agency was empowered to weigh various considerations. In this case, the reviewing agency had imposed conditions on the proposed project, and the court was satisfied that these conditions would ensure sustainable development and intergenerational equity.

---

9   *WildEarth Guardians v. United States Bureau of Land Mgmt.*, 870 F.3d 1222 (10th Cir. 2017).
10   *Gloucester Resources Limited v Minister for Planning* [2019] NSWLEC 7.
11   Footnote 10, para. 527.
12   See, e.g., *Gray v Minister for Planning* [2006] 152 LGERA 258; *Coast and Country Association Queensland Inc v Smith* [2016] QCA 242.
13   *Australian Coal Alliance Incorporated v Wyong Coal Pty Ltd* [2019] NSWLEC 31.

c) Inadequate Justification in Europe and New Zealand

The above cases can be contrasted to a recent UK decision, *HJ Banks & Company Ltd v Secretary of State for Housing Communities and Local Government*, in which an administrative court found that a UK agency had provided inadequate justification for its decision to deny planning permission for a coal mining project based on concerns about GHG emissions. In particular, the court found that the agency had failed to explain how power generation would be replaced by less carbon-intensive sources rather than imported coal if the coal mine were not approved (footnote 2).

(See Part Two, Section I.A.1.a. Challenges to Extraction Leases for further discussion of this case.)

A 2013 decision from the Supreme Court of New Zealand, *West Coast ENT Inc. v. Buller Coal Ltd.*, held that the Government of New Zealand was precluded from accounting for indirect GHG emissions from coal end use when considering applications for coal mining because those emissions fell outside of the government's jurisdiction.[14] This decision was grounded in the unique legislative history of the statute under which such authorizations were issued.

In *Greenpeace Nordic Ass'n and Nature and Youth v. Ministry of Petroleum and Energy*, a Norwegian district court found that the government's approval of oil and gas licenses did not violate the Norwegian constitution.[15] The court also touched on the adequacy of the EIA conducted for those license approvals. The plaintiffs argued that the EIA was inadequate because the government had failed to address whether the licensing decisions were consistent with the need to reduce GHG emissions. The court found that the government had adequately assessed emissions and climate change impacts and that this was legally sufficient.

In January 2020, the Borgarting Court of Appeal upheld the decision of the district court.[16] The court considered that the alleged environmental damage from oil and gas combustion could fall within the ambit of the Norwegian constitutional right to an environment conducive to health. However, the court was reluctant to review a political decision. It also reasoned that the extent to which the licenses would increase GHG emissions was unclear. That decision is now on appeal before the Supreme Court.[17]

---

[14] For example, New Zealand legislators had indicated that the climate change effects of GHG were appropriately addressed at the national policy level. They had stated one objective of the bill was to remove climate change considerations from decision-making concerning "industrial discharges of greenhouse gases," *West Coast ENT Inc. v. Buller Coal Ltd.* [2013] NZSC 87.

[15] *Greenpeace Nordic Ass'n and Nature and Youth v. Ministry of Petroleum and Energy*, Case No. 16-166674TVI-OTIR/06 (Oslo District Court) (4 January 2018) (unofficial translation).

[16] *Greenpeace Nordic Ass'n and Nature and Youth v. Government of Norway*, Case No. 18-060499ASD-BORG/03 (Borgarting Court of Appeal) (22 January 2020) (unofficial translation).

[17] The Supreme Court granted leave to appeal on 20 April 2020. See *Greenpeace Nordic Ass'n and Nature and Youth v. Government of Norway, Ministry of Petroleum and Energy*, Case No. 20-051052SIV-HRET (Supreme Court) (20 April 2020) (order in Norwegian).

(See also Part One, Section II.A.4. The Right to a Healthy Environment in Nigeria and Norway for a full case summary.)

d) Cumulative Emissions in North America

Some US decisions have also begun to flesh out requirements for evaluating cumulative emissions from government decisions pertaining to fossil fuel production. For example, US courts have considered whether an agency is required to disclose emissions from all of its recent and pending coal mining approvals when deciding whether to grant a new coal lease.

Recently, in *WildEarth Guardians v. Zinke,* a US district court found that the EIA conducted for oil and gas leasing was inadequate because in its review of a lease sale—encompassing 473 leases—the reviewing agency had failed to quantify the aggregate emissions from reasonably foreseeable oil and gas leasing in the region.[18]

A Canadian decision dealt with the reasonableness of the government's assertion that tar sands development would not have a significant impact on GHG emissions and climate change. In *Pembina Institute for Appropriate Development and Others v Attorney General of Canada and Imperial Oil,* the Federal Court of Canada held that the government had failed to adequately support its finding of no significant impact in its estimate that tar sands development would generate 3.7 million tons of CO_2e per year.[19]

There are no US decisions directly addressing whether a specific quantity of GHG emissions rises to the level of a "significant impact," but there some cases that address the criteria for evaluating significance in this context (footnote 18).

e) Involving the Public in Kenya

Public participation is another issue. In *Save Lamu et al. v. National Environmental Management Authority and Amu Power Co. Ltd.,* Kenya's National Environment Tribunal denied a license for the construction of a coal-fired power plant, which had been approved by the National Environmental Management Authority.[20] The plant in question would have been the first coal-fired power plant in Kenya. The tribunal found that the issuing authority had violated the EIA and audit regulations by granting the license without meaningful public participation. Furthermore, the tribunal found that it had properly considered the effects of neither climate change nor Kenyan climate change law in its assessment.

---

[18] *WildEarth Guardians v. Zinke,* No. 1:16-cv-01724 (D.D. C. 8/25/16).
[19] *Pembina Institute for Appropriate Development and Others v Attorney General of Canada and Imperial Oil,* [2008] FC 302.
[20] *Save Lamu et al. v. National Environmental Management Authority and Amu Power Co. Ltd.* (2019) Tribunal Appeal No. Net 196 (Kenya).

The tribunal ordered a new EIA that would include "all approved and legible detailed architectural and engineering plans for the plant and its ancillary facilities (such as the coal storage and handling facility and the ash pit with its location in relation to the sea shore), in consideration of the Climate Change Act 2016, the Energy Act 2019 and the Natural Resources (Classes of Transactions Subject to Ratification) Act 2016 in so far as the project will utilise seawater for the plant and/or if applicable."[21]

B.   Asia and the Pacific Approaches

Despite global efforts to reduce fossil fuel reliance, coal consumption grew in 2016–2017, driven primarily by demand in Asia.[22] "Leave it in the ground" litigation is thus fertile terrain for challenging fossil fuel expansion.

1.   Challenging Coal Mining

Permitting cases can result in a wide range of orders, which can all be impactful. A court need not halt a project entirely for there to be an impact on regulating responses to climate change. Courts and tribunals can still make a range of orders that positively impact mitigation action.

a)   *Statutory Grounds in Indonesia*

In 2013, residents in Samarinda, Indonesia sued the central and local governments for failing to appropriately evaluate or monitor coal mines in *Komari, et al. v. Mayor of Samarinda, et al.*[23] The residents argued that the law required the minister of energy and mineral resources, the minister of environment and forestry, and the governor of East Kalimantan to act to reduce GHG.[24] The residents claimed that the defendants' lack of commitment to climate change meant they had failed to evaluate and monitor coal mining permits, resulting in severe environmental degradation.

The District Court agreed, finding that the government had failed to meet its statutory obligations to take climate change into account when granting permits. The government had also failed to monitor and inspect mining operations. The court considered that the defendants had negligently failed to ensure a healthy environment, which impacted the public interest. However, the court did not cancel permits. Instead, it directed the government to review its coal mining policy. The policy review, the court declared, should cover (i) the licensing process; (ii) evaluation of existing permits; (iii) environmental protection; and (iv) supervision, inspection, and enforcement.[25]

[21]   Footnote 20, para. 155.

[22]   International Energy Agency. 2018. *Coal 2018: Analysis and Forecasts to 2023*. Paris.

[23]   District Court of Samarinda, Decision No. 55/Pdt.G/2013/PN.Smda., *Komari et al. v. Mayor of Samarinda et al.* (2014).

[24]   PR No. 61 of 2011 concerning National Action Plan related to Greenhouse Gases.

[25]   Footnote 23, pp. 141–143.

When the courts ask governments to review policies to ensure they align with climate change commitments, they spark change and prompt action. Courts can send a clear message on justice.

b) Constitutional Rights in Pakistan

In Pakistan, a 7-year-old girl relied on her constitutional rights to challenge a provincial government's decision to develop a coalfield in the Thar Desert. In *Ali v. Federation of Pakistan*, Ali argued that exploiting the Thar coalfields would release approximately 327 billion tons of CO_2. This amount is over 1,000 times Pakistan's estimated annual GHG emissions. She asserted that increased CO_2 emissions would contribute to an unstable global climate system, leading to continued and increasingly catastrophic climate events.

The petition sought outcomes much broader than a standard procedural review of the Government of Sindh's decision to grant a mining lease to Sindh Carbon Energy Ltd.[26] In this regard, it did not expressly challenge the decision of the Sindh Environmental Protection Agency (EPA) to approve the project's environmental and social impact assessment of January 2014.[27] Instead, the petition argued for a rights-based evaluation of the decision based on constitutional and international legal principles. It contended that the constitutional rights to life, human dignity, equal protection of the law, among others incorporate several doctrines and principles—e.g., the doctrine of public trust, international environmental principles of sustainable development, the precautionary principle, EIA, and intergenerational and intragenerational equity. The case is undecided.

(See Part One, Section II.B.3.a. The Energy Sector in Pakistan for a full case summary of *Ali v. Federation of Pakistan & Another* as well as Part One, Section I.B.2.b. Environmental Damage and Future Generations in South Asia; Part One, Section IV.B.2. International Commitments in Pending Cases in South Asia; and Part Three, Section III.B.2. Coal-Fired Electricity in Pakistan for further discussion of this case.)

This petitioner's arguments reflected the reasoning of the Lahore High Court in *Imrana Tiwana v. Province of Punjab*.[28] In that case, the court expanded the meaning of environmental justice. It said that environmental justice was an amalgam of (i) "the constitutional principles of democracy, equality, social, economic and political justice"; and (ii) "the fundamental right to life, liberty and human dignity" under article 14 of Pakistan's constitution.[29] The court stated that these fundamental rights included the "international environmental principles of sustainable development, precautionary principle, environmental impact assessment, inter and intra-generational equity and public trust doctrine" (footnote 29).

---

[26] Details about the mining lease grant obtained at Oracle Power PLC. Thar Coalfield Block VI.
[27] Details about approval of the EIA obtained at Oracle Power PLC. Thar Coalfield Block VI.
[28] *Imrana Tiwana v. Punjab Province*, 2015 LHC 2551.
[29] Footnote 28, p. 37.

(See Part Two, Section V.B.2.a. More Highways, More Emissions in Pakistan for a full case summary of *Imrana Tiwana v. Province of Punjab*; and Part Five, Section III.B.1. Failure to Consult in South Asia for further discussion of this case.)

2. Oil Exploration in Protected Marine Areas in the Philippines

Litigants and courts need not make climate change a central issue for a case to have significance to climate change litigation.

In *Resident Marine Mammals of the Protected Seascape Tañon Strait et al. v. Secretary Angelo Reyes et al.*, two petitions challenged the government's decision to allow exploration drilling for oil in the Philippines.[30] The government granted a service contract allowing the exploration, development, and exploitation of petroleum resources within Tañon Strait, a protected seascape under the National Integrated Protected Areas System Act of 1992 (RA 7586).

The petitions sought to protect marine life, such as cetaceans, mangroves, fish, and crustaceans. They argued that the service contract and environmental permit should be nullified. Named petitioners under the first petition were "Resident Marine Mammals of the Protected Seascape Tañon Strait," joined and represented by their legal guardians (the Stewards).[31] Fisherfolk filed the second petition.

Both petitions alleged that the project's seismic survey had drastically reduced the supply of fish. They also alleged there was little to no public consultation with stakeholders before the government granted the project environmental clearance. The petitioners did not make climate change central to their arguments, and the Supreme Court did not mention the issue in its decision.

Dolphins. In a recent Philippine case, petitioners challenged oil drilling in the Tañon Strait on behalf of marine mammals and argued that it would affect fish stocks (photo by Flavio Gasperini).

---

30 *Resident Marine Mammals of the Protected Seascape Tañon Strait et al. v. Secretary Angelo Reyes et al.*, G.R. Nos. 180771 and 181527, 21 April 2015.
31 Footnote 30, p. 3.

The court's decision focused on the legality of the oil drilling contract. It observed that section 2 Article XII of the 1987 Constitution of the Philippines requires the President to sign a service contract for oil exploration and extraction and report it to Congress. As that had not occurred, the court held that the agreement had violated the constitution and was, therefore, null and void.

Further, any activity falling outside the scope of a management plan for a protected area requires an EIA. The court, therefore, ruled that the contract violated the National Integrated Protected Areas System Act, which prohibits the exploitation of natural resources in protected areas. Only a law could permit the exploitation and use of this resource within a protected marine area. Thus, the court's reliance on local environmental permitting requirements safeguarded the seascape.

(See Part One, Section I.B.1.b. Transcendental Importance and the Standing of Mammals in the Philippines for further discussion of this case.)

3. Gas Drilling in Bangladesh

BELA Vs. Bangladesh concerned a challenge to the government's joint venture agreement with Niko Resources (Bangladesh) Limited (Niko) for gas exploration at the Tengratila Gas Field in Bangladesh.[32] Two severe blowouts and fires occurred due to Niko's drilling. Over 100 billion cubic feet of gas leaked, and the fires caused loss of life, property, cattle, trees, and fisheries within the agreement area. The incidents exhausted the Chhatak (West) gas reserves—a government committee calculated the value of loss of gas as up to $11.8 million.

BELA argued that the agreement was invalid, having been procured through flawed processes. It sought orders restraining government payments to Niko and contended that the government had failed to take action to recover compensation for environmental damage.

The Supreme Court of Bangladesh held that the joint venture agreement was valid. However, it directed Niko to pay compensation according to decisions in the Joint District Court, or to mutual agreement between the parties. The dispute was later resolved in Niko's favor by the International Centre for Settlement of Investment Disputes.[33]

BELA Vs. Bangladesh occurred before the Paris Agreement and before countries had submitted their NDCs. The parties did not argue about the climate consequences of over 100 billion cubic feet of gas leaking into the atmosphere. Changing awareness of the need to reduce emissions may change how such cases are argued and decided.

---

[32] *BELA Vs. Bangladesh*, WP No. 6911 of 2005, D-/16-11-2009.
[33] *Niko Resources (Bangladesh) Ltd. Vs. Bangladesh Petroleum Exploration & Production Company Limited & Ors*, ICSID Case Nos. ARB/10/11 and ARB/10/18, Award, 11 September 2014.

II. Power Plant Cases

A. Global Approaches

1. Beyond Coal: The Economic Case

Transitioning communities away from coal to cleaner sources of energy has climate, public health, and economic benefits. Sierra Club, an environmental organization in the US, launched a major effort to reduce US reliance on coal in 2010—the Beyond Coal Campaign. The campaign has already helped shut down more than 50% of the coal-fired power plants operating in the US, resulting in significant emissions reductions.

In the first phase of the campaign, a coalition of environmental advocates and lawyers focused on blocking permits for new coal-fired power plants. At hearings before public utility commissions and other state agencies of jurisdiction, the campaign now broadly challenges coal at the state and local levels.

The campaign deploys economic arguments to promote the retirement of coal plants and increased use of renewable energy. For example, in *In the Matter of Xcel Energy's 2016–2030 Integrated Resource Plan*, the campaign's advocacy led a state public utilities commission to approve an energy plan for a utility company. It required retiring two coal plants, as well as maximizing wind and solar energy sources and energy efficiency.[34]

The plan, which the commission approved with modifications, doubles the amount of renewable energy and cuts carbon emissions by 60% in the state where the utility company operates. In requiring the utility company to increase its reliance on renewable energy, the state public utilities commission reasoned that the "acquisition of wind and possibly solar resources in the next five years represents the least-cost method of meeting" the utility's resource needs.[35] The commission also noted that retiring the utility company's existing coal-fired plants "is part of virtually every least-cost planning scenario."[36]

The campaign's economic argument—that coal is more expensive than other, cleaner energy sources, and that the costs of pollution control and regulatory compliance should not be passed on to ratepayers—has also been successful in other states. For example, in a legal proceeding before the Washington Utilities and Transportation Commission, the state public utilities commission rejected a utility company's request to increase its electricity rates.[37]

---

[34] *In the Matter of Xcel Energy's 2016–2030 Integrated Resource Plan*, E-002/RP-15-21 Minn. Pub. Util. Comm'n (2017).

[35] Footnote 34, p. 7.

[36] Footnote 34, p. 8.

[37] *Washington Utilities and Transportation Commission v. Pacific Power & Light Company*, UE-152253 Washington Util. & Trans. Comm'n (2016).

Instead, the commission ordered the company to increase its depreciation schedule for two coal-fired plants.

In reaching its decision, the commission found that "there are increasing legal, economic, and policy considerations limiting the long-term viability of coal-fired generation plants," and that the current depreciation schedule for two of the company's coal-fired plants "are possibly overstated and not consistent with these general policy and economic trends."[38]

The commission also rejected the company's request to earn a profit on capital investment at one of the utility's coal plants, noting that "the Company has failed to demonstrate that it adequately examined the changing circumstances in coal and natural gas prices that" would have made the investment "a prudent or imprudent decision."[39]

Although the campaign does not rely on climate change-related arguments specifically, it is motivated by climate concerns. The campaign has been so successful that it has been adopted in Europe, by Europe Beyond Coal.

2. Greenhouse Gas Emissions from Power Plants

Electricity generation from the combustion of fossil fuels accounts for a significant portion of GHG emissions. The following cases offer a range of legal approaches to limiting emissions from power plants. European cases revolve around emission allowances under the European Union's carbon emission trading scheme. One Australian court considered whether an implied limit on CO_2 emissions exists under common law. Courts in other jurisdictions have analyzed federal agencies' statutory authority to regulate GHG emissions under federal law. Courts have also required climate change impact assessments to guarantee that the goals of NDCs under the Paris Agreement are met.

a) Cap-and-Trade Systems in Spain

The EU Emissions Trading Scheme, a cap-and-trade system that limits emission allowances for European companies, triggered some cases when it was launched in 2005. One common suit involves companies suing national governments to increase their assigned emission allowances. This type of emission allowance challenge may point to a kind of case emblematic to cap-and-trade systems more generally.

In re Unión Fenosa Generación, S.A., for example, an energy company challenged the Spanish government's approval of the company's emission allowances assignment.[40] The challenge was based on the national law regulating the market

---

[38] Footnote 37, p. 87.

[39] Footnote 37, p. 92.

[40] *In re Unión Fenosa Generación, S.A.,* Judgment No. 6903/2008 of Sept. 30, 2008.

for GHG emissions trading. The company argued that its emission allowances for two of its power plants were too low.

The highest court of ordinary jurisdiction, the Supreme Tribunal, granted the company's request for an increase in the emission allowances for one combined cycle power plant. This decision was because the plant had been incorrectly considered a "new entrant" to the emissions market under the regulation's timetable. However, the court denied the plaintiff's request for an increase in its emission allowances for its coal-fired power plant in La Coruña, one of the five worst emitters in Spain.

b) Implied Limits in Australia and the United States

In *Macquarie Generation v Hodgson*, an Australian court of appeal found that a state-owned electricity generation company was not subject to an implied common law limit on its CO_2 emissions.[41] Environmental activists had filed suit against the power company, alleging that the company's CO_2 emissions caused harm in violation of federal environmental protection law.

The lower court ruled for the plaintiffs, finding that the company was required to reduce its emissions to a level achieved by exercising reasonable care for the interests of others and the environment. In reversing the lower court's decision, however, the court of appeal reasoned that no actionable nuisance had been alleged. Thus, common law principles were not applicable to the permit for the company's operations granted under a statute.

Federal agencies can also play a role in regulating GHG emissions. However, in *Utility Air Regulatory Group v. EPA*, the Supreme Court of the US determined that a federal agency had exceeded its statutory authority in seeking to regulate GHG emissions from small sources not otherwise regulated under federal air pollution law.[42] The court held that federal air pollution law, namely the Clean Air Act, did not authorize the agency to require smaller, unregulated stationary sources of pollution to obtain a certain type of permit based solely on their potential GHG emissions.

In reaching its decision, the court reasoned that the agency's interpretation of federal air pollution law expanded the agency's regulatory authority. This expansion of regulatory authority was inappropriate without explicit permission from the US Congress. Thus, the court made a decision that preserved the "separation of powers" principle. However, the court upheld the agency's ability to require larger polluters that already required these permits to also comply with "best available control technology" for GHG.

---

[41] *Macquarie Generation v Hodgson* [2011] NSWCA 424.
[42] *Util. Air Regulatory Grp. v. E.P.A.*, 573 US 302, 134 S. Ct. 2427, 2431, 189 L. Ed. 2d 372 (2014).

c) Emissions and the Paris Agreement in South Africa

The Paris Agreement is relevant for limiting GHG emissions from power plants. In *Earthlife Africa Johannesburg v the Minister of Environmental Affairs and others*, the High Court of South Africa directed the government to consider a climate change impact assessment report for a proposed 1,200-megawatt (MW) coal-fired power station.[43] The court found that a climate change impact assessment was necessary and relevant to ensuring that South Africa meets the emissions trajectory outlined in its NDC to the Paris Agreement.

(See Part Two, Section II.B.2. Changing Attitudes in Indonesia for further discussion of this case. See also Part Two, Section I.A.2. Environmental Impact Assessment Cases for further discussion of EIA cases and coal plants; and Part One, Section IV. The Role of the Paris Agreement for further discussion of judicial treatment of the Paris Agreement.)

B. Asia and the Pacific Approaches

1. Impact Assessments in South Asia

In *Balachandra Bhikaji Nalwade v. Union of India*, Nalwade challenged a 1,200-MW coal thermal power station in the Indian state of Maharashtra because of its impacts on his mango orchards.[44] He argued that the Ministry of Environment and Forests, and the National Environment Appellate Authority had erroneously relied on an incomplete assessment when they granted project clearance. The assessment was not based on a detailed study, the petitioner claimed, and was thus inconclusive about the effects on mango and cashew plants.

The High Court of Delhi reasoned that the UN Framework Convention on Climate Change (UNFCCC) required parties to anticipate, prevent, and minimize the causes of climate change. Where there were threats of serious or irreversible damage, parties to the convention should not postpone intervention because of a lack of scientific certainty. Further, the operation of the precautionary principle within Indian law made it mandatory for the government to anticipate, prevent, and attack the causes of environmental degradation.

The court directed the Expert Appraisal Committee to reexamine the approval in light of the full impact assessment report. The committee, the court continued, should keep in mind the principle of sustainable development. The court made power plant commencement and grid integration conditional upon the Expert Appraisal Committee's approval.

---

[43] *Earthlife Africa Johannesburg v the Minister of Environmental Affairs and others*, Case no. 65662/16 (Mar. 8, 2017).

[44] *Balachandra Bhikaji Nalwade v. Union of India*, 170 (2009) DLT 251.

The project ultimately proceeded. However, the case showed the power of the court to impose additional considerations on project approval.

In *Environmental Foundation Limited v Anura Wijepala, Chairman Ceylon Electricity Board and 15 Others*, petitioners challenged the government's EIA-based approval for the Sampur coal power plant at Trincomalee, Sri Lanka.[45] Environment Foundation Limited argued that the government had failed to consider the potential environmental impacts of a coal power plant on the surrounding marine environment. It also argued that coal power generation contributed to climate change and that the government must reduce emissions and create emission standards given its commitments under the UNFCCC, the Kyoto Protocol, and the Paris Agreement.

The plaintiff withdrew its case in 2017 after the Sri Lankan solicitor general said that the government would not proceed with the Sampur coal power project. The court issued a decision to that effect.

2. Changing Attitudes in Indonesia

Four plaintiffs challenged an environmental permit issued for the Celukan Bawan Coal-Fired Power Plant expansion in Bali, Indonesia in *Ketut Mangku Wijana, et al. v. Governor of Bali et al.*[46] The plaintiffs argued that neither the project EIA nor the governor of Bali's decision took climate change impacts into account. In their view, the climate and atmosphere should form part of the environment. They contended that project impacts on the climate system should be treated as significant environmental impacts, which the EIA should consider.[47]

The plaintiffs maintained that the EIA should evaluate how the project's predicted carbon emissions would affect Indonesia's national carbon emissions. Such modeling would enable the government to test whether the project aligned with Indonesia's NDCs under the Paris Agreement. Given Bali's vulnerability to rising sea levels, the plaintiffs also argued that the EIA should assess the impact of sea level rise and storm surge on local businesses and activities.

Experts supporting the plaintiffs submitted an *amicus curiae* brief, inviting the court to consider international best practices.[48] Experts cited *Earthlife Africa Johannesburg v the Minister of Environmental Affairs and others* (footnote 43). In that 2017 case, the High Court of South Africa directed the government to

---

[45] *Environmental Foundation Limited v Anura Wijepala, Chairman Ceylon Electricity Board and 15 Others* SCFR 179/2016.

[46] Administrative Court of Denpasar, No. 2/G/LH/2018/PTUN.DPS, *Ketut Mangku Wijana et al. v. Governor of Bali et al.*

[47] In Indonesia, EIAs are called Analisis Mengenai Dampak Lingkungan (AMDAL).

[48] *Amici Curiae* brief was submitted by multiple parties on 26 June 2018 by Indonesian Center for Environmental Law, Earthjustice, Environmental Law Alliance Worldwide, Client Earth, Center for Environmental Rights, Environmental Defenders' Offices of Australia, Environmental Justice Australia, The Access Initiative, and Research Center for Climate Change University Indonesia.

consider a climate change impact assessment report for a proposed 1,200-MW coal-fired power station. The court felt the assessment was necessary and relevant to ensuring that South Africa met the emissions trajectory outlined in its NDCs.

(See Part Two, Section II.A.2.c. Emissions and the Paris Agreement in South Africa for a full case summary of this *Earthlife Africa Johannesburg v the Minister of Environmental Affairs and Others*.)

The plaintiffs' arguments in *Ketut Mangku Wijana et al. v. Governor of Bali et al.* did not persuade the court. It held that they lacked standing and that new technology could mitigate the risk of pollution.[49] The court further ordered that the power plant expansion should not stop during the appeals process. The plaintiffs were unsuccessful with their appeals to the High Administrative Court of Denpasar and the Supreme Court.

While the plaintiffs did not achieve their desired outcome in the court, this litigation impacted norms and values.[50] The case and public concern attracted political attention. In September 2018, Bali's new governor, Wayan Koster, announced his preference for green energy. He reportedly stated he would pressure the power plant owners to phase out coal and replace it with gas.[51]

3. Statutory Rights in Bangladesh

In *Centre for Human Rights Movement Vs. Government of Bangladesh*, petitioners challenged the government's plans to build a 1,300-MW coal-based thermal power station near the Sundarbans, a mangrove forest in the delta of the Bay of Bengal.[52] The petitioners alleged that the power plant would breach the Bangladesh Environment Conservation Act. They further argued that the Sundarbans was the world's largest mangrove forest, a listed World Heritage Site, and protected under the Wetland Act. The case was accompanied by much political pressure and has not progressed.

4. Transboundary Assessments in the Federated States of Micronesia

On 3 December 2009, the Government of the Federated States of Micronesia (FSM) formally requested that the Czech Republic conduct a transboundary EIA for the proposed expansion and modernization of the Prunéřov II coal-fired

---

[49] M. Taylor. 2018. Indonesian Court Rejects Bid to Stop Coal Power Plant Expansion. *Reuters*. 17 August.

[50] H.M. Osofsky and J. Peel. 2013. The Role of Litigation in Multilevel Climate Change Governance: Possibilities for a Lower Carbon Future? *Environmental and Planning Law Journal*. 30 (4). pp. 303–328.

[51] T. Apriando. 2019. Local People Challenge Coal Plant Expansion in Bali. *China Dialogue*. 4 September; W. Nurhayat and C.A. Siahaan. 2018. Gubernur Bali yang Baru Minta PLTU Celukan Bawang Pakai Gas. *Kumparan*. 8 September.

[52] Writ Petition No. 1212 of 2011.

power plant in the Czech Republic.[53] The Government of the FSM asserted that the lignite-fired power plant was one of the biggest industrial sources of CO_2 emissions globally and would contribute to global warming. Global warming, in turn, would lead to the destruction of the country's entire environment.[54] Although the Czech Ministry of the Environment accepted the request, the minister later approved the Prunéřov II expansion.

The FSM government's request seeking the review within the framework of the Espoo Convention predated the Paris Agreement. The authors are not aware of similar requests for transboundary EIAs from Asia and the Pacific countries.

5. Coal-Fired Power Stations in the Philippines

In 2010, the Philippine Supreme Court issued innovative Rules of Procedure for Environmental Cases with the writ of *kalikasan* (nature).[55] The writ protects the right to a healthy environment and functions as an extraordinary remedy. It provides relief from actual or threatened violations to one's constitutional right to a balanced and healthful ecology. However, the breach or threatened violation must be unlawful and cause substantial environmental damage that would prejudice the life, health, or the property of inhabitants in two or more cities or provinces.[56] Parties may file their petition in the Supreme Court or Court of Appeals.

Relief is swift. The courts must give an order within 3 days and judgment within 60 days.[57] Courts may grant a wide range of reliefs, including a temporary environmental protection order. Courts are also directed to apply the precautionary principle where "there is a lack of full scientific certainty in establishing a causal link between human activity and environmental effect."[58]

In *Paje v. Casino et al.*, petitioners sought a writ of *kalikasan* for an environmental clearance granted for a 300-MW coal-fired power plant in Subic, a coastal municipality in the Philippines.[59] The petitioners argued that the power plant would cause environmental damage and pollution, which would adversely affect the residents in two provinces. While the claim did not specifically focus on climate change, some of their assertions echoed climate change arguments as they challenged the use of coal for power generation. The petitioners claimed that the plan to discharge heated water into Subic Bay would warm the local marine environment, harming aquatic organisms and depleting marine oxygen levels.

---

[53] The Government of the FSM sought this review under the Espoo Convention and the Czech Act on Environmental Impact Assessment. Collection of Laws No. 100 of 2001.

[54] A. Yatilman. 2009. Letter request for a transboundary EIA proceeding from the plan for the modernization of the Prunéřov II power plant. 3 December.

[55] Government of the Philippines, Supreme Court. 2010. Rules of Procedure for Environmental Cases, A.M. No. 09-6-8-SC.

[56] Footnote 55, section 1, rule 7, part III.

[57] Footnote 55, sections 5 and 15, rule 7, part III.

[58] Footnote 55, section 1, rule 20, part V.

[59] *Paje v. Casino et al.*, G.R. Nos. 207257, 207276, 207282 & 207366, 3 February 2015.

The Supreme Court refused the petition on the basis that the petitioners had failed to call adequate evidence to prove their case. The court noted that future petitioners might use a writ of *kalikasan* to challenge an environmental clearance provided

(i) the defects in granting the clearance were reasonably connected or had a causal connection to the actual or threatened environmental damage; and

(ii) the parties had exhausted (or are exempt from exhausting) all administrative remedies or primary jurisdiction.

Defects might occur, e.g., where there were serious or substantial misrepresentations or fraud in the application for an environmental clearance that would cause environmental impacts of significant magnitude.[60]

Given its emphasis on environmental protection, the writ could be useful in the Philippines for challenging fossil fuel projects or stopping pollution that contributes to climate change. However, there are few instances of litigants successfully attaining a writ.

III. Pipelines and Fossil Fuel Transport Projects

A. Global Approaches

1. Statute-Based Challenges to Siting and Permitting

Recent cases challenging oil and natural gas pipelines, coal rail facilities, and other fossil fuel transportation projects have focused primarily on issues relating to EIAs. The cases generally allege that the approving government body failed to adequately consider project-related GHG emissions in the EIA.

a) Cases Dismissed in the United States

In the US, a small but growing number of cases have also challenged the approval of natural gas pipelines because the approving body failed to ensure that development was in the public interest as required by federal law. The cases have pointed to, among other things, the approving body's failure to consider the GHG emissions associated with the upstream production and downstream combustion

---

[60] Footnote 59, p. 20.

of natural gas to be transported via the pipeline.[61] At the time of writing, at least one of the cases remained undecided,[62] while several had been dismissed on procedural and other grounds (e.g., for lack of standing).[63]

Another notable US case—challenging natural gas pipeline development under a federal law protecting religious freedom—was also recently dismissed on procedural grounds. In *Adorers of the Blood of Christ v. Federal Energy Regulatory Commission*, a vowed religious order of Roman Catholic women challenged the approval of a pipeline crossing their land.[64] The order argued that the approval violated their right to free exercise of religion because pipeline development would "contribute to global warming in a manner contrary to their religious beliefs," which required them to "protect and preserve the Earth as God's creation."[65] That argument was not addressed, either at first instance or on appeal, with the courts dismissing the case for lack of jurisdiction.[66]

b) *Natural Gas Pipelines in the United States*

Some cases seeking to advance natural gas pipeline development have also recently come before the US courts. The cases generally involve state attempts to block pipeline projects on environmental grounds unrelated to climate change. Many arise in the context of federal environmental laws, such as the Clean Water Act, which requires certain pipeline projects to obtain a state water quality certificate demonstrating compliance with applicable water quality standards. Authorities in at least four states have refused to certify pipeline projects, often on the grounds that there is insufficient information to assess the project's water quality impacts, or that the available information indicates that the project will violate water quality standards.[67]

In cases challenging the refusals, the courts have typically deferred to state authorities' judgment on these issues, viewing them as falling within the

---

[61]   *Delaware Riverkeeper Network v. Fed. Energy Regulatory Comm'n*, No. 18-1128 (D.C. Cir. filed May 9, 2018); *Otsego 2000, Inc. v. Fed. Energy Regulatory Comm'n*, No. 18-1188 (D.C. Cir. filed Jul. 16, 2018); *Appalachian Voices v. Fed. Energy Regulatory Comm'n*, No. 17-1271 (D.C. Cir. filed Dec. 22, 2017); *Sierra Club v. US Dep't of Energy*, No. 15-1489 (D.C. Cir. filed Dec. 22, 2015).

[62]   *Delaware Riverkeeper Network v. Fed. Energy Regulatory Comm'n*, No. 18-1128 (D.C. Cir. filed May 9, 2018).

[63]   *Otsego 2000, Inc. v. Fed. Energy Regulatory Comm'n*, 2019 US App. LEXIS 14060 (D.C. Cir. 2019).

[64]   *Adorers of the Blood of Christ v. Fed. Energy Regulatory Comm'n*, 283 F. Supp. 3d 342 (E.D. Pa. 2017), aff'd, 897 F.3d 187 (3d Cir. 2018), *cert. denied*, 139 S. Ct. 1169 (2019).

[65]   Footnote 64, 897 F.3d, pp. 190 and 193.

[66]   Footnotes 64, p. 198.

[67]   Authorities in Connecticut, Oregon, New Jersey, and New York have denied water quality certificates for pipeline projects. See Letter from Connecticut Department of Energy and Environmental Protection to Islander East Pipeline Company, LLC (Dec. 19, 2016); Letter from Oregon Department of Environmental Quality to Jordan Cove LNG, LLC and Pacific Connector Gas Pipeline, LP (May 6, 2019); Letter from New Jersey Department of Environmental Protection to PennEast Pipeline Company (Feb 1, 2018); Letter from New York State Department of Environmental Conservation to Millennium Pipeline Company LLC and TRC Environment Corp. (Aug. 30, 2017).

authorities' unique expertise.[68] The courts have, however, insisted that state authorities provide a detailed factual basis for their decisions.[69]

2. Property Appropriation in the United States

The construction of gas pipelines and transportation projects can require the seizure of private property. In the US, land trusts and private landowners cannot affirmatively challenge companies' seizure of their property for gas pipeline construction. But such landowners have attempted to defend their lands from seizure.

A vigorous defense can take two forms: (i) aggrieved parties can defend against a company's bid to seize their property in state or federal district court; and (ii) such parties can challenge a company's government-issued "certificate of public convenience and necessity." This certificate is the source of the company's authority for both constructing interstate pipelines and condemning lands necessary for those pipelines in federal appellate court.

In *Appalachian Voices v. Federal Energy Regulatory Commission*, a US federal appellate court upheld a company's "certificate of public convenience and necessity," which authorized the company to construct a 488.5-kilometer (km) natural gas pipeline.[70] Environmental groups challenged the certificate, arguing, among other things, that the federal agency that issued the certificate did not adequately consider the pipeline's harms. These harms included downstream GHG emissions from the combustion of the gas transported by the pipeline. The plaintiffs also argued that the company's exercise of eminent domain under the Natural Gas Act—a federal statute—was unconstitutional. The court reasoned that the constitutional requirements were met by the agency's public convenience and necessity determination under the Natural Gas Act.

Other cases rooted in federalism claims may be more successful, e.g., where a state challenges a private company's authority to seize state land.[71]

3. Environmental Impact Statements in the United States

EIA laws have provided a legal basis for lawsuits challenging government approvals of pipelines and other natural gas transportation infrastructure where climate change impacts have not been adequately accounted for. As with the EIA cases involving fossil fuel production, many lawsuits involving fossil fuel transportation

---

[68] See, e.g., *Constitution Pipeline Co., LLC v. N.Y. Dep't of Envtl. Conservation*, 868 F.3d 87, 103 (2d Cir. 2017).

[69] See, e.g., *Islander E. Pipeline Co. v. Conn. Dep't of Envtl. Prot.*, 482 F.3d 79, 95 (2d Cir. 2006), appeal after remand, sub nom. *Islander E. Pipeline Co., LLC v. McCarthy*, 525 F.3d 141, 150-151 (2d. Cir. 2008).

[70] *Appalachian Voices v. Fed. Energy Regulatory Comm'n*, No. 17-1271 (D.C. Cir. Feb. 19, 2019).

[71] See, e.g., *PennEast Pipeline Company, LLC v. A Permanent Easement for 1.74 Acres et al.*, 19-1191 (filed 3rd Cir. 2019).

have included questions about the scope of emissions that must be considered when reviewing a proposed project. In particular, courts have decided whether upstream emissions from the production of the transported fuels and downstream emissions from the combustion of the transported fuels qualify as "indirect effects." Indirect effects would have to be disclosed in EIA documents.

Two of the earliest decisions in this category involved the EIAs for US rail projects intended to transport coal. In *Mid States Coalition for Progress v. Surface Transportation Board*, a US appellate court held that the reviewing agency must disclose downstream emissions from the combustion of the coal. In *North Plains Resource Council, Inc. v. Surface Transportation Board*, a US appellate court held that the agency must consider upstream emissions from the mining of the coal.[72]

Construction of a gas pipeline in the United States. Litigation is now challenging decisions to approve gas pipelines over the failure to take increased GHG emissions into account (photo by the National Parks Conservation Association).

Courts have also required consideration of downstream combustion emissions in the context of oil and natural gas pipelines. Most notably, in *Sierra Club v. FERC*, a US appellate court found that downstream emissions from natural gas combustion were an indirect effect of a proposed pipeline project where the end use of the natural gas was known.[73] No US decision has yet been issued finding inadequate analysis of upstream (i.e., production) emissions in the context of the pipeline project. There are, however, at least two decisions finding adequate analysis because the agency incorporated quantitative analysis of upstream emissions in its review.[74]

B.   Asia and the Pacific Approaches: Pipeline Emissions in the Philippines

To date, litigants in Asia and the Pacific have not used climate change to object to fossil fuel pipelines or transport projects. Although litigants have sued over damage caused by oil spills and gas pipeline leaks, they have not raised climate change as an issue for adjudication.

The Supreme Court of the Philippines granted its first writ of *kalikasan* (nature) to stop a fossil fuel pipeline leak in Manila in *West Tower Condominium Corp v. First Philippine Industrial Corporation et al.*[75] The respondent's 117-km-long

---

72   *Mid States Coal. for Progress v. Surface Transp. Bd.*, 345 F.3d 520, 549 (8th Cir. 2003); N. Plains Res. Council at 1082 (9th Cir. 2011).
73   *Sierra Club v. Fed. Energy Regulatory Comm'n*, 827 F.3d 59 (D.C. Cir. 2016).
74   *Indigenous Environmental Network v. US Dept. of State*, No. 4:17-cv-00029 (D. Mont. 11/8/18); *Sierra Club v. DOE*, No. 15-1489 (D.C. Cir. 8/15/17).
75   *West Tower Condominium Corp v. First Philippine Industrial Corporation et al.*, G.R. No. 194239, 16 June 2015.

pipeline system transported a range of fuels such as diesel, gasoline, and kerosene throughout Manila. In 2010, the pipeline leaked, affecting residents in two barangays as well as the West Tower condominium.[76]

At first instance, the Court of Appeals awarded a writ of *kalikasan* with a temporary environmental protection order. It ordered the respondent to (i) cease operating the leaking pipeline, (ii) check the pipeline's structural integrity, and (iii) implement measures to prevent any incidents resulting from leaks and report on those measures. The petitioners also requested the creation of a special trust fund to answer for similar contingencies. The Supreme Court refused to grant a trust fund, reasoning that the petitioned trust fund went beyond special trust funds as contemplated by the Rules of Procedure for Environmental Cases.

While this case did not explicitly plead or rely on climate change, it had ramifications for reducing fossil fuel emissions from pipeline leaks. (See Part Three, Section II.B.2. Liability for Nuisance from a Pipeline Leak in the Philippines for further discussion of this case.)

IV. Renewable Energy

A. Global Approaches

1. Challenges to Renewable Energy Project Siting and Permitting

This section discusses recent court challenges to renewable energy projects brought by residents and community groups concerned about the projects' adverse impacts on the local environment. When adjudicating such challenges, the courts have emphasized the need to weigh any local adverse impacts against the broader social benefits of renewable energy development, including in mitigating climate change. To justify the approval of projects, many have relied on government climate change policies as well as broader goals around sustainable development.

a) Wind Turbines in Australia

In a leading Australian case—*Taralga Landscape Guardians Inc v Minister for Planning and Another*—the New South Wales Land and Environment Court upheld the approval of a turbine wind energy project consisting of 62 turbines in rural New South Wales.[77] A community association comprising landowners and residents from the surrounding community challenged the approval, arguing that the project would have negative visual and noise impacts, and also threaten local flora and fauna.

---

[76] Barangays are the smallest administrative division in the Philippines. They equate to a borough, ward, village, district, or inner-city suburb.
[77] *Taralga Landscape Guardians Inc v Minister for Planning & Anor* [2007] NSWLEC 59.

While acknowledging the potential impacts, the court concluded that the project's benefits outweighed the impacts. The court based its decision, in part, on the principles of sustainable development, which it described as "central to any decision-making process concerning the development of new energy resources."[78] The court placed particular emphasis on the principle of intergenerational equity, which it interpreted as requiring, among other things, high-emitting energy sources to be replaced with lower-emitting alternatives to mitigate climate change. The court noted that federal and state climate change policies support increased use of wind and other low emission renewable energy sources.

According to the court, while renewable energy development would inevitably result in some local adverse impacts, those impacts must be balanced against "the broader public good of increasing the supply of renewable energy" and mitigating the effects of climate change for current and future generations.[79]

In subsequent decisions, Australian courts approved renewable energy projects based on their potential to reduce GHG emissions, even where the emissions reduction potential was relatively small. In *Russell & Ors v Surf Coast SC & Anor*, the Victorian Civil and Administrative Tribunal (VCAT) upheld the approval of a 14-turbine wind energy project proposed for development on agricultural land in Victoria.[80] Residents challenged the approval on several grounds, including that the project's purported emissions reduction benefits had been overstated and did not justify its significant adverse impacts. To support that argument, the residents pointed to the low average capacity factor of wind turbines (relative to baseload generation) and the fact that they only operate intermittently.[81]

While accepting this, the tribunal concluded that the project would still have climate change benefits, citing the state government estimates that it could avoid the emission of 80,000 metric tons of CO_2 per year.[82] Reasoning that state policy supported low-carbon energy development, the tribunal held that the emissions reduction potential must be given "considerable weight." This potential justified the approval of the project, although it would have adverse impacts on the local landscape.[83]

b) Wind Turbines in New Zealand

A similar approach has also been taken in other jurisdictions. In *Genesis Power Limited v Franklin District Council*, the Environment Court of New Zealand approved an 18-turbine wind energy project, which had previously been rejected by local authorities.[84] The project developer and a federal government body (i.e.,

---

[78]   Footnote 77, p. 73.
[79]   Footnote 77, pp. 3 and 80.
[80]   *Russell & Ors v Surf Coast SC & Anor* [2009] VCAT 1324.
[81]   Footnote 80, p. 23.
[82]   Footnote 80, pp. 27–28.
[83]   Footnote 80, pp. 28–30.
[84]   *Genesis Power Limited & the Energy Efficiency and Conservation Authority v Franklin District Council* [2005] NZRMA 541.

the New Zealand Energy Efficiency and Conservation Authority) challenged the rejection under the law governing approval of renewable energy projects.

In upholding the challenge, the court noted that the law aimed to "promote the sustainable management of natural and physical resources," which were threatened by climate change.[85] The court held that, in evaluating renewable energy projects, "particular regard" must be had to the need to mitigate climate change and the role renewable energy could play therein.[86] The court expressly rejected claims that the mitigation benefits need not be considered because the wind energy project was small.[87] According to the court, while the project would contribute just 0.8% of New Zealand's then renewable energy target, it would still assist in achieving the country's climate change goals, avoiding GHG emissions associated with fossil fuel-based electricity generation.[88]

c) Wind Turbines in the United Kingdom

Courts in the UK have also emphasized the need to consider climate change benefits when assessing renewable energy projects. In *Newark & Sherwood District Council & Anor v Secretary of State for Communities and Local Government & Anor*, two local councils challenged the approval of a single wind turbine.[89] The councils argued, among other things, that the approving inspector had failed to consider the turbine's limited generating capacity when assessing its climate change benefits.[90] That argument was rejected by the High Court of Justice, which upheld the inspector's conclusion that the turbine would make a "valuable contribution" to mitigating climate change, despite its small size.[91]

The court based its decision on a government policy document, which indicated that "significant weight" should be given to the benefits of renewable energy projects, "whatever their scale."[92] The court concluded that, while the turbine would make only a small contribution to renewable generation, its climate change benefits were "sufficient" to outweigh its adverse impacts.[93]

It should be noted that the project at issue in *Newark & Sherwood District Council & Anor v Secretary of State for Communities and Local Government & Anor* was expected to have only limited adverse environmental impacts. However, in subsequent cases, the UK courts have approved projects found to be highly damaging.

---

[85] Footnote 84, p. 59, para. 227.
[86] Footnote 84, p. 58, para. 226.
[87] Footnote 84, pp. 57–59, paras. 224–228.
[88] Footnote 84, pp. 15–18, paras. 64–65.
[89] *Newark & Sherwood District Council & Anor v Secretary of State for Communities and Local Government & Anor* [2013] EWHC 2162 (Admin).
[90] Footnote 89, pp. 57–58.
[91] Footnote 89, p. 66.
[92] Footnote 89, p. 62.
[93] Footnote 89, pp. 60–66.

In *Wildland Ltd and The Welbeck Estates v Scottish Ministers*, the Court of Session upheld the approval of a 22-turbine wind energy project likely to have "significant impacts" on sensitive wildlands in Scotland.[94] The court held that the approving ministers appropriately balanced those impacts against the project's benefits, including its potential to reduce GHG emissions and thus further the Scottish government's efforts to tackle climate change, which justified project approval.[95]

d) Solar Projects in the United States

Litigants have also challenged solar projects. In *Clean Water Action v. Jackson Township*, a US state court dismissed a challenge to an amusement park company for installing a 21-MW solar array on its property.[96] The plaintiffs alleged that the land use ordinances that permitted the solar array conflicted with the township master plan. In reaching its decision, the court noted that the solar array would meet substantially all of the company's energy needs and reduce reliance on carbon-emitting sources of power.

The court found that the land use ordinances were consistent with the goals of the township master plan and that promoting "reliance upon renewable energy . . . is a legitimate objective of zoning."[97] Although the court acknowledged that the plaintiffs advanced legitimate environmental arguments, the court upheld the solar array approval. The court reasoned that solar energy was "an inherently beneficial use, which is of value to the community, serves a public good, and promotes public welfare."[98] The court also found that the use of land for solar arrays was consistent with "natural use of the land" and that it was "within the prerogative of the legislative body to consider the environmental advantage of renewable solar energy and to balance that against other environmental impacts."[99]

2. Challenges to Renewable Energy Policies

Litigants have challenged not only specific renewable energy projects but also government policies requiring or encouraging project development. This section discusses several recent US and European cases in which the courts have considered the scope of governments' authority to adopt renewable energy policies.

a) Renewables in the United States

The US cases have focused primarily on state governments' authority to issue renewable energy policies. In these cases, courts have generally construed state authority broadly, upholding various policies alleged to exceed states' regulatory jurisdiction, and/or encroach on areas under federal regulation.

---

94 *Wildland Ltd and The Welbeck Estates v Scottish Ministers* [2017] CSOH 113.
95 Footnote 94, pp. 17–20 and 45.
96 *Clean Water Action v. Jackson Township*, OCN-L-1251-15 PW (N.J. Super. Ct. 2017).
97 Footnote 96, p. 15.
98 Footnote 96, p. 13.
99 Footnote 96, p. 16.

In *Southern California Edison Company v. Public Utilities Commission of the State of California*, a California court upheld a state program—the Electric Program Investment Charge—requiring utilities to levy a surcharge on customers to fund renewable energy research, development, and demonstration projects.[100]

The program was established by the California Public Utilities Commission—a body authorized under the state constitution to regulate electric utilities. Southern California Edison challenged the program as exceeding the authority of the California Public Utilities Commission. In dismissing the challenge, the California Court of Appeals emphasized that the commission has vast jurisdiction under both the state constitution and legislation to "take any action . . . cognate and germane to utility regulation."[101] The court held that the establishment of the program fell squarely within that authority since it was intended to facilitate the development of new technologies to provide utility customers with cheaper, safer, and more reliable electricity services.

In *Allco Finance Ltd. v. Klee*, a solar energy developer (Allco) challenged two Connecticut state programs that require utilities to obtain electricity from renewable sources.[102] One of the programs—Connecticut's Renewable Energy Procurement program—authorized the state energy agency to solicit bids for renewable generation and direct utilities to enter into contracts with the winning bidder(s). Allco alleged that this program was preempted by federal law because it compelled utilities to enter into contracts with renewable generators and thus involved the regulation of wholesale electricity sales.

This fell, Allco claimed, within the exclusive authority of federal regulators. That view was rejected by the US Court of Appeals for the Second Circuit, which pointed to the program documents indicating that utilities were "not obligate[d]" to accept any bid and could contract with winning bidders "at the[ir] discretion."[103] The court thus held that the Renewable Energy Procurement program did not compel or otherwise regulate wholesale electricity sales in violation of federal law.

The court in *Allco Finance Ltd. v. Klee* also dismissed a challenge to Connecticut's Renewable Portfolio Standard program, which required state utilities to obtain an increasing share of their electricity from renewable sources. Utilities could demonstrate compliance with that requirement by purchasing renewable energy certificates from qualifying generators in a specific geographic region. Allco argued that, due to this geographic restriction, the program discriminated against its out-of-region facilities in violation of the US constitution.

---

100 *S. Cal. Edison Co. v. Pub. Util. Comm'n of State of Cal.*, 2014 Cal. App. Unpub. LEXIS 3758 (Cal. Ct. App. 2014).
101 Footnote 100, pp. 17–18.
102 *Allco Finance Ltd. v. Klee*, 861 F.3d 82 (2d Cir. 2017), *cert. denied*, 138 S. Ct. 926 (2018).
103 Footnote 102, p. 98.

The court also rejected that argument. Finding that renewable energy certificates produced by in- and out-of-region generators constituted different products, the court held that Connecticut's Renewable Portfolio Standard program "does no more than treat different products differently in a nondiscriminatory fashion."[104] The court further held that the program's differential treatment of in- and out-of-region generators was justified based on Connecticut's interest in encouraging the development of local renewable generating facilities that would, among other things, contribute to an improvement in the state's air quality.

b) Renewables in Europe

The European Court of Justice considered similar issues in *Ålands Vindkraft AB v Energimyndigheten*.[105] The case concerned a 2011 Swedish law requiring electricity suppliers and certain consumers to purchase certificates. Awarded by the national energy agency, these certificates were based on the amount of renewable electricity produced in Sweden. The owner of a Finnish wind farm, which had been denied certificates for renewable electricity produced outside Sweden, challenged the law on the basis that it hindered trade between EU member states in violation of the Treaty on the Functioning of the EU.

The European Court of Justice agreed that the law could limit imports of renewable electricity into Sweden from other EU member states because Swedish-based generators would likely bundle the sale of certificates with electricity. Where this occurred, electricity suppliers and consumers requiring certificates would be forced to buy renewable electricity from Swedish-based generators, rather than import it. Nevertheless, the court held that the law did not violate the Treaty on the Functioning of the EU because the import restriction was "justified by overriding requirements relating to protection of the environment," including the need to promote renewable energy development to reduce GHG emissions.[106]

British cases have focused on governments' authority to weaken existing renewable energy policies. In *Secretary of State for Energy and Climate Change v Friends of the Earth & Others*, solar energy installers and community groups challenged a proposal to vary the UK's Feed-in-Tariff program, which required electricity suppliers to pay small-scale solar and other low-carbon generators above-market rates for any electricity they produce.[107] After a surge in solar installations in the UK, the secretary of state for energy and climate change proposed to reduce the rate for new and certain existing installations.

The UK Court of Appeal held that, in applying the reduced rate to existing installations, the secretary of state had exceeded its authority. The court reasoned

---

[104] Footnote 102, p. 103.
[105] Case C-573/12, *Ålands Vindkraft AB v Energimyndigheten* [2014] ECLI:EU:C:2014:2037.
[106] Footnote 105, pp. 77–82.
[107] *Secretary of State for Energy and Climate Change v Friends of the Earth & Ors* [2012] ECA Civ 28.

that the Feed-in-Tariff program was intended to encourage the installation of small-scale low-carbon-generating facilities. As such, the program guaranteed the owners of such facilities a fixed rate for their electricity.

Describing that guarantee as "fundamental" to the program, the court ruled that the rate could not be retroactively reduced because doing so would take away the owners' entitlement to payment at the fixed rate, thereby depriving them of their "vested rights" under the program.[108]

B.   Approaches from Asia and the Pacific

The Intergovernmental Panel on Climate Change (IPCC) has identified the role renewables play in reducing the global carbon budget, despite their environmental, physical, or financial impacts. Like people elsewhere, not everyone in Asia and the Pacific wants a renewable energy project nearby. Consequently, most renewable energy litigation in the region focuses on the environmental and other impacts of renewable energy projects.

Such litigation can be challenging for courts. They must balance competing interests and needs, and also discern the best course of action to develop sustainably and meet climate goals.

1.   Hydropower in South Asia

Kali Gandaki "A" hydroelectric power station in Nepal. Although hydropower is a lower-carbon technology, litigants have challenged the environmental impacts of large-scale hydro projects (photo by Samir Jung Thapa/ADB).

Large-scale hydropower can have widespread impacts. Hydropower projects can affect land use, wildlife, and riparian ecology. Many communities oppose hydro-based projects because people are often resettled to make way for them. Communities not forced to move are affected in other ways, such as by impacts on downstream river flows.

In *Alaknanda Hydro Power Company Ltd. v. Anuj Joshi and Ors.*, the Supreme Court of India noted the importance of holistically assessing the impacts of multiple hydroelectric projects.[109] The Central Electricity Authority approved the 200-MW Srinagar Hydro Electric Project in 1985. After the initial approval, the project scope increased to 300 MW, with a higher dam wall and larger dam size. The Central Electricity Authority also approved the transfer of the environmental clearance to new project proponents.

---

[108] Footnote 107, pp. 40 and 42.
[109] *Alaknanda Hydro Power Company Ltd. v. Anuj Joshi and Ors.*, (2014) 1 SCC 769.

The respondents challenged the project in 2009, arguing that it should comply with public consultation procedures required under the 2006 EIA regulations. Between 1985 and 2014, the government had also liberalized its energy policy and encouraged private participation in energy development. The court discussed the findings in the interministerial committee. It recommended that pending the Ganga Basin Management Plan, no new hydropower projects would be approved beyond the 69 identified projects within the Alaknanda and Bhagirathi river basins.[110]

The court was concerned about the government's failure to assess the cumulative impacts of multiple hydropower projects on one river basin. It found there was no scientific assessment of the cumulative effects of the projects' components, e.g., blasting, deforesting, and building dams. These components, among others, had caused environmental injury. The court directed the government to stop all environmental and forest-clearing approvals for hydroelectric power projects in the State of Uttarakhand until further orders.

The court also questioned whether the various hydro-based projects had contributed to catastrophic flooding in North India in 2013. A multiday cloudburst had caused floods and landslides, killing around 5,700 people.[111] The court directed the government to form an expert body to study whether, and to what extent, the approved hydroelectric power projects had contributed to (i) the environmental degradation within the state, and (ii) the 2013 flooding tragedy.[112]

(See Part Four, Section II.B. Asia and the Pacific Approaches: Failing to Assess Cumulative Impacts in South Asia for further discussion of this case.)

2. Wind Power in South Asia

Projects must ensure they seek all relevant approvals. Maintaining a good relationship with the surrounding community also helps minimize litigation risks.

Community members in India sought relief from the short- and long-term adverse effects of a wind farm in *Kallpavalli Vrishka Pempakamdarula & Ors v. Union of India & Ors.*[113] Community members did not initially object to Enercon (India) Limited's 55-turbine wind farm when it was approved in 2007. The villagers assumed the effects would be minimal. They also thought it would result in jobs, which it did not.

Other expectations were not met. For example, Enercon built a 15-meter wide road when it only had the approval to construct a 3-meter wide road. Furthermore, Enercon's contractors cut down 30,000 trees—as well as thousands

---

[110] Footnote 109, p. 808, para. 49.

[111] *BBC*. 2013. India Floods: More than 5,700 People 'Presumed Dead'. 15 July.

[112] Footnote 109, p. 809, para. 52.2.

[113] *Kallpavalli Vrishka Pempakamdarula & Ors. v. Union of India & Ors.*, Original Application No. 92 of 2013 (National Green Tribunal, 25 August 2015).

of smaller trees—and built the road through the village. Construction extensively damaged topography and ecology, and depleted traditional water bodies.

Villagers claimed that the 74-meter high turbines disbursed rain clouds, and also dried out and killed their pasturelands, impairing their capacity to graze sheep and goats. After raising their concerns about the project impacts on their lands and livelihood, the villagers and Enercon reached a community agreement. The company, however, later breached that agreement.

In defending the case, Enercon and the Ministry of New and Renewable Energy argued that windmills caused no ill effects and that they were an accepted method of reducing global carbon emissions. For that reason, the ministry stated that it promoted wind energy. It also emerged that the applicants did not own the land on which the road or wind farm was built.

The National Green Tribunal (NGT) found that there was no evidence that operating the wind turbines caused environmental impacts. However, it concluded that the project construction had damaged public land. So, the NGT ordered the wind farm operator to replant trees, pay environmental compensation to the government, and prevent plastic pollution.

Companies implementing wind energy projects in India have challenged grid rules that do not compensate them for injecting additional energy onto the grid. In *Renew Wind Energy (AP) Private Limited v. Karnataka Electricity Regulatory Commission & Ors.*, the appellant sought compensation for injecting electricity into the grid in violation of the regulations.[114] The appellant operated an 18-MW wind farm in the state of Karnataka. The wind farm injected electricity into the grid without prior agreement or approval from the electricity regulatory commission. The electrical grid could not store or use the extra energy injected. The tribunal held that the appellant was not entitled to compensation for the additional energy, which could not be stored or benefited from.

3. Renewable Energy Purchase Requirements in South Asia

Meeting net zero carbon emissions by 2050 will require widespread and drastic reductions in carbon emissions.[115] However, government policy to promote renewable energy is controversial for some. In India, companies have challenged regulations requiring them to purchase renewable energy.

Hindustan Zinc Ltd. v. Rajasthan Electricity Regulatory Commission concerned petitions against regulations requiring regulated parties to buy renewable energy.[116] Appellants manufactured metal and nonmetal products and built

---

[114] *Renew Wind Energy (AP) Private Limited v. Karnataka Electricity Regulatory Commission & Ors.,* 2017 ELR (APTEL) 1223.

[115] Intergovernmental Panel on Climate Change (IPCC). 2018. Summary for Policymakers. In V. Masson-Delmotte et al., eds. *Global Warming of 1.5°C. An IPCC Special Report.* In press. pp. 15–16.

[116] *Hindustan Zinc Ltd. v. Rajasthan Electricity Regulatory Commission,* (2015) 12 SCC 611.

captive power plants dedicated to supplying their operations. The Rajasthan Electricity Regulatory Commission, Jaipur approved regulations requiring captive power plants and open-access consumers to purchase minimum quantities of renewable energy or pay a surcharge where they fail to meet the minimum purchase requirement.[117]

Before the High Court of Rajasthan, 28 petitioners mounted similar arguments.[118] Some petitions argued that the commission had exceeded its statutory powers in passing the renewable energy regulations. Other petitions argued that the commission lacked authority to direct the petitioners to purchase renewable energy or to levy a surcharge because companies did not hold distribution licenses. Therefore, the petitions contended that the regulation should be declared inapplicable to captive power plants and open-access consumers.

The State of Rajasthan asserted that it had passed the regulations to promote renewable energy generation for environmental protection and reduction of GHG emissions. It also argued that regulations that oblige end users to buy a minimum percentage of renewable energy to promote its generation—and reduce GHG emissions—align with global climate goals.

The High Court of Rajasthan upheld the regulation, issuing its decision in *Ambuja Cement v. Rajasthan Electricity Regulatory Commission* (footnote 118). It accepted that the government had passed the regulation to promote renewable energy. The court noted that coal dominated India's energy, with thermal sources generating 71% of the nation's power in 2003. It also quoted part 5.12.1 of the National Electricity Policy, which outlines an "urgent need" to promote the generation of nonconventional energy sources and advocates for efforts to "reduce the capital cost" of renewable energy projects (footnote 118). On that basis, the court considered that boosting the production of renewable energy would reduce GHG emissions and serve the greater public interest.

The court held that the commission was empowered to impose the obligation on captive power plants and open-access consumers to purchase renewable energy to protect the ecology from environmental degradation. It dismissed the argument that the regulations restricted the petitioners' constitutional rights under articles 14 and 19(1)(g) and 14 of the constitution.

The Supreme Court of India also upheld the regulations in *Hindustan Zinc Ltd. v. Rajasthan Electricity Regulatory Commission* (footnote 116). It considered that the regulations had been passed to protect the environment and prevent pollution through the use of renewable sources of energy. The court also observed that

---

[117]   Open access allows large electricity consumers to choose suppliers directly from the transmission and distribution network rather than buy electricity directly from a local electricity distribution company. See D. Singh. 2017. Newer Challenges for Open Access in Electricity: Need for Refinements in the Regulations. *Brookings*. 28 April.

[118]   Lower instance case reported as *Ambuja Cement v. Rajasthan Electricity Regulatory Commission*, 2012 ELR (Rajasthan) 1146.

thermal energy was one of the leading contributors to the GHG that led to global warming. Finally, the court held that the goal of using renewable energy to reduce pollution was in the larger public interest, and the same would prevail over the interests of the specific industries.

4. Waste-to-Energy Plants in South Asia

Waste-to-energy (WTE), briefly explained in Box 2.1, converts waste into an energy source. Litigation involving WTE plants has focused on emissions and impacts to the surrounding ecology.

In *Sukhdev Vihar Residents Welfare Association and Ors. v. Respondent: The State of NCT of Delhi and Ors.*, community members objected to the location and impacts of a proposed waste-to-energy (WTE) plant.[119] The petitioners argued that waste incineration caused air and water pollution, having disastrous impacts on the

---

Box 2.1: What Is Waste-to-Energy?

Advocates and detractors do not agree on whether waste-to-energy (WTE) is renewable energy. WTE relies on the disposal of waste, which is arguably not renewable because items are often generated from nonrenewable resources. In a sustainable world, citizens would not throw garbage away. Items would be created to have residual value for composting, recycling, or reuse.[a]

Biomass—organic material from plants and animals—forms a significant component of municipal solid waste in the form of food scraps, garden waste, and wastepaper. Advocates argue that the biomass component of waste, given its biological origin, makes WTE a renewable energy. Biogas and methane emissions—by-products of biomass decomposition—need to be managed. The World Bank projects that South Asia and East Asia will generate 661 million tons of waste per year, while the Pacific will generate 714 million tons.[b] Therefore, WTE may play a role in reducing emissions from landfills, especially in the short-term, while economies transition to more sustainable product usage cycles.

Project Drawdown estimates that reducing waste in landfills might avoid up to 2.2 gigatons of CO_2 emissions.[c] Additionally, technology and sorting in WTE production can remove recyclable and toxic inputs and capture emissions. These processes can make WTE a lower emission form of energy production compared with fossil fuel energies.[d] However, WTE requires tight regulation to ensure it does not result in high greenhouse gas emissions and environmental pollutants.

---

[a] P. Hawken, ed. 2017. *Drawdown: The Most Comprehensive Plan Ever Proposed to Reverse Global Warming.* 1st edition. New York, NY: Penguin Books. p. 31.

[b] World Bank. 2020. Trends in Solid Waste Management. *What a Waste 2.0: A Global Snapshot of Solid Waste Management to 2050.*

[c] Drawdown. Landfill Methane Capture; P. Hawken, ed. 2017. *Drawdown: The Most Comprehensive Plan Ever Proposed to Reverse Global Warming.* 1st edition. New York, NY: Penguin Books. p. 33.

[d] Footnote a, p. 32.

Source: Authors.

---

[119] *Sukhdev Vihar Residents Welfare Association & Ors. v. Respondent: The State of NCT of Delhi & Ors.*, Original Application No. 22 (THC) of 2013 (National Green Tribunal, 2 February 2017).

environment and local ecology. They alleged that the respondent's incinerator emitted more CO_2 per MW per hour than any fossil fuel-based power source, including coal and fuel power plants, meaning the plant would contribute to global climate change.

The NGT considered the importance of the precautionary principle and sustainable development principles in resolving this case. It also recognized the importance of managing Delhi's 14,100 metric tons of daily waste. The plant could process 3,000 metric tons of municipal solid waste (MSW) per day, with the potential to handle an additional 1,000 metric tons MSW. The plant also used the fly ash (a by-product of incineration) to manufacture fly ash bricks, leaving no waste residue.

The NGT noted that the proponent developed the project under the Clean Development Mechanism. It concluded that there was no doubt that such plants should be permitted to continue, but only if they do not cause pollution or environmental degradation. Further, the NGT considered that the concept of "not in my backyard" must be subservient to the public interest, which included processing waste.

The NGT found that there was a period during which the plant had exceeded emission standards due to deficient waste segregation and technology, for which it should pay compensation. However, the NGT dismissed the petition on the ground that it was time-barred by the Indian Limitation Act, 1963. The NGT also required strict supervision of the plant, including its emissions, and

(i)   directed the National Capital Territory of Delhi and all local authorities to make it mandatory for all construction projects (public or private) to use the bricks manufactured from fly ash;
(ii)   directed the government to provide more landfill sites;
(iii) recommended that the government contribute to establishing more WTE plants at appropriate locations; and
(iv)   directed the relevant agencies to reduce the height of landfill sites, expedite their bio-stabilization, and recover reusable material from landfill sites (particularly inert and plastic waste) and use it in road construction.

The value of this judgment lies in the NGT's proactive orders, driven by its broad understanding of the critical environmental issues in India. The NGT understood the potential environmental impacts of the plant but balanced those with the need of the greater good—to manage MSW and generate low-emission energy. It did not ignore the emissions breaches. Indeed, it required strict compliance with emissions standards, and it fined the plant for its violation.

The NGT's orders demonstrate a holistic approach to legal problem-solving. The NGT understood the links between poor waste management and climate change. This awareness and experience in managing environmental matters underpinned the additional orders it made, which supported the government's broader goals to manage waste and convert it into energy.

This approach to legal problem-solving within environmental law, coupled with proactive orders on allegedly lax government agencies, has become a defining feature of South Asian jurisprudence.[120]

V. Transportation Policies and Projects

This section discusses legal challenges brought by plaintiffs seeking further government consideration of the climate change impacts associated with transportation-related policies and projects. These suits concern both emissions stemming from the use of vehicles and the construction of transportation-related projects such as highways and airport runways.

A. Global Approaches

1. Fuel Standards for Vehicles in the United States

In the US, several suits have challenged whether a federal agency has sufficiently considered climate impacts in setting corporate average fuel economy standards—standards that require a given model year of vehicle to attain a certain ratio of miles per gallon. The obligation to issue these standards stems from the Energy Policy and Conservation Act. Courts have resisted designating the level of environmental review necessary to issue fuel economy standards. They have, however, found that the act and environmental review requirements obligated the agency to consider the impacts of climate change.

As other countries target to limit their GHG emissions, particularly to comply with the goals of the Paris Agreement, they may choose to enact similar laws for fuel efficiency. How US courts have interpreted obligations to consider climate change as part of the environmental review of fuel standards could inform the judicial review of similar standards in other countries.

In *Center for Biological Diversity v. National Highway Traffic Safety Administration*, a US federal appellate court held that the National Highway Traffic Safety Administration failed to adequately consider climate change impacts in its EIA of a rule that set corporate average fuel economy standards for light-duty trucks.[121] The court also found that the failure of the National Highway Traffic Safety Administration to monetize the benefits of GHG emissions reduction was arbitrary and capricious and contrary to the Energy Policy and Conservation Act.

---

[120] Courts in the US have also addressed WTE issues. In *State of California, et al. v. US EPA*, Case No. 18-cv-03237-HSG, the court found that the EPA failed to meet its statutory obligation to restrict climate-warming methane and various conventional pollutants that spew from MSW landfills across the country. See E. Gilmer. 2019. Court Orders EPA to Address Landfill Emissions. *Scientific America.* 7 May.

[121] *Center for Biological Diversity v. National Highway Traffic Safety Administration*, 538 F.3d 1172 (9th Cir. 2008).

By statute, the agency was responsible for issuing standards that "shall be the maximum feasible average fuel economy level that the Secretary decides the manufacturers can achieve in that model year." The agency had not completed the necessary analysis because the agency did not monetize the benefits of GHG emissions in making its determination. The court instructed the agency to conduct a new EIA and promulgate new standards as expeditiously as possible.

Center for Biological Diversity v. National Highway Traffic Safety Administration demonstrates that while US courts can be deferential to agency decision-making, they still hold agencies to procedural requirements to adequately consider climate change impacts as part of their decision-making.

2. Highway Projects in the United States

The construction and expansion of highway projects is also a source of direct and indirect GHG emissions. In the US, some plaintiffs have challenged whether agencies approving such projects have adequately considered the emissions related to these projects. It is part of the statutory duties of the agencies to conduct a review of the environmental impacts of major federal actions that significantly affect the environment.

As discussed, courts have held agencies to procedural requirements to consider climate change in their decision-making. However, courts have also upheld assessments that provide little or no analysis of the significance of GHG emissions generated from specific projects to the global problem of climate change.

In *North Carolina Alliance for Transportation Reform, Inc. v. US Department of Transportation*, several environmental groups challenged the construction of a federal highway project in North Carolina.[122] The plaintiffs alleged that an environmental impact statement (EIS) for the project had failed to evaluate its indirect effects (of increasing vehicle miles traveled and related GHG emissions), thus failing to account for the cumulative impact of these emissions on climate change. A federal trial court held that although federal environmental law—specifically the National Environmental Policy Act (NEPA)—required an analysis of air quality, NEPA did not expressly refer to climate change or GHG emissions. Thus, such an analysis of emissions was not necessary.

This aspect of the court's decision has been effectively overruled. However, the court also concluded that the defendants had provided a rational basis for their decision not to analyze the potential effect of GHG emissions on global climate change. The defendants argued in part that another federal trial court had previously found that analysis of emissions on a different highway was not useful

---

[122] *North Carolina Alliance for Transportation Reform, Inc. v. US Department of Transportation*, 713 F. Supp. 2d 491 (M.D.N.C. 2010).

on a project-level basis because no national regulatory thresholds had been established.[123]

In *Pacificans for a Scenic Coast v. California Dep't of Transportation*, three environmental advocacy organizations commenced a lawsuit in a federal trial court against federal and state agencies that authorized a freeway-widening project in the City of Pacifica, California.[124] The plaintiffs alleged, among other things, that the environmental review conducted under the NEPA for the project had failed to determine the significance of the project's GHG emissions. They claimed it had also failed to describe, estimate, or calculate the emissions associated with the project's construction phase. While a federal district court found the government's environmental review of the project sufficient and consistent with the required procedures, the court did not specifically discuss how the project was adequate in considering GHG emissions (footnote 124).

3. Airport Expansions

Given the large contribution of air travel to GHG emissions, recent cases in at least three different countries have challenged proposals to expand airports. Thus far, these cases have not been successful.

a) *Climate Obligations in the United Kingdom*

NGOs filed suit against the secretary of state for transport, alleging inadequate consideration of climate change impacts of the expansion of Heathrow International Airport. The case, *R (Friends of the Earth) v Secretary of State for Transport & Others*, was filed in the High Court of Justice Queen's Bench Division and heard on appeal by the Court of Appeal.[125]

The claimants argued that the secretary's national policy statement supporting the expansion of Heathrow Airport (airports national policy statement) violated the Planning Act 2008 (the 2008 Act) and the Human Rights Act 1998. The claimants argued that the two statutes require the secretary to pursue sustainable development and consider mitigating and adapting to climate change. The claimants also argued that the two statutes gave rise to implicit obligations to heed the advice of the Committee on Climate Change, the government's obligations under the Paris Agreement, and its commitment to review its national climate change targets in light of the Paris Agreement.

---

[123] *Audubon Naturalist Society of The Central Atlantic States, Inc. v. US Department of Transportation*, 524 F. Supp.2d 642, 708 (D.Md.2007).

[124] *Pacificans for a Scenic Coast v. California Dep't of Transportation*, 204 F. Supp. 3d 1075 (N.D. Cal. 2016).

[125] *R (Friends of the Earth) v Secretary of State for Transport & Others* [2020] EWCA Civ 214. The lower instance decision is *Plan B Earth and Others v Secretary of State for Transport* [2019] EWHC 1070 (Admin).

The High Court dismissed the suit, concluding that the secretary was not obliged to evaluate international climate commitments in settling the airports national policy statement. Weighing factors like the Paris Agreement, climate science, or the future need for more ambitious targets were optional.

The Court of Appeal reversed the High Court's decision in February 2020 in *R v Secretary of State for Transport & Others*.[126] It held that the airports national policy statement was invalid because it did not consider the government's "firm policy commitments on climate change."[127] Before producing the policy statement, the government had ratified the Paris Agreement, and various ministers had issued firm statements reiterating the government's policy of adhering to the Paris Agreement. Such actions meant that the Paris Agreement was "clearly part of 'government policy' by the time" the government designated the policy statement."[128]

While the court conceded that the government was not obliged to conform to policy statements, the legislative scheme under the 2008 act required the executive to take account of its policy commitments when producing a policy statement. Failure to do so rendered the airports national policy statement invalid and the government's decision to approve the new runway unlawful. Reconsideration of the policy statement should evaluate the impacts of the aviation industry and post-2050 impacts of emissions.

b) Emissions Reduction Targets in Austria

In re Vienna-Schwechat Airport Expansion, the Austrian Constitutional Court upheld the approval of construction of a third runway at Vienna's main airport against a climate-related challenge.[129] The plaintiffs had persuaded a panel of the Austrian Federal Administrative Court to overturn the government of Lower Austria's approval of the construction of the runway. The panel concluded that "authorizing the runway would do more harm to the public interest than good, primarily because it would be contrary to Austria's national and international obligations to mitigate the causes of climate change.

Of the authorities cited by the panel, the most important was Austria's Climate Protection Act of 2011, which set emissions reduction targets for various sectors, including the transport sector. Because a third runway was expected to increase Austria's annual CO_2 emissions, the panel concluded that it would be at odds with the provisions of the 2011 Act as well as with Austria's constitution and its international commitments under EU law and the Paris Agreement" (footnote 129).

In June 2017, the Austrian Constitutional Court overturned the panel's decision. The court cited multiple errors that had led the lower court to improperly give

126 *R (Friends of the Earth) v Secretary of State for Transport & Others* [2020] EWCA Civ 214.
127 Footnote 126, para. 283.
128 Footnote 126, para. 228.
129 *In re Vienna-Schwechat Airport Expansion* [2018] W109 2000179-1/291E (Austria Admin. Ct.).

weight to climate change and land use considerations in the balancing test it had used to consider the public's interest in a third runway. In March 2018, the lower court issued a new decision that approved the construction of the third runway.

c) A Right to an Environment in Ireland

In *Friends of the Irish Environment CLG v Fingal County Council*, an environmental group challenged the Fingal County Council's decision to issue a 5-year extension to the Dublin Airport Authority for their planning permission to construct a new runway.[130] The court declined to grant any of the relief sought by the applicant because it had failed to assert a viable claim for standing under section 42 of the Planning and Development Act 2000, Article 11 of the Consolidated EIA Directive, or the "Aarhus Convention" (the UN Economic Commission for Europe Convention on Access to Information, Public Participation in Decision-Making, and Access to Justice in Environmental Matters adopted on 25 June 1998 in the Danish city of Aarhus).

(See Part One, Section I.A.2. Standing and Climate Change in Australia and Europe for further discussion of this case.)

In a historic first, however, the High Court issued a judgment recognizing a personal constitutional right to an environment under the Irish constitution. This right, which is "consistent with the human dignity and well-being of citizens at large is an essential condition for the fulfilment of all human rights. It is an indispensable existential right that is enjoyed universally, yet which is vested personally" and may be protected under article 40.3.1° of the constitution.[131]

The court elaborated that this right was not so "utopian" as to prevent enforcement. Enforcement relies on identifying specific duties and obligations, which might be defined over time. The High Court concluded, however, that the applicant had no right under the Planning and Development Act to participate in the council's decision to grant a 5-year extension to the Dublin Airport Authority. Further, as the extension did not disproportionately interfere with the applicant's right to an environment, there was no violation of a constitutional right.

(See also Part One, Section 1. Standing for a discussion of standing issues.)

B.   Asia and the Pacific Approaches

1.   Curbing Vehicle Pollution to Reduce Emissions

Air pollution from transportation is a significant issue in Asia (see Box 2.2). Most transport litigation in Asia has focused on reducing traffic pollution and congestion to reduce harmful pollutants. Road users have also sued governments

---

[130] *Friends of the Irish Environment CLG v Fingal County Council* [2017] IEHC 695.
[131] Footnote 130, pp. 292–293, para. 264.

over decisions to impose emissions testing or ceilings on license numbers. While these cases may not have focused on the climate impacts of traffic emissions, they still have resulted in lowered emissions.

Box 2.2: Air Pollution from Transportation in Asia

Air pollution from transportation severely damages health and contributes to global greenhouse gas (GHG) emissions. In 2017, the transport sector emitted 24% of global CO_2 emissions from fuel combustion, making it the third-largest emitting sector.[a] To date, per capita emissions from road traffic in Asia have not significantly contributed to the region's carbon emissions.

The 2014 Intergovernmental Panel on Climate Change (IPCC) report on transport noted that many cities in India and the People's Republic of China use less than 2 gigajoules (GJ)/capita per year compared with over 100 GJ/capita in several cities in the United States.[b] Further, the International Energy Agency reported that Asia's transport sector contributed less than one-sixth of its total CO_2 emissions by combustion in 2017 (footnote a). However, GHG emissions from traffic will likely grow as expanding middle classes demand the luxury of their own car.

---

[a] International Energy Agency. 2019. *Statistics: CO₂ Emissions from Fuel Combustion: Highlights*. Paris. p. 11.
[b] R. Sims et al. 2014. Transport. In O. Edenhofer et al., eds. *Climate Change 2014: Mitigation of Climate Change. Contribution of Working Group III to the Fifth Assessment Report of the Intergovernmental Panel on Climate Change.* Cambridge University Press: Cambridge, United Kingdom and New York, NY. p. 611.

Source: Authors.

---

a) Fuel Standards and Mandamus Orders in South Asia

The Supreme Court of India famously made a series of orders requiring the government to reduce traffic congestion and vehicular pollution in *MC Mehta v. Union of India*.[132] MC Mehta sued the national government in 1985, seeking action over Delhi's chaotic traffic and vehicular pollution.[133] He relied on his constitutional right to life.

The court agreed that Delhi's vehicular pollution impacted residents' quality of life. It concluded that the constitutional right to life meant that there was a duty to reduce pollution and manage chaotic traffic. The court held it was essential for all road users to understand their environmental impact.

Since 1994, the Supreme Court has issued numerous orders in this case, requiring the government to take action in accordance with its continuing mandamus procedure. First used in the 1980s, the continuing mandamus procedure enables the court to keep a matter open so that it can monitor a government agency's

---

[132] *M.C. Mehta v. Union of India*, (1991) SCR (1) 866, 1991 SCC (2) 353.
[133] *M.C. Mehta v. Union of India*, Writ Petition (Civil) 13029/1985.

progress against orders and issue fresh orders where needed.[134] In 1995, the court directed the government to convert all state-owned vehicles to compressed natural gas.[135] The court also directed that all buses in Delhi be converted to compressed natural gas by 1 April 2001 and that cars failing to comply with new fuel standards could be sold after 1 April 2017.[136]

Courts in Bangladesh and Sri Lanka have also used continuing mandamus orders to act on vehicular pollution and fuel standards. In *M. Farooque Vs. Government of Bangladesh*, the Supreme Court of Bangladesh ordered the government to establish a national standard for petroleum based on international standards in 2002.[137] It directed that the standard should ensure the reduction and removal of toxic and hazardous constituents from fuel. The court kept the matter open for monitoring. It directed the government to submit reports of actions and results every 6 months and to publish the court's directions in print and electronic media for "two days twice in a week for one month."

In *Geethani Wijesinghe v Patali Champika Ranawake, Ministry of Environment and Natural Resources*, the petitioner sued the Government of Sri Lanka over its failure to implement the regulations and air quality standards.[138] She argued that her constitutional right to life included the right to breathe air of a quality that supports life. In response to the Supreme Court's initial decision in 2007, the government issued new standards for emissions for vehicles in 2008.[139]

> " The definition of "sustainable development" which Brundtland gave more than 3 decades back still holds good. The phrase covers the development that meets the needs of the present without compromising the ability of the future generation to meet their own needs.
>
> In *Narmada Bachao Andolan v. Union of India* this Court observed that sustainable development means the type or extent of development that can take place and which can be sustained by nature/ecology with or without mitigation. In these matters, the required standard now is that the risk of harm to the environment or to human health is to be decided in public interest, according to a "reasonable person's" test.
>
> Source: *M.C. Mehta v. Union of India*, (1998) 6 SCC 63 and 2017 SCC OnLine SC 291.

---

[134] *Hussainara Khatoon (3) v. State of Bihar*, (1980) 1 SCC 93 is an early example of the continuing mandamus procedure. The Supreme Court of India coined the term "continuing mandamus" in *Vineet Narain v. Union of India*, (1998) 1 SCC 226; AIR 1998 SC 889. See also M. Poddar and B. Nahar. 2017. 'Continuing Mandamus'—A Judicial Innovation to Bridge the Right-Remedy Gap. *NUJS L. Rev.* 10 (3). pp. 555–608.

[135] Order mentioned in *M.C. Mehta v. Union of India*, (1998) 6 SCC 648.

[136] *M.C. Mehta v. Union of India*, (1998) 6 SCC 63 and 2017 SCC OnLine SC 291.

[137] *M. Farooque Vs. Government of Bangladesh* 22 BLD 345 (2002).

[138] *Geethani Wijesinghe v Patali Champika Ranawake, Ministry of Environment and Natural Resources* SCFR 87/2007.

[139] Government of Sri Lanka. 2008. *Amendment to the National Environmental (Air Emission, Fuel and Vehicle Importation Standards) Regulations, No. 1 of 2003*. Colombo.

The court later made orders regarding the Strategic Plan for Traffic Management in Greater Colombo area. In 2014, the court closed the case after the government had prepared draft fuel quality regulations.[140]

These cases predate concerns about climate change. Consequently, they did not link the imposition of fuel standards with emissions reductions in the transport sector. However, actions to reduce vehicular pollution have positive mitigation outcomes. Further, continuing mandamus orders provide a useful remedy when monitoring government action or inaction over time. While regional courts have not yet applied the continuing mandamus order to climate change matters, there may be cases in which litigants persuade courts of the benefits of monitoring and directing government action on climate action over time.

b) Mobile Billboards and Traffic Congestion in South Asia

Litigants argued that mobile billboards worsened traffic, impacting health and the environment in *Outdoors Communication v. PWD and Municipal Corporation of Delhi*.[141] The Municipal Corporation of Delhi permitted private operators to manage mobile billboards on Delhi's streets. The Public Works Department argued that mobile billboards intensified traffic congestion and breached the law established in the *MC Mehta* case, which banned billboards because they were hazardous and disturbed traffic.

The court held that the billboards breached the law established in the MC Mehta case and the Delhi Municipal Corporation Act, 1957. The court contemplated modern society's tug-of-war between demanding traffic decongestion and clamoring for more—more water, more energy, and more resources. Against this backdrop, global warming received scant attention, and traffic congestion damaged health and lives. Governments, it said, must balance the delivery of services and facilities as a matter of public policy.

A view from Charminar, India. Courts in Asia have considered the links between air pollution from traffic congestion and climate change (photo by Carlos Castillo).

But, decisions enabling industries to "cut their losses or make more profits at the cost of public health is not a sign of good governance."[142] Such decisions, it held, contravened the government's constitutional mandate "to secure the health of the people, improve public health, and protect and improve the environment."[143] The "larger interest of the environment and of the public would override all individual concerns."[144]

---

140 *Environmental Foundation Ltd. v Minister for Environment & Ors. 2014 SC FR No. 87/07.*
141 *Outdoors Communication v. PWD and Municipal Corporation of Delhi, 2007 (2) CTLJ 179 (Del).*
142 Footnote 141, para. 139.
143 Footnote 141, para. 118. See articles 39(e), 47, and 48(A) of the Constitution of India.
144 Footnote 141, para. 165.

c)   License Ceilings in South Asia

Asian governments have also imposed license ceilings to limit road traffic and vehicular pollution. In *Manushi Sangthan, Delhi v. Govt. of Delhi & Ors.*, rickshaw drivers challenged the government ceiling on rickshaw licenses.[145] The drivers argued that rickshaws provided immediate employment for up to 800,000 unskilled workers and that the ceiling was unsustainable and arbitrary. They asserted that the government should prioritize rickshaws as a form of public transport, especially given that 85% of the public relies on them. Caps were not created for cars.

The court noted that the Delhi Master Plan required segregated roads, separate bicycle tracks, and bus corridors. It acknowledged these measures might cause hardship and generate controversy. But two critical factors supported these measures. Firstly, "Planet Earth seems to be running out of options unless 'unorthodox' and sometimes unpopular policies are pursued."[146] It considered the signs of global warming self-evident, depriving each succeeding generation of environmental beauty, abundance, and benefits. Secondly, it concluded that governments could not prioritize road access for one class of vehicle only, particularly when that class demonstrably contributed to road congestion.

The court agreed that the rickshaw license cap was arbitrary and set the decision aside. However, it ordered the government to constitute a special task force to explore all the questions about road traffic in Delhi. It mandated the task force to consider options for minimizing congestion, reducing vehicular pollution, and ensuring equitable access to the roads by all classes of vehicles. The court directed the National Capital Territory of Delhi to issue a notification and provide adequate budgetary support.

d)   Vehicle Emissions Testing in Fiji

Fiji Taxi Union disputed the Land Transport Authority's decision to test exhaust emissions with an electronic smoke detection machine in *State v Land Transport Authority, Ex parte Fiji Taxi Union*.[147] The union argued that the Land Transport Authority had exceeded its power. While concerned about air pollution, the court focused on the agency's power to use equipment in aid of its statutory functions. It concluded that the machine was an aid in assessing a vehicle's safety and environmental soundness.

Neither the court nor the applicants mentioned climate change. However, arguments over an agency's capacity to use a particular technology may grow, especially as technology improves and governments seek to improve reporting and compliance.

---

145 *Manushi Sangthan, Delhi v. Govt. of Delhi & Ors.*, 2010 SCC OnLine Del 580.
146 Footnote 145, para. 72.
147 *State v Land Transport Authority, Ex parte Fiji Taxi Union* [2004] FJHC 252.

2. Road and Highway Projects

a) *More Highways, More Emissions in Pakistan*

Litigants have also challenged emissions resulting from expressway projects. For example, in *Imrana Tiwana v. Province of Punjab*, petitioners challenged an expressway because of concerns about the project's EIA, including the credibility of its emissions forecasts.[148] The Lahore Development Authority (LDA) proposed the 7 km expressway, which the Environmental Protection Agency (EPA) approved.

The petitioners argued that the project's EIA failed to meet legal requirements and that the EPA's environmental permitting procedure was defective. The LDA had prepared the EIA by following the guidelines for a hatchery project rather than a major road project. It also had not sought public comment on the expressway. Furthermore, the LDA had started construction before receiving environmental approval.

In reviewing the EIA, the EPA had failed to establish an advisory committee or even an EIA review committee. Petitioners also argued (successfully) that the EPA lacked autonomy because it was attached to the provincial government, undermining its capacity to review the EIA independently.

While the petitioners did not specifically raise any climate change arguments, they asserted that the EIA data on present and anticipated vehicular emissions were unsubstantiated, violating procedural requirements. They also challenged the EIA's estimate that the project would result in decreased emissions.

The High Court of Lahore did not conduct a merits review. Instead, it focused on two constitutional dimensions: (i) the essential nature of environmental justice to fundamental rights, and (ii) the powers and autonomy of elected local government. It, therefore, did not consider emissions, technical viability, or climate impacts of the expressway project.[149]

The court observed that the global community designed EIAs to function as a sustainable development tool. EIAs integrate "environmental considerations into socio-economic development and decision-making processes."[150] The court considered public participation an "integral part of EIA" and "akin to environmental democracy."[151] The court held that the LDA's failure to seek public comment or await the EPA's approval before commencing construction was a fatal flaw. It set aside the EIA for the construction phase because it violated the right to life and dignity of the citizenry. It further considered that the approval offended environmental justice and due process, which were protected under articles 4 and 10A of the Constitution of Pakistan.

---

[148] *Imrana Tiwana v. Province of Punjab*, PLD 2015 Lahore 522. pp. 17, 18, and 23.
[149] Footnote 148, p. 34, para. 20.
[150] Footnote 148, p. 47, para. 35.
[151] Footnote 148, p. 53, para. 41.

While the court did not address the EIA's alleged failure to account for changes in vehicular emissions, the petitioners raised this dimension in their case. Although the petitioners did not succeed on this argument, they achieved their goal to halt the project.

(See Part Two, Section I.B.1.b. Constitutional Rights in Pakistan; and Part Five, Section III.B.1. Failure to Consult in South Asia for further discussion of this case.)

b) Road Sharing in the Philippines

Petitioners argued that road sharing presented a sustainable response to climate change in *Segovia et al. v. Climate Change Commission et al.*[152] The petitioners proposed that Philippine roads should be shared by dividing them lengthwise. An all-weather sidewalk and bicycling lane would use one half of the road. Only Filipino-made vehicles should use the road on the other side.

The petitioners sought a writ of *kalikasan* (nature) and continuing mandamus orders to realize their vision of road sharing. They argued that the government's failure to reduce personal and official fossil fuel consumption violated atmospheric trust. Road sharing, they argued, met the objectives of Philippine environmental laws, including the Climate Change Act and Clean Air Act.[153] The petitioners also asked the court to direct the Office of the President, cabinet officials, and cabinet employees to take public transportation half the time and cut their fuel consumption by 50%.

Pedestrian walkways along the EDSA highway in Manila. Petitioners in the Philippines argued that 50% of roads should be dedicated to pedestrian use to reduce GHG emissions from transportation (photo by Veejay Villafranca/ADB).

The Supreme Court dismissed the petition, finding that the petitioners had not proved that there was a breach of law or a failure to act. Although air quality in Manila did not meet the standards set under the national guidelines, the court was satisfied with the government's progress in reducing particulate matter. Further, the petitioners' novel approach toward road sharing did not persuade the Supreme Court. It considered that the road sharing request was an attempt to control how the executive actualized legislation or policy.

(See Part One, Section II.B.3.b. The Transport Sector in the Philippines; and Part One, Section III.B.3. Transport Emission Reduction Commitments in the Philippines for further discussion of this case.)

---

[152] *Segovia et al. v. Climate Change Commission et al.*, G.R. No. 211010, 7 March 2017.

[153] The petitioners cited Republic Act No. (RA) 97291 (Climate Change Act) and RA 87492 (Clean Air Act); Executive Order No. 774; Administrative Order No. 254, s. 2009; and Administrative Order No. 171, s. 2007.

c) Road Projects Impacting Biodiversity in Nepal

The Supreme Court of Nepal stopped a road project through Chitwan National Park due to defects in the EIA and concerns over impacts to an ecosystem under stress due to climate change. Home to critically endangered species like the single-horned Asiatic rhinoceros and Bengal tiger, the Chitwan National Park is a UNESCO World Heritage Site.[154]

In *Simkhada vs Office of the Prime Minister*, the petitioners argued that the project EIA and initial environmental examination breached the requirements imposed by the Environment Protection Act, 2053 (1997) and the National Parks and Wildlife Conservation Act, 2029 (1973).[155] They also argued that the planned route would cut through the park, interfering with the habitats of protected species, undermining environmental conservation. Such impacts violated the petitioners' constitutional rights to life and a clean and healthy environment.

The court highlighted the importance of protecting the constitutional right to a clean and healthy environment in response to climate change. Nepal, explained the court, faces numerous challenges conserving biodiversity and the environment. Climate change-induced calamities are complicating conservation efforts. Such factors made it "all the more necessary" to protect the constitutionally guaranteed right to a clean and healthy environment and to realize "environmentally sustainable development" through planned conservation efforts.[156]

The court concluded that the planned road would have significant impacts on the park's biodiversity and environment, violating the constitution. Additionally, the respondents had failed to secure consent for the road from the World Heritage Committee, Chitwan National Park Office, and Department of National Parks and Wildlife Conservation as required under the National Parks and Wildlife Conservation Act. Noting the government's obligation to take stewardship over the heritage of the park, the court held that the EIA report and government's decision were defective.

(See Part Two, Section IV.B.1 International Commitments in Settled Cases in South Asia for further discussion of this case.)

3. Airports and a Failure of Due Process in South Asia

While Asia and the Pacific countries have seen relatively few cases challenging airport construction or upgrade, there is a recent important case from India.

---

[154] UNESCO. Chitwan National Park.
[155] *Advocate Ramchandra Simkhada and Others vs Office of the Prime Minister and Council of Ministers, Government of Nepal and Others*, Writ Petition No. 068-WO-0597 (Supreme Court of Nepal, 13 February 2019).
[156] Footnote 155, p. 46.

In *Hanuman Laxman Aroskar v. Union of India,* the appellants challenged the government's environmental clearance for a greenfield international airport at Mopa in Goa.[157] The challenge focused on the proponent's failure to disclose the need to cut down 54,676 trees and the project's impact on ecologically sensitive zones within Maharashtra. The applicants challenged the proponent's failure to take note of wildlife in the surrounding forests or to collect baseline soil, air, and water samples within Maharashtra, even though nearly 40% of that state was within the study area.

The court reasoned the relevance of the 2030 Agenda for Sustainable Development for India, particularly Sustainable Development Goals (SDGs) 13 and 16. SDG 13 encourages climate action, while SDG 16 focuses on protecting ecosystems and promoting sustainable development. The court considered that environmental health preserved life, a constitutional right in India. In light of the government's commitment to these goals, the court concluded that India's EIA regulation links with "India's quest to pursue the SDGs."[158]

The court further highlighted the government's commitment under the Paris Agreement to establish new carbon sinks of 2.5–3 billion tons of CO_2 equivalent by 2030 through new forest and tree cover. Given the proponent's failure to disclose vital information about the environmental impacts on trees and ecosystems, the court concluded there was a failure of due process.

Accordingly, the court directed the EIA review committee to (i) revisit its recommendation to approve the project's environmental clearance, in light of the court's concerns; and (ii) impose sufficient extra conditions to address the court's concerns if it proposed to approve the project. The court made no specific direction to the committee to take climate change impacts into account when reconsidering the EIA, but this direction seems implicit. The court expressly discussed the connection between India's EIA regulation and the 2030 Agenda for Sustainable Development. It further highlighted India's pledge to establish new sinks under the Paris Agreement. Honoring the spirit of the court's concerns requires consideration of how to mitigate the airport's climate and environmental impacts.

(See Part Five, Section III.B.1. Failure to Consult in South Asia for further discussion of this case.)

In January 2020, the Supreme Court determined that the airport project could proceed.[159] It was satisfied that the project proponent had sought to remedy its failures by considering additional information. It also noted that the EIA review committee and previous court orders had imposed mitigatory conditions. The court appointed the National Environmental Engineering Research Institute to oversee compliance with the court's directions.

---

157   *Hanuman Laxman Aroskar v. Union of India,* 2019 SCC OnLine SC 441.
158   Footnote 157, p. 88.
159   *Hanuman Laxman Aroskar v. Union of India,* MA No. 965 of 2019 (Supreme Court of India, 16 January 2020).

VI. Nuclear Facilities

A. Global Approaches

Litigants have also challenged governments' approval of new nuclear generating facilities and their adoption of policies aimed at supporting existing generators. This section highlights three recent US cases involving such challenges.

1. A Cost-Effective Choice in the United States

New Energy Economy, Inc. v. New Mexico Public Regulation Commission involved a challenge to the New Mexico Public Regulation Commission's approval of a utility plan to retire two existing coal-fired generators and replace part of their capacity with nuclear generation.[160] The plaintiff—a nonprofit group that advocates for carbon-free energy development—argued that the utility had not adequately considered the possibility of using renewable energy, which is "less costly and less risky" than nuclear.[161]

That argument was rejected by the New Mexico Supreme Court, which found that the utility had modeled the costs of using various energy sources, including wind and solar. The court noted that, based on the modeling, the commission had found nuclear to be the "most cost-effective" choice and stated that it would not "second-guess" that finding.[162]

2. Environmental Attributes in the United States

In *Coalition for Competitive Electricity v. Zibelman*, owners of fossil fuel-fired power plants challenged a New York state program designed to compensate nuclear facilities for their zero-emission attributes.[163] Electricity providers and municipalities mounted a similar challenge to subsidies in New York and Illinois for nuclear power plants in *Electric Power Supply Association v. Star*.[164] Both cases challenged wholesale electricity sales and prices, which fell under the exclusive authority of federal regulators.[165]

While acknowledging that the subsidies depressed wholesale electricity rates, the courts held that the programs did not infringe on federal regulatory authority. The courts emphasized that the subsidy programs neither set wholesale prices nor

---

[160] *New Energy Econ., Inc. v. N.M. Pub. Regulation Comm'n*, 416 P.3d 277 (N.M. 2018).

[161] Footnote 160, p. 287.

[162] Footnote 160, p. 288.

[163] *Coal. for Competitive Elec. v. Zibelman*, 906 F.3d 41 (2d Cir. 2017), aff'g 272 F. Supp. 3d 554 (S.D.N.Y. 2017), *cert. denied*, 2019 US LEXIS 2652 (2019).

[164] *Elec. Power Supply Assoc. v. Star*, 904 F.3d 518 (7th Cir. 2018), *reh'g denied* 2018 US App. LEXIS 28509 (7th Cir.2018), *cert. denied*, 139 S.Ct. 1547 (2019).

[165] Footnote 163, p. 48 and footnote 164, pp. 522–524.

required providers to participate in wholesale markets.[166] The courts viewed the programs as dealing solely with the environmental attributes of generation, the regulation of which was expressly reserved to the states under federal law.[167]

B. Asia and the Pacific Approaches: Nuclear Controversy in South Asia

In its Special Report on Global Warming of 1.5 °C, the IPCC outlined the energy supply mix needed to achieve 1.5°C pathways. In short, the share of energy derived from low-carbon-emitting sources needs to grow, and the overall share of fossil fuels without carbon capture and storage must decline.[168] The IPCC identified nuclear energy as a low-carbon-emitting source of energy. However, nuclear energy is controversial.

The memory of the nuclear power plant disasters at Three Mile Island, Chernobyl, and Fukushima looms large. Many worry about safety and security risks, waste disposal challenges, and water requirements.[169]

Against this backdrop, local community members objected to the government's decision to approve the Kudankulam Nuclear Power Plant in *Sundarrajan v. Union of India*.[170] They argued that the proposed plant threatened their constitutional right to life, and their safety and security. They complained that the planning for both disaster management, and storage and disposal of radioactive waste was inadequate.

The court graciously acknowledged the community's concerns about nuclear energy. After a thorough review of national policy and law and international treaties, the court concluded that the plant should proceed, albeit with conditions. Such conditions should work to ensure safety and public trust in the project.

The court considered the policymakers' preference for including nuclear energy in India's fuel mix, currently dominated by coal. Shifting to atomic energy would reduce reliance on fossil fuels and enable sustainable economic growth. Further, the court noted that it could not shape national policy unless it tampered with fundamental constitutional principles or the constitution's basic structure.

In balancing the public interest and human rights, the court noted that the expert committees were satisfied by the safety measures and action, and that radiation would not cause harm. The court stated that electricity was the "heart and soul of modern life, a life meant not for the rich and famous alone but also the poor and

---

[166] Footnote 163, p. 50–52; footnote 164, pp. 523–524.
[167] Footnote 163, p. 52; footnote 164, p. 524.
[168] J. Rogelj et al. 2018. Mitigation Pathways Compatible with 1.5°C in the Context of Sustainable Development. In V. Masson-Delmotte et al., eds. *Global Warming of 1.5°C. An IPCC Special Report*. In press. p. 130.
[169] *Union of Concerned Scientists*. 2018. Nuclear Power & Global Warming.
[170] *Sundarrajan v. Union of India*, (2013) 6 SCC 620.

downtrodden."[171] Electricity provided the means of livelihood. In short, the court considered that the "nuclear power plant is being established not to negate [the] right to life but to protect the right to life" as guaranteed under the constitution.[172]

VII. Water and Aquatic Environments

A. Global Approaches

While reviewing challenges to water extraction permits and allocation determinations, courts around the world have considered climate change's impact on water availability—including issues of sustainability—and pointed to the precautionary principle. Courts have also relied on climate science and climate models to determine the appropriate use of water resources. In at least one case, a court hinged its decision on water allocation on the public's right to clean water. Sustainable water use needs to ensure that the resource is available to all for varied needs. Climate change will make that goal more challenging by intensifying water insecurity. To date, litigation has focused on water sharing or protecting water resources to safeguard ecosystem function.

1. Water Management in Australia

Australian courts have limited commercial water extraction in cases where climate change would render proposed levels of extraction unsustainable. In *David Kettle Consulting v Gosford City Council*, the Land and Environment Court of New South Wales upheld the appeal of permit conditions for water extraction at a water bottling plant. [173] The permit restricted both the rate of water extraction and total extraction levels at a water bottling plant of one of the world's major Coca-Cola bottlers—Coca-Cola Amatil. Coca-Cola Amatil challenged the permit restrictions.

The court affirmed that the permit should be without conditions until 2011. However, the court analyzed the impacts of climate change on rainfall to decide that the extraction rates and levels should be reevaluated in 2011. More timely data would be available, and the permit would be up for renewal. Although the court did not consider its "conclusion in precise terms as being a response to the precautionary principle," the court did cite the "precautionary principle" and noted intergenerational equity, conservation of biological diversity, and ecological integrity as relevant guidelines for its approach.

In *Alanvale Pty Ltd v Southern Rural Water Authority*, an administrative tribunal upheld a water management agency's decision to deny licenses for groundwater

---

171   Footnote 170, para. 182.
172   Footnote 170, para. 184.
173   *David Kettle Consulting v Gosford City Council* [2008] NSWLEC 1385.

extraction. The tribunal reasoned that climate change creates a risk of over-allocating groundwater supply due to rainfall scarcity.[174]

(See Part Four, Section II.A.1. Climate Change Impacts on Projects in Australia for a full case summary of *Alanvale Pty Ltd v Southern Rural Water Authority*.)

However, in *Paul v Goulburn Murray Water Corporation and Others*, the same administrative tribunal upheld a local water authority's decision to grant two licenses for groundwater extraction.[175] A landowner challenged the licenses, arguing that the use of water would be unsustainable given climate change's projected reduction of water availability. The tribunal acknowledged that there was some uncertainty about climate change impacts, and thus the application of the precautionary principle may be appropriate. However, the tribunal found that based on the technical evidence before it, the water use permitted under the licenses would be sustainable.

2. Climate Models as Evidence in the United States

Environmental groups have relied on climate models showing reduced water levels to challenge water diversion permits. In *Alliance for the Great Lakes v. Illinois Department of Natural Resources*, environmental groups challenged a state agency's order permitting a district to divert an additional 1,589.9 billion liters of water from Lake Michigan.[176] Plaintiffs claimed that in failing to properly determine the volume of the diversion and impose conservation practices as conditions, the district violated state law. The plaintiffs further argued that limiting diversion "to the least extent possible" is "particularly important because scientific models project that climate change will produce a drop of two feet in the average water level of the Great Lakes during this century."[177] The case has been filed but not decided.

3. The Right to Clean Water in Colombia

The Constitutional Court in Colombia barred regulatory authorities from allowing resource extraction that would threaten the public's right to clean water in 2016. In *Decision C-035/16 (Alberto Castilla Salazar and Others v. Colombia)*, the court held that various articles of Law No. 1450 of 2011 and Law No. 1753 of 2015 were unconstitutional because they threatened *páramos*, high-altitude ecosystems.[178] The court highlighted that *páramos* provide up to 70% of Colombia's drinking water and yet have limited regulatory protection, making them fragile.

---

174 *Alanvale Pty Ltd v Southern Rural Water Authority* [2010] VCAT 480.

175 *Paul v Goulburn Murray Water Corporation and Others* [2010] VCAT 1755.

176 Complaint for Illinois Administrative Review, *Alliance for the Great Lakes v. Illinois Department of Natural Resources*, LMO-14-5 (Cir. Ct. Cook Cty. filed Apr. 14, 2017).

177 Footnote 176, para 6.

178 Corte Constitucional [C.C.] [Constitutional Court], Febrero 8, 2016, Sentencia C-035/16 (Colom.); UN Environment Programme. 2017. *The Status of Climate Change Litigation: A Global Review*. Nairobi, Kenya.

In describing them as carbon capture systems, the court noted that *páramos* are capable of absorbing and holding more carbon than a similarly sized tropical rainforest. The impugned statutory provisions allowed for development within the *páramos*, endangering the public's right to clean water. The court also held that the articles excused government agencies from justifying decisions to allow environmentally damaging resource extraction within the *páramos*, which was unconstitutional.

Climate change impacts on water security influenced the court's decision to uphold constitutional rights. The court stressed the value of water continuing to flow from the *páramos* given predicted climatic change. The case shows that climate change adaptation can be a relevant factor to weigh when interpreting constitutionally protected rights even if those rights do not specifically reference climate change (footnote 178).

B.   Asia and the Pacific Approaches

1.   Water Security

a)   *The Potential for Conflict in the Region*

Fresh water constitutes 2.53% of the earth's water supply.[179] Only 1.2% of the world's water is accessible as surface and other fresh water—the ice caps and glaciers store almost 69% of global fresh water.[180] By 2050, water demand within Asia and the Pacific is projected to increase by about 55%.[181] Domestic water use, manufacturing, and thermal electricity generators will drive this increased thirst for water (footnote 181).

Asia and the Pacific is heavily reliant on agriculture. Asia uses around 80% of its water resources to grow food, and most Asian countries rely on groundwater for farming.[182] More food is needed too. By 2050, developing countries will need to grow 100% more food using diminishing water resources.[183] Yet, current data estimate that more than 75% of the Asian region is water insecure (footnote 182). By 2050, up to 3.4 billion people in Asia could be living in water-stressed areas.[184]

---

[179]   I. Shiklomanov. 1993. World Fresh Water Resources. In P. Gleick, ed. *Water in Crisis: A Guide to the World's Fresh Water Resources.* Oxford: Oxford University Press; and ADB. 2016. *Agriculture Placing Huge Demands on Water: Asia's Thirst for Food.* Infographic. Manila.

[180]   I. Shiklomanov and J. Rodda, eds. 2003. World Water Resources at the Beginning of the Twenty-First Century. *International Hydrology Series.* Cambridge: Cambridge University Press. p. 13; and Government of the United States, United States Geological Survey. The Distribution of Water On, In, and Above the Earth.

[181]   Organisation for Economic Co-operation and Development. 2012. *Environmental Outlook to 2050: The Consequences of Inaction.* Paris.

[182]   ADB. 2015. *Water and Climate Change: Asia's Vulnerability to Climate Change Adds Extra Dimension to Asia's Water Challenges.* Manila; and footnote 179.

[183]   ADB. 2016. *Asian Water Development Outlook 2016: Strengthening Water Security in Asia and the Pacific.* Manila.

[184]   P. Burek et al. 2016. *Water Futures and Solutions: Asia 2050.* Laxenburg, Austria: International Institute for Applied Systems Analysis.

Figure 2: Agriculture Placing Huge Demands on Water: Asia's Thirst for Food

Agriculture is placing the biggest demands on water in Asia and the Pacific, as rising populations, rapid urbanization, and energy, industrial, and domestic use have left water stocks in a critical state.

ADB

FINITE SUPPLY AND COMPETING DEMANDS

EARTH'S WATER SUPPLY

2.5% freshwater

97.5% saline water

Estimated increases in Asia's water usage by 2030:
- 65% – industrial water use
- 30% – domestic use
- 5% – agriculture use

65% / 30% / 5%

Agriculture will need to produce 60% more food globally, and 100% more in developing countries using diminishing water resources

60% / 100%

FOOD AND DRINKS

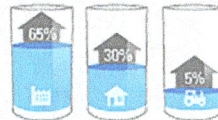

2–4 LITERS
Daily drinking requirement of an average person

2,000–5,000 LITERS
Average quantity of water needed to produce one person's daily food

By 2050, 60% of Asia-Pacific's population will be living in cities.

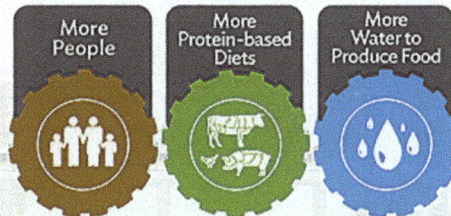

More People | More Protein-based Diets | More Water to Produce Food

ASIA AND IRRIGATION

WATER USAGE

AROUND 80%
of Asia's freshwater is used to irrigate crops, much of which **IS USED INEFFICIENTLY**

80%

Most Asian countries rely heavily on groundwater for farming

BIGGEST IRRIGATED AREAS USING GROUNDWATER

INDIA
39 MILLION HECTARES

PRC*
19 MILLION HECTARES

*PRC = People's Republic of China

FACTORS RESTRAINING IRRIGATION PERFORMANCE

- finite resources
- outdated system designs
- institutional inefficiencies
- weak governance

PROJECTED CLIMATE CHANGE IMPACTS TO AGRICULTURE

- increasing frequency and severity of droughts and unpredictable rainfall threaten agriculture
- elevated temperatures increase irrigation water demand, reduce yields
- salination of groundwater in coastal aquifers
- direct flood damage to crops

SOURCES:
- Asian Development Bank. 2009. Meeting the Water and Climate Change Challenge
- Asian Development Bank. Water for All
- Human Appropriation of the World's Fresh Water Supply. Retrieved from http://www.globalchange.umich.edu/

Factors such as population growth, increasing urbanization and water pollution, and excessive groundwater extraction underpin Asia's water insecurity. Meeting the increased demand for water in Asia and the Pacific will require improving water productivity and management, e.g., by using recycled and desalinated water.[185] The region must also limit groundwater overuse and make agricultural water use more efficient.

See Figure 2 for a brief overview of competing demands for water resources, irrigation in the region, and projected climate change impacts to agriculture.

Conflicts over water are not new.[186] Without action, climate change and population growth will trigger intense competition for water, potentially leading to war.[187] A recent study found that the Ganges–Brahmaputra and Indus river basins are in the world's top five most vulnerable hot spots for water conflict.[188] Some of these conflicts may end up on the steps of the court. Understanding the links between water, energy, food, and climate will be critical for developing appropriate responses to water insecurity (footnote 182).

b) Safeguarding Water Resources in Pakistan and the Philippines

Within Asia, litigation objecting to water extraction focuses on sustainable use to safeguard resources for current and future uses. Available cases from Asia have not yet explicitly assessed the climate impacts of water extraction, including anticipated changes in rainfall and water security. Nevertheless, Asian courts have been clear about the need to protect water resources for future generations.

This report found only one example of water extraction litigation in Niue, an island country in the South Pacific Ocean, which is one of ADB's newest developing member countries.[189]

In Pakistan, the High Court of Sindh stopped Nestlé Milkpak Limited (Nestlé) from building a water bottling factory in *Sindh Institute of Urology and Transplantation v. Nestlé Milkpak Limited*.[190] The secretary to the Government of Sindh granted Nestlé a 99-year lease to build a factory in "Education City," an area that was supposed to be reserved for educational organizations. The plaintiffs objected to the lease, primarily on the ground that Nestlé would extract large quantities of groundwater, leaving the plaintiffs and other organizations at Education City without water. Nestlé argued that the lease was sound and that

---

[185] Footnote 183, p. xvii.

[186] Pacific Institute. Water Conflict Chronology (accessed 1 January 2020).

[187] P. Ratner. 2018. Where Will the 'Water Wars' of the Future Be Fought? *World Economic Forum.* 23 October.

[188] F. Farinosi et al. 2018. An Innovative Approach to the Assessment of Hydro-Political Risk: A Spatially Explicit, Data Driven Indicator of Hydro-Political Issues. *Global Environmental Change.* 52 (9). pp. 286–313.

[189] See *Coe v Vaiea Farm Ltd* [2018] NUHC 2.

[190] *Sindh Institute of Urology and Transplantation v. Nestlé Milkpak Limited*, 2005 CLC 424 (Karachi).

Deosai National Park, Pakistan. The park is a significant watershed, feeding three river systems in Pakistan. Asian courts have recognized citizens' fundamental right to water and protected water resources against unfettered exploitation (photo by Mehtab Farooq).

an EIA was unnecessary. The EPA (a defendant) argued that producing bottled water did not require environmental approval as the project was "not likely to cause any adverse environment effects."

Finding that the natural resource of water is in the public trust, the court granted an injunction preventing Nestlé from building its water bottling factory at Education City. The court considered that "no civilized society" should allow "unfettered exploitation" of its natural resources. Water "is a Nectar [sic], sustaining life on earth and without water, the earth would be desert." Water use must, therefore, be safeguarded for "present and future generations through careful planning or management as appropriate."

The Philippine Court of Appeals also recognized the fundamental connection between water and life in *SWIM (Save Waters of Indang, Cavite Movement Inc.) v. PTK2 H20 Corporation*.[191] Petitioners sought a writ of *kalikasan* (nature) and a temporary environmental protection order against an approved water supply contract granted to the respondent.

The court concluded that water was an essential element of life and an environmental resource. Therefore, the respondent's excessive water extraction could dangerously impact not only the riparian ecosystem but also local livelihoods, and should thus not be permitted.

---

[191] *SWIM (Save Waters of Indang, Cavite Movement Inc.) v. PTK2 H20 Corporation*, CA-G.R. SP No. 00028, 30 January 2015.

> No civilized society shall permit the unfettered exploitation of its natural resources by anyone particularly in respect of the water which is a necessity of…life. Ground water is a national wealth and belongs to entire society. It is a Nectar [*sic*], sustaining life on earth and without water, the earth would be desert, I find myself in agreement with Principle to Stockholm Declaration, 1972 as reproduced above in para. 13 of this order that the natural resources of the earth including the air, water, land, flora and fauna especially representative samples of natural eco-systems must be safeguarded for the benefit of present and future generations through careful planning and management as appropriate.
>
> Source: *Sindh Institute of Urology and Transplantation v. Nestlé Milkpak Limited*, 2005 CLC 424 (Karachi).

2. Protecting Water from Contamination

Given the need to protect existing water resources, courts have been willing to protect water from contamination based on constitutional rights.

a) *Constitutional Rights in Fiji and South Asia*

A few states in Asia and the Pacific include a specific right to water within their constitutions. The Government of Fiji, for instance, must take reasonable measures to progressively realize the right of its people to clean and safe water in adequate quantities.[192] Citizens of Maldives also have a constitutional right to clean water.[193] Other countries, such as Bangladesh, use legislation to guarantee a right to water. The Bangladesh Water Act, 2013 grants citizens a right to potable water and water for hygiene and sanitation.[194]

In the absence of this explicit right, other courts have extended the constitutional right to life to include the right to clean water. In *Subhash Kumar v. State of Bihar and Others*, the Indian Supreme Court held that the right to life includes the right to enjoy pollution-free water.[195]

(See Part One, Section II.B.1.a. Life, Dignity, and Equality in South Asia for further discussion of this case.) Any citizen may sue to remove water pollution. In *A.P. Pollution*

---

[192] Constitution of the Republic of Fiji, 2013. Chapter 2, art. 36(1).
[193] Constitution of the Republic of Maldives, 2008. Chapter II, art. 23.
[194] *Bangladesh Water Act*, 2013. sec. 3.
[195] *Subhash Kumar v. State of Bihar and Others*, (1991) 1 SCC 598, para. 7.

Control Board II v. M.V. Nayudu, the Supreme Court further observed that the right to access drinking water was fundamental to life and that the state had a duty under article 21 of the constitution to provide clean drinking water to its citizens.[196]

The Supreme Court of Pakistan also declared that the country's constitutional right to life includes a right to water. In *General Secretary, West Pakistan Salt Miners Labour Union v. The Director, Industries and Mineral Development, Punjab,* the petitioners challenged the grant of mining leases dangerously close to the area's primary water source.[197] The court considered that water was the source of life all over the world and a fundamental right.

b) *Water as a Human Right in Southeast Asia*

Appellants argued that water was a basic right in *Malaysian Trade Union Congress & Ors v Menteri Tenaga, Air dan Komunikasi & Anor.*[198] The case focused on the appellants' right to access the ministerial decision allowing a water concessionaire to increase tariffs. Ultimately, the court did not make any pronouncements on the constitutional right to water in Malaysia.

(See Part One, Section I.B.1.d. for further discussion of this case.)

Water is a fundamental human right in Indonesia.[199] A recent petition disputed a water resource law allowing commercial exploitation of water. The Constitutional Court of Indonesia reasoned that the country's 1947 constitution protected the basic right to access water, along with the human right to a healthy environment.[200] Given these rights, the state should only permit commercial water exploitation where all other water needs had been met.

The Philippine Commission on Human Rights has also declared that access to safe water is a human right, critical for nourishing and ensuring the highest attainable standard of health and living.[201] It made this announcement during the Manila water crisis in 2019. In March 2019, Manila Water (a private water concessionaire) stopped water supply to around 52,000 households in Metro Manila and the Province of Rizal. A public uproar ensued. Residents desperately sought water, even filling up their water containers from fire engines. Local groups petitioned the regulator to penalize Manila Water for the shortage.[202]

---

[196] *A.P. Pollution Control Board II v. M.V. Nayudu,* (2001) 2 SCC 62.

[197] *General Secretary, West Pakistan Salt Miners Labour Union v. The Director, Industries and Mineral Development, Punjab,* 1994 SCMR 2016.

[198] *Malaysian Trade Union Congress & 13 Ors v Menteri Tenaga, Air dan Komunikasi & Anor* [2014] 2 CLJ 525.

[199] Constitutional Court of the Republic of Indonesia, Case No. 85/PUU-XI/2013, pronounced on 18 February 2015.

[200] Constitution of the Republic of Indonesia, 1945. Chapter XA, arts. 28H(1) and 28I(4).

[201] J. Mateo. 2019. Access to Water is a Human Right—CHR. *The Philippine Star.* 15 March.

[202] R. Villanueva. 2019. Manila Water Sued. *The Philippine Star.* 26 March.

Manila Water later explained that low rainfall and delayed water infrastructure projects had depleted the water supply. Low supply and high demand meant that Manila Water could not deliver water to its customers.[203] On 24 April 2019, the government regulator fined Manila Water ₱1.13 billion for failing to provide 24-hour water supply to customers.[204] This crisis was an early indicator of the water scarcity that many megacities in Asia and the Pacific will face.

3. Water Justice Is Climate Justice in Pakistan

Water justice was central to the decision in *Leghari v. Federation of Pakistan*.[205] Ashgar Leghari sued the government over its failure to implement immediate remedial adaptation measures. As a farmer, Leghari had experienced firsthand the devastation of water instability and scarcity. In its decision, the court perfectly explained the nexus between life, water, and climate change:

> Water is life. Water is a human right and all people should have access to clean and affordable water. Water has interconnectedness with people and resources and is a commons that should be held in public trust. This brings us to Water Justice, a sub-concept of Climate Justice. Water justice refers to the access of individuals to clean water. More specifically, the access of individuals to clean water for survival (drinking, fishing, etc.) and recreational purposes as a human right. Water justice demands that all communities be able to access and manage water for beneficial uses, including drinking, waste removal, cultural and spiritual practices, reliance on the wildlife it sustains, and enjoyment for recreational purposes (footnote 203).

The court's decision to classify water justice as a sub-concept of climate justice was cutting edge. It acknowledged how climate change would impact the right to adequate and clean water. It also provided a useful grounding for future cases needing to balance the right of different parties to water in the coming era of climate change.

(See Part One, Section II.B.2.a. Climate Justice in the Philippines and Pakistan for a full case summary of *Leghari v. Federation of Pakistan*; and Part Four, Section I.B.1.a. Climate and Water Justice in Pakistan for further discussion of this case.)

---

203 K. Sabillo. 2019. EXPLAINER: Why Is There a Water Shortage in Metro Manila? *ABS-CBN News*. 12 March.
204 R. Rivas. 2019. MWSS Slaps Manila Water with P1.13-Billion Fine for Supply Crisis. *Rappler*. 24 April.
205 *Leghari v. Federation of Pakistan*, PLD 2018 Lahore 364.

VIII. Land Use Change

A. Global Approaches

1. Deforestation

Deforestation contributes to climate change. Trees capture CO_2, reducing the level of GHG in the atmosphere. Thus, cutting or burning trees reduces carbon capture capacity. Furthermore, trees release the CO_2 they have stored when they are cut or burned. While deforestation reduces carbon stocks, sustainable management—such as planting and forest rehabilitation—can maintain or even increase carbon stocks.[206] In addition, forests play a critical role in increasing countries' adaptive capacity and resilience to climate change impacts. For some countries, such as Brazil, deforestation is a leading cause of GHG emissions. This section describes legal attempts to limit deforestation by highlighting examples from Brazil and the International Court of Justice (ICJ).

a) Environmental Policy in Brazil

Brazilian courts have upheld agency and federal prosecutorial efforts to limit deforestation. Federal legislation in Brazil enacts a "polluter pays" principle and strict liability for environmental offenses.[207] The Brazilian Superior Court of Justice has relied on these legal provisions to enforce climate action.

For example, in *Maia Filho v. Federal Environmental Agency*, the Superior Court of Justice upheld the federal environmental agency's penalty for the use of fires in harvesting sugarcane, a practice that releases GHG emissions.[208] The court determined that the fine was valid under the National Environmental Policy Act, 1981, a federal law that restricts burning for agricultural purposes. The court interpreted the National Environmental Policy Act in light of climate change, reasoning that climate change informed how the objectives of environmental protection—established in the text and environmental norms of the Constitution of Brazil—should be applied.

In *Public Prosecutor's Office v. H Carlos Schneider S/A Comércio e Indústria & Others*, the Superior Court of Justice upheld the trial court's decision that a group responsible for draining and clearing a mangrove forest had to restore the forest.[209] A labor company had cleared the mangrove forest in an urban area and built a landfill and other structures. The Superior Court of Justice ordered the company to remove any structures and restore the mangrove area.

---

[206] UNFCCC. 2019. *Land Use, Land-Use Change and Forestry (LULUCF)*.

[207] Geetanjali Ganguly et al. 2018. *If at First You Don't Succeed: Suing Corporations for Climate Change*, 38 Oxford J. of Legal Studies 841, 863.

[208] S.T.J., Recurso Especial no. 1000731 RO 2007 / 0254811-8, Relator: Ministro Antônio Herman Benjamin, 25 August 2009.

[209] S.T.J., Recurso Especial no. 650728 SC 2003 / 0221786-0, Relator: Ministro Antônio Herman Benjamin, 23 October 2007.

In reaching its decision, the court reasoned that mangrove forests provide vital ecological, economic, and social functions. The court noted that given the value mangrove forests add, "it is everyone's duty... to ensure the preservation of mangrove forests, an ever-increasing need, especially in times of climate changes and increasing sea levels."[210] Brazilian federal and constitutional law provided the legal basis for the court to declare the destruction of the mangrove area as illegal and to issue an injunction to restore it.

(See Part Three, Section V.A. Global Approaches: Restoring Forests in Brazil for further discussion of this case.)

b) Lost Sequestration Services in Nicaragua

Forests provide carbon sequestration services by removing CO_2 from the atmosphere. Thus, deforestation may lead to liability for lost environmental services. *Certain Activities Carried Out by Nicaragua in the Border Area (Costa Rica v. Nicaragua)* was the first claim for compensation for environmental damages heard by the ICJ. It awarded Costa Rica compensation for the loss of environmental goods and services sustained when Nicaragua excavated two channels on its territory.[211] Excavating the channels necessitated the clearing of almost 300 trees and 6.19 hectares of vegetation. Costa Rica argued that the trees and vegetation had provided services like gas and air quality regulation and that losing these services should be compensable.[212]

The ICJ concluded that the excavation works extensively impaired the land's capacity to provide environmental goods and services. As Nicaragua's actions caused the loss of environmental services, it should compensate Costa Rica. In valuing the loss of carbon sequestration services, the ICJ reasoned that there was a continuing loss and adjusted compensation accordingly.

(See Part Six, Section I. Global Approaches: Transboundary Harm in South America for further discussion of this case.)

c) National Obligation under the Paris Agreement in Colombia

Finally, in *Future Generations v. Ministry of the Environment*, the Colombian Supreme Court ordered the government to reduce deforestation in the Amazon to zero by 2020 to comply with its constitutional duty to combat climate change under the Paris Agreement.[213]

---

210 Footnote 207, unofficial translation.
211 *Certain Activities Carried Out by Nicaragua in the Border Area (Costa Rica v. Nicaragua) and Construction of a Road in Costa Rica along the San Juan River (Nicaragua v. Costa Rica)*, Judgment, ICJ Reports 2015. p. 665.
212 *Certain Activities Carried Out by Nicaragua in the Border Area (Costa Rica v. Nicaragua): Compensation Owed by the Republic of Nicaragua to the Republic of Costa Rica*, Compensation, Judgment, ICJ Reports 2018. para 64.
213 Corte Suprema de Justicia [C.S.J.] [Supreme Court], Abril 5, 2018, M.P: L. Villabona, Expediente: 11001-22-03-000-2018-00319-01 (Colomb.).

(See also Part One, Section II.A.3. The Rights of Nature in Colombia for a full case summary of *Future Generations v. Ministry of the Environment and Others*; and Part One, Section IV.A.1. Reducing Deforestation in Colombia for further discussion of this case.)

2. Emissions-Related Case in the United States

Land use and land use planning can impact GHG emissions. For example, in *Bay Area Citizens v. Association of Bay Area Governments*, a state appellate court affirmed an ambitious regional and local approach to reducing GHG emissions. California regional agencies developed a regional transportation plan to reduce GHG emissions from cars and light trucks, which the court upheld.[214] The petitioners who challenged the plan argued that it was "draconian" and should have relied on emissions reductions expected from preexisting statewide mandates for reducing emissions.[215]

The appellate court determined that the planning agencies did not have to count statewide emissions reductions in developing their regional plan. The court reasoned that the state legislature intended for the regional plans to result in additional emissions reductions. It "makes no sense," the court decided, that the legislature would launch "a major new climate protection initiative requiring regional agencies to develop regional land use and transportation strategies through an elaborate planning process that in the end would be superfluous because the Agencies could meet...regional emissions reduction targets simply by invoking reductions already expected from preexisting statewide mandates."[216]

3. Adaptive Capacity Cases in Europe

Adapting to climate change may require governments to restructure existing funding programs. For example, in *Neuzelle Agricultural Cooperative v Head of Administrative Services of Oder-Spree Rural District Authority*, the European Court of Justice upheld two amendments to an economic support scheme for farmers the European Council had enacted to increase adaptation finance.[217] The amendments reduced all direct payments beyond a certain amount and redirected those savings toward measures to address new challenges to the agriculture sector, including "climate change and the increasing importance of bio-energy, as well as the need for better water management and more effective protection of biodiversity."[218]

The amendments noted that parties to the Kyoto Protocol, the EU, and its member states are called upon to "adapt its policies in the light of climate

---

[214] *Bay Area Citizens v. Association of Bay Area Governments*, 248 Cal. App. 4th 966 (2016).
[215] Footnote 212, p. 976.
[216] Footnote 212, p. 977.
[217] Judgment of 14 March 2013, *Neuzelle Agricultural Cooperative v Head of Administrative Services of Oder-Spree Rural District Authority*, C-545/11, EU:C:2013:169.
[218] Footnote 215, para. 9.

change considerations" (footnote 216). The European Court of Justice reasoned that the purpose of the original provision was to establish support schemes for farmers and that the decreases in direct payments, as well as the percentage of reductions, were valid and did not violate any principles of EU law.

B.   Asia and the Pacific Approaches

This section covers emissions from land conversion and urban emissions. (See also Part One, Section I. Standing discusses the importance of forests and the impacts of deforestation.) Countries need to manage not only forests but also agricultural land.

1.   Timber Licenses in the Philippines

In the landmark Philippine case of *Oposa v. Factoran*, the petitioners contested all existing timber license agreements in the Philippines.[219] They sought orders to cancel these licenses and prevent the government from approving renewed or new licenses. The constitutional right to a balanced and healthful ecology underpinned this claim.

The petitioners asserted that deforestation had shrunk Philippine forest cover from 53% to around 12% of the country's land area between 1968 and 1993. This deforestation resulted in a host of environmental tragedies, including water shortages, water table salinization, recurrent droughts, flooding, and increasing velocity of typhoon winds. Petitioners also argued that deforestation reduced the earth's capacity to process CO_2, leading to global warming. Petitioners represented their generation as well as generations yet unborn based on the concept of intergenerational equity—the first known example of petitioners representing future generations.

The court agreed there was a violation of the petitioners' rights. The right to a balanced and healthful ecology falls within the declaration of principles and state policies, and not under the bill of rights within the Philippine constitution. Nevertheless, the court considered it fundamentally important. Such a right concerns self-preservation and self-perpetuation—rights that are assumed to have existed from the inception of humankind. With this right comes a solemn state obligation to preserve a balanced and advance a healthful ecology to avoid the day when future generations "inherit nothing but parched earth incapable of sustaining life."[220]

The court set aside the licenses. They were not contracts and did not give rise to property rights.

(See Part One, Section I.B.1.a. Class Actions and Future Generations in the Philippines for a full case summary of *Oposa v. Factoran. Oposa* is also discussed

---

[219]   *Oposa v. Factoran*, G.R. No. 101083, 30 July 1993.
[220]   Footnote 217, per Davide, Jr., J.

in Part One, Section II.B.1.b. Quality of Life in Southeast Asia; Part One, Section II.B.2.a. Climate Justice in the Philippines and Pakistan; Part Two, Section VIII.B.1. Timber Licenses in the Philippines; and Part Five, Section VI.A. Children and Deforestation.)

2. Sustainable Buildings in India

Global emissions from construction and buildings are sizable. In 2014, for example, the construction and manufacturing industries contributed around 20% of global CO_2 emissions. Residential buildings and commercial and public services contributed about 9%.[221] In response, some of ADB's developing member countries have identified measures to control emissions from the building sector.[222]

Society for Protection of Environment & Biodiversity v. Union of India & Ors concerned a challenge to India's Model Building Bye Laws, 2016 and amendment to its EIA notification (regulation).[223] The bylaws contained a section on climate-resilient construction. However, the amending regulation and bylaws exempted residential building construction projects less than 150,000 m² from obtaining environmental permitting. Applicants argued that the exemption would cause unregulated building and construction, having a "disastrous effect on environment."[224]

The National Green Tribunal (NGT) observed that India's construction industry emits 22% of its total annual CO_2 emissions. It noted that the regulation would exempt particular construction projects from complying with national laws on water and air. The exemption, said the NGT, would also impair India's international commitments to reduce its carbon emissions under the Paris Agreement and pursue sustainable development in line with the Rio Declaration on Environment and Development, 1992. As such, the NGT quashed the exemption.

---

[221] H. Ritchie and M. Roser. 2020. CO₂ and Greenhouse Gas Emissions. *Our World in Data*.

[222] J.A. Amponin and J.W. Evans. 2016. Assessing the Intended Nationally Determined Contributions of ADB Developing Members. *ADB Sustainable Development Working Paper Series*. No. 44. Manila: ADB.

[223] *Society for Protection of Environment & Biodiversity v. Union of India & Ors*, Misc. Applications Nos. 148 of 2017, 3 of 2017, 445 of 2017, 879 of 2017, 55 of 2017, and 620 of 2017 (National Green Tribunal, 8 December 2017).

[224] Footnote 221, para. 4.

PART THREE

CASES AGAINST PRIVATE ENTITIES

Although governments are typically the defendants in climate litigation, some private entities have been challenged in the state, local, federal, and regional courts. This growing number of lawsuits against private entities leverage human rights, nuisance, and negligence claims. In considering the human rights obligations of private actors and corporations, international human rights bodies, courts, and lawyers making their case have relied on human rights principles enshrined in their respective jurisdictions' constitutions. In the case of negligence and nuisance claims, courts are being asked to apply both common law principles and civil law provisions to decide whether fossil fuel companies and other corporations are liable for climate-related damages.

Other types of cases against private entities have focused on corporate compliance within carbon markets, damage to forests as a result of business activity, corporate transparency, and false advertising. As carbon markets become a more established mechanism to achieve mitigation results, courts have stepped in to ensure the efficacy of the carbon marketplace. Judicial review may also serve to hold fossil fuel companies and other corporations accountable for damage to forests, and to their investors for managing climate change risks. This growing number of cases against private entities has exposed private parties to new types of legal risk.

I.   Human Rights and the United Nations

In a handful of cases, plaintiffs have used human rights law to sue fossil fuel companies and other corporations for their contributions to GHG emissions. The core international human rights treaties do not directly address the obligations of private parties to respect human rights. However, international bodies, national governments, and courts are beginning to recognize standards for non-state actors and incorporate these standards into international and domestic law. Some are enshrined in the United Nations (UN) Guiding Principles on Business and Human Rights (the "Ruggie Principles"), proposed by UN Special Representative John Ruggie and endorsed by the UN Human Rights Council (Council) in June 2011.[1] Ruggie Principles 18 and 19 state that business should

---

[1]   *United Nations Human Rights Council (UNHRC) Resolution 17/4, Human Rights and Transnational Corporations and Other Business Enterprises*, A/HRC/Res/17/4 (6 July 2011). For more information about these principles and the scope of private actors' human rights obligations with respect to climate change mitigation and adaptation, see M. Burger and J. Wentz. 2015. *Climate Change and Human Rights*. Nairobi: UN Environment Programme.

identify and assess any actual or potential adverse human rights impacts with which they may be involved either through their own activities or as a result of their business relationships, . . . include meaningful consultation with potentially affected groups and other relevant stakeholders, . . . and integrate the findings from their impact assessments across relevant internal functions and processes, and take appropriate action.[2]

Since 2011, the Council has issued further resolutions that clarify the human rights obligations of the private sector. The Human Rights and Climate Change resolution of 2017 indicates that "human rights obligations and responsibilities as enshrined in the relevant international human rights instruments" provide roles for businesses "to promote, protect and/or respect, as would be appropriate, the rights and best interests of children, when taking action to address the adverse effects of climate change."[3] The Human Rights and Climate Change resolution of 2018 adds that businesses should promote and respect the rights of women and girls.[4]

The Council resolution of 2019 encourages businesses to provide forums for public participation. The resolution affirms that businesses should "carry out human rights due diligence, including with regard to human rights relating to the enjoyment of a safe, clean and healthy environment and by conducting meaningful and inclusive consultations with potentially affected groups and other relevant stakeholders."[5] The resolution further encourages businesses to exchange best practices for addressing adverse human rights impacts, especially when they pertain to environmental human rights defenders (footnote 5).

More recently, the Special Rapporteur on Human Rights and the Environment identified five key responsibilities businesses have in relation to climate change:

(i)   reduce GHG emissions from their activities and their subsidiaries;
(ii)   reduce GHG emissions from their products and services;
(iii)   minimize GHG emissions from their suppliers;
(iv)   publicly disclose their emissions, climate vulnerability, and the risk of stranded assets; and
(v)   ensure that people affected by business-related human rights violations have access to effective remedies.[6]

---

2   UN Human Rights Office of the High Commissioner. 2011. *Guiding Principles on Business and Human Rights: Implementing the United Nations "Protect, Respect and Remedy" Framework.* New York and Geneva. p. 19.

3   UNHRC Resolution 35/20, *Human Rights and Climate Change*, A/HRC/Res/35/20 (7 July 2017). p. 4.

4   UNHRC Resolution 38/4, *Human Rights and Climate Change*, A/HRC/Res/38/4 (16 July 2018). p. 4.

5   UNHRC Resolution 40/11, *Human Rights and Climate Change*, A/HRC/Res/40/11 (2 April 2019). p. 6.

6   D.R. Boyd. 2019. *Report of the Special Rapporteur on the Issue of Human Rights Obligations Relating to the Enjoyment of a Safe, Clean, Healthy and Sustainable Environment*, A/74/161 (15 July), pp. 19–20.

A. Global Approaches: Human Rights in Nigeria and the Netherlands

There are at least two human rights cases that have been filed outside of the Asia and Pacific region against private emitters. The first was *Gbemre v. Shell Petroleum Development Company of Nigeria Ltd. and Others*, where the Federal High Court of Nigeria held that Shell's practice of methane flaring during natural gas production in Nigeria violated Nigerian citizens' rights to life, health, and a clean environment under the Nigerian constitution and the African Charter on Human and Peoples' Rights.[7] The court found that the Nigerian government had also violated human rights by allowing the flaring to occur and ordered the immediate cessation of flaring activities.

(See Part One, Section II.A.4. The Right to a Healthy Environment in Nigeria and Norway for a full case summary of *Gbemre v. Shell Petroleum Development Company of Nigeria Ltd. and Others*.)

More recently, in *Milieudefensie et al. v Royal Dutch Shell Plc.*, environmental groups have filed a lawsuit in the Netherlands, alleging that Shell's contributions to climate change arising from its production and promotion of fossil fuels violated its duty of care under domestic law and human rights obligations.[8]

(See Part Three, Section III.A. Global Approaches: A Duty of Care in the Netherlands for a full case summary of *Milieudefensie et al. v Royal Dutch Shell Plc.*)

B. Asia and the Pacific Approaches

Human rights-based litigation against private entities for climate change is uncommon in Asia and the Pacific. Within Asia, litigants are more likely to rely on constitutional environmental rights, also known as environmental constitutionalism.[9] Such cases—which argue that the constitutional right to life incorporates environmental protection—trace their origins to the 1972 Stockholm Declaration on the Human Environment.[10] The declaration provides that humans have a "fundamental right to freedom, equality and adequate conditions of life, in an environment of a quality that permits a life of dignity and well-being."[11]

Courts reasoned that the declaration—along with the constitutional protection of life and directive principles on environmental protection—obliged a state to

---

[7] *Gbemre v. Shell*, FHC/B/CS/53/05 (2005).

[8] *Milieudefensie et al. v Royal Dutch Shell Plc.*, File No. 90046903 (Hof Hague 2019).

[9] For a more detailed discussion on environmental constitutionalism in Asia, see J.R. May and E. Daly. 2017. *Judicial Handbook on Environmental Constitutionalism*. Nairobi: UN Environment Programme.

[10] See *Virender Gaur and Ors. v. State of Haryana and Ors.*, (1995) 2 SCC 577; *S. Jagannathan v. Union of India*, (1997) 2 SCC 87.

[11] United Nations Conference on the Human Environment. 1972. *Declaration of the United Nations Conference on the Human Environment*. Stockholm. 5–16 June.

protect the environment as a fundamental component of protecting citizens' right to life.[12] *Virender Gaur and Ors. v. State of Haryana and Ors.* in India, represents an early example of such reasoning.[13]

(See Part One, Section I.B.2.b. Environmental Damage and Future Generations in South Asia for a full case summary of *Virender Gaur and Ors. v. State of Haryana and Ors.*; Part One, Section II.B.1.a. Life, Dignity, and Equality in South Asia; and Part Three, Section I.B.1. Human Rights and Climate in the Philippines for further discussion of this case.)

However, no constitutions are protecting a preindustrial climate—the climate of the Holocene to which civilization is adapted.[14] Further, few courts have extended the constitutional right to life to include climate justice or protection.[15] As such, litigants in Asia have explored human rights cases.

1.   Human Rights and Climate in the Philippines

One such case in Asia is a petition filed by environmental groups in the Philippines entitled In re Greenpeace Southeast Asia and Others.[16] In 2015, Greenpeace Southeast Asia and the Philippine Rural Reconstruction Movement petitioned the Commission on Human Rights (CHR) of the Philippines on behalf of 13 organizations and 20 individuals. They alleged that 47 carbon majors knowingly contributed to the root causes of climate change and thus violated the human rights of Filipinos.[17] In particular, the petitioners asked whether the top 50 CO_2 emitters in the world between 1751 and 2010—collectively accounting for 21.71% of the world's CO_2 emissions—have violated, or threaten to violate, among others, the human right to life and the highest attainable standard of physical and mental health, and self-determination.

In December 2019, the CHR found that there was sufficient evidence to conclude that the carbon majors have contributed to dangerous anthropogenic climate change, for which they can be held legally and morally responsible.[18] The CHR could not impose legal liability under existing international human rights law, which should serve as a benchmark for domestic courts when assessing climate liability. It reasoned that national courts could hold companies responsible under

---

[12]   *Virender Gaur and Ors. v. State of Haryana and Ors.*, (1995) 2 SCC 577; *Air India Statutory Corporation v. United Labour Union*, AIR 1997 SC 645.

[13]   *Virender Gaur and Ors. v. State of Haryana and Ors.*, (1995) 2 SCC 577.

[14]   J. Hansen et al. 2008. Target Atmospheric CO_2: Where Should Humanity Aim? *The Open Atmospheric Science Journal.* 2. p. 226.

[15]   See, e.g., *Leghari v. Federation of Pakistan*, PLD 2018 Lahore 364.

[16]   Case No. CHR-NI-2016-0001, Commission on Human Rights Philippines.

[17]   The carbon majors are investor-owned producers of oil, gas, coal, and cement. They include Chevron, ExxonMobil, Rio Tinto, Lukoil, and Massey Coal.

[18]   J. Paris. 2019. CHR: Big Oil, Cement Firms Legally, Morally Liable for Climate Change Effects. *Rappler.* 11 December; and T. Challe. 2020. Philippines Human Rights Commission Found Carbon Majors Can Be Liable for Climate Impacts. *Sabin Center for Climate Change Law: Climate Law Blog.* 10 January.

domestic laws. Consideration of legal and moral responsibility should also extend to state-owned fossil fuel companies, said the CHR.

The CHR stressed the potential for criminally prosecuting carbon majors where behaviors amount to crimes, especially fraud, obstruction, and willful obfuscation. In circumstances where countries do not have laws to hold corporations to account for their behavior, the CHR urged countries to create strong legal frameworks.[19]

Speaking at COP25 in December 2019, CHR Commissioner Roberto Cadiz cautioned companies against continuing with business as usual in the absence of legal liability.[20] "Moral responsibility is as strong as legal responsibility," he warned (footnote 19). Moral responsibility could evolve into legal liability where countries enact laws in alignment with international treaty obligations. For example, Commissioner Cadiz alluded to the potential conversion of the UN Guiding Principles on Business and Human Rights into a binding treaty.[21]

The emphasis on the interaction between human rights and climate change makes this decision momentous. It advocates that domestic courts consider international human rights standards in resolving climate litigation. This recommendation resonates with existing Asian judicial approaches in environmental law.

The introduction to this section highlighted the decision of *Virender Gaur and Ors. v. State of Haryana and Ors.* (footnote 13). In extending the constitutional right to life, the Supreme Court of India referenced international principles articulated in the Stockholm Declaration of 1972 (footnote 11). As with environmental law, domestic courts can also look to international principles to set a standard where relevant and appropriate.

(See Part One, Section I.B.2.b. Environmental Damage and Future Generations in South Asia for a full case summary of *Virender Gaur and Ors. v. State of Haryana and Ors.*; Part One, Section II.B.1.a. Life, Dignity, and Equality in South Asia; and Part Three, Section I.B. Asia and the Pacific Approaches for further discussion of this case.)

2. Human Rights and the Environment in Fiji

Although constitutional-based claims dominate jurisprudence in Asia and the Pacific, there are examples of rights-based judicial approaches to resolving environmental issues. Such approaches are useful when plaintiffs have no

[19] J. Paris. 2019. CHR: Big Oil, Cement Firms Legally, Morally Liable for Climate Change Effects. *Rappler*. 11 December.

[20] COP 25 was the 25th Conference of the Parties under the UNFCCC held in Madrid on 2–13 December 2019. See UNFCCC. UN Climate Change Conference – December 2019.

[21] UNHRC Resolution 17/4, *Human Rights and Transnational Corporations and Other Business Enterprises*, A/HRC/RES/17/4 (6 July 2011); footnote 2; and International Chamber of Commerce. 2019. What is the Importance of the United Nations' Guiding Principles on Business and Human Rights? News release. 19 November.

apparent recourse to constitutional or statutory protection, a common problem with climate change litigation.

A Fijian magistrates' court relied on inalienable human rights when deciding to terminate a private commercial operation for persistent environmental abuses in *Nasinu Town Council v Khan*.[22] Over 20 years, residents complained that the defendant's business was littering, spilling oil, emitting toxic fumes and noise pollution, and thus impacting their health and safety. The court's major concern was the residents' rights and suffering. It considered that the defendant's actions had impacted the residents' health and, therefore, their inalienable rights to life, liberty, happiness, safety, and sustainable development. Sustainable development, said the court, was a new era of law. Quoting from *Bulankulama and Others v Secretary, Ministry of Industrial Development and Others*, a Sri Lankan decision, the court noted:

> Human beings are at the centre of concerns for sustainable development. They are entitled to a healthy and productive life in harmony with nature (Principle 1, Rio De Janeiro Declaration). In order to achieve sustainable development, environmental protection shall constitute an integral part of the development process and cannot be considered in isolation from it. (Principle 4, Rio De Janeiro Declaration).[23]

Because the case related to nature and society, the Fiji magistrate's court distinguished it from a "normal injunction case."[24] It concluded that the residents had a right to live "in a pollution free, safe and healthy environment" (footnote 24). The court granted several injunction orders for the illegal operations to cease and for the defendant to clean up the polluted area.

3. Constitutional Rights and Private Entities in South Asia

Litigants' preference for environmental constitutionalism makes private entities vulnerable to liability for climate action based on constitutional rights. Asian courts frequently demonstrate a preference for melding broader human rights with national constitutional rights.

Residents in India relied on their constitutional rights to sue a chemical factory in *Matthew Lukose & Others v. Kerala State Pollution Control Board & Others*.[25] The claim sought emissions reductions or factory closure but not financial compensation. Petitioners sued Travancore-Electro Chemicals Industries Limited for discharging lime slurry (a chemical used to treat wastewater) into neighboring streams and spewing excessive amounts of CO_2, carbon monoxide, and sulfur dioxide. The petitioners also sued the Kerala State Pollution Control Board for authorizing the discharge but failing to ensure the company's compliance with board directions.

---

[22]   *Nasinu Town Council v Khan* [2011] FJMC 82.
[23]   *Bulankulama and Others v Secretary, Ministry of Industrial Development and Others* 2000 3 Sri LR 243.
[24]   Footnote 22, para. 63.
[25]   *Matthew Lukose & Others v. Kerala State Pollution Control Board & Others*, (1990) 2 KLJ 717.

The court concluded that the excessive emissions of Travancore-Electro Chemicals Industries breached the national air pollution act, amounting to an "invasion of the [constitutional] right to life." This right to life, said the court, was more than a mere immunity from death. It must include the right to an environment that is adequate for human health and well-being. The court underscored the importance of having a proper environment management policy, enforceable through sanctions. Failing to protect against environmental deficit and degradation would lead to "global warming, greenhouse effect and depletion of ozone layer."

The court noted that the National Aeronautics and Space Administration models predicted global warming due to CO_2 pollution and that the UN Environment Programme proposed to establish the Intergovernmental Panel on Climate Change. Citing *Corfu Channel (United Kingdom v. Albania)*, an action in the International Court of Justice (ICJ) concerning damage at sea and the right of innocent passage, the court observed that "every state is obliged to prevent its territories [from] being used against the interest of other states."[26]

In light of "socio-ecological bankruptcy and ecosystem disruption," the court declared a need to conduct environmental audits, strengthen enforcement, and sanction provisions.[27] It suggested the creation of a national environmental agency with planning, enforcement, and sanctioning powers. The court gave the company 3 months to comply with the Kerala State Pollution Control Board's emission limits or face closure.

II. Nuisance

Plaintiffs have begun to use tort law as a litigation tool. State and local governments, indigenous peoples, environmental groups, property owners, and professional associations have all brought nuisance claims against GHG emitters. These cases typically have one of two goals: (i) force GHG emitters to reduce their emissions, or (ii) shift the costs of adapting to climate change to fossil fuel companies. While the majority of these cases have arisen in the US, other jurisdictions have seen nuisance claims as well.

A. Global Approaches

1. Nuisance Cases in the United States

Two landmark cases in the US—*American Electric Power v. Connecticut* and *Native Village of Kivalina v. ExxonMobil Corp.*—were both suits against energy

---

[26] Footnote 25, p. 724, para. 14; and *Corfu Channel (United Kingdom v. Albania)*, Merits, Judgment, ICJ Reports 1949, p. 22.

[27] Footnote 25, p. 725, para. 18.

producers based on a theory of public nuisance under federal common law. In *American Electric Power v. Connecticut*, a consortium of states, cities, and NGOs sued four private power companies and the Tennessee Valley Authority over CO_2 emissions.[28] The plaintiffs argued that the emissions constituted a public nuisance under US federal common law because they contributed to global warming. The plaintiffs sought orders requiring the power companies to reduce their emissions.

The US Supreme Court dismissed the lawsuit on the grounds that federal common law claims in this area have been displaced by the Clean Air Act, a federal law that authorizes the Environmental Protection Agency (EPA) to regulate GHG emissions from power plants and other sources. The court reasoned that Congress had granted EPA the power to determine how GHG should be regulated, and it was inappropriate for the judiciary to issue their own rules.

Similarly, in *Native Village of Kivalina v. ExxonMobil Corp.*, a federal appellate court held that a public nuisance claim against some fossil fuel companies—including ExxonMobil, BP, and Chevron—was also displaced by the Clean Air Act.[29] The plaintiffs—Inupiat, indigenous peoples from Kivalina, Alaska—alleged that direct emissions associated with the energy companies' operations contributed to climate change and had resulted in the erosion of the Arctic sea ice that protected the Kivalina coast from storms. The plaintiffs sought money damages of $95 million–$400 million for the costs of relocating residents. However, the court concluded that the Clean Air Act had displaced federal common law claims seeking damages as well as injunctions.

In US cases against emitters and fossil fuel companies, proving causation is a plausible hurdle. However, the law is still unsettled on this matter.

2. Ongoing State and Local Government Lawsuits in the United States

Since 2017, US state and local governments have filed some state lawsuits against fossil fuel companies, seeking compensation for adaptation costs associated with sea level rise, wildfires, upland floods, and other climate impacts. These suits are at various stages of procedural development.

In California, two lawsuits filed in state court by the cities of San Francisco and Oakland alleged that five of the world's largest oil companies promoted fossil fuel use when they knew their products would contribute to dangerous global warming and cause sea level rise.[30] The San Francisco and Oakland cases originally sought an abatement remedy under California state law to fund

---

[28]   *Am. Elec. Power Co. v. Connecticut*, 564 US 410 (2011).

[29]   *Native Vill. of Kivalina v. ExxonMobil Corp.*, 696 F.3d 849 (9th Cir. 2012).

[30]   *City of San Francisco v. BP*, No. 3:17-cv06012-WHA (N.D. Cal. Apr. 3, 2018); *City of Oakland v. BP*, No. 3:17-cv-06011-WHA (N.D. Cal. Apr. 3, 2018).

adaptation measures, including the construction of seawalls and elevation of low-lying property and buildings.

The San Francisco and Oakland cases were removed to federal court, where a federal district court first determined that any climate change nuisance suit necessarily arose under federal law. Therefore, the court dismissed the public nuisance suits, deciding that the cities' claims were displaced by the Clean Air Act pursuant to *American Electric Power Co. v. Connecticut and Native Village of Kivalina v. ExxonMobil Corp.*

(See Part Three, Section II.A.1. Nuisance Cases in the United States for the full case summary of two cases.)

The court also found that a federal common law nuisance claim for climate harms would interfere with the President's foreign affairs power. The cities appealed, and a decision is pending in a US federal appellate court.

Other Californian cities and counties filed similar suits that alleged public nuisance and other tort, statutory, and public trust claims—including negligence, strict liability, trespass, failure to warn, and design defect. These suits sought abatement and requested disgorgement of profits, compensatory damages, and punitive damages for sea level rise and other climate impacts, including wildfire and drought. Unlike the San Francisco and Oakland cases, these other lawsuits were remanded to state court after a federal judge reasoned that they should be governed by state law rather than federal law.[31] The remand order is currently being appealed in federal appellate court. If the federal appellate court affirms the remand, a state court might have the opportunity to consider the merits of local government plaintiffs' nuisance claim.

Other state and local governments, including the City of New York, City of Baltimore, King County in Washington, three local governments in Colorado state, State of Rhode Island, and Pacific Fishermen's Association, have also sued to shift the costs of climate harms back to fossil fuel companies. These cases are at various stages.

3. Transboundary Nuisance Claims in Germany

The US is not the only jurisdiction in which plaintiffs have sought to recover the costs of adapting to climate change from fossil fuel companies. For example, in *Lliuya v RWE AG* (also discussed in Part One, Section I.A.3. Private Citizens in Foreign Jurisdictions in Europe and New Zealand), German courts are considering the potential liability of a GHG emitter for climate impacts based on a theory of nuisance.[32]

---

[31] *County of San Mateo v. Chevron Corporation, et al.,* No. 18-15499 (filed 9th Cir. 2017). For updates, see Sabin Center for Climate Change Law. County of San Mateo v. Chevron Corp. (accessed 1 January 2020).

[32] *Lliuya v RWE AG,* District Court of Essen, Dec. 15, 2016, Case No. 2 O 285/15, ECLI:DE:LGE:2016: 1215.2O285.15.00. For an unofficial English translation, see Sabin Center for Climate Change Law. Lliuya v. RWE AG (accessed 29 April 2020).

Saúl Lliuya, a Peruvian farmer, sued RWE AG (Germany's largest electricity producer) for nuisance under paragraph 1004 of the German Civil Code. Lliuya asked the court to declare RWE AG partly responsible for melting glaciers and the enlargement of Palcacocha (a glacial lake) near his town, Huaraz, on the grounds that it is a large GHG emitter and contributor to climate change. He sought reimbursement for personal adaptation costs plus €17,000 (about $19,000) for the Huaraz community association to build siphons, drains, and dams to protect the town from flooding. The claimed €17,000 (about $19,000) equated to "0.47 percent of both (1) the estimated cost of protective measures; and (2) RWE's estimated annual contribution to global GHG emissions."[33]

The District Court of Essen dismissed the case for several reasons, including on account of two causation issues. First, the plaintiff presented insufficient evidence. Lliuya had asked the court to specify RWE's precise annual contribution to global emissions rather than submitting an estimate. Second, the court found that no "linear chain of causation" linked the alleged injury and RWE's emissions.[34] Rather, the court reasoned that many emitters had created the risk of flood confronting the Peruvian town. As such, the root cause of the risk could not be ascribed to RWE in particular (footnote 34).

However, the Higher Regional Court in Hamm overturned the district court's decision. It reasoned that the distance between emissions and impacts did not necessarily rule out the application of nuisance law and that the case should proceed. The appeal is now in the evidentiary phase (footnote 32).

B.   Asia and the Pacific Approaches

The authors are not aware of climate change nuisance cases against private entities in Asia and the Pacific. However, courts in Asia have established equitable outcomes in nuisance cases that are worth discussing. Many jurisdictions lack effective remedies for environmental nuisance. In such circumstances, rights-based approaches may be useful and appropriate.

1.   Public Nuisance from a Chemical Factory in Sri Lanka

The Court of Appeal of Sri Lanka considered the right of community members to sustainable development and intergenerational equity in the context of environmental nuisance. In *Singalanka Standard Chemicals Ltd v Thalangama Appuhamilage Sirisena and Others*, a petitioner appealed a magistrate's decision to close its chemical factory.[35] Residents had alleged that emissions and discharges from the factory constituted a public nuisance, leading to the magistrate's closure

---

[33]   UN Environment Programme. 2017. *The Status of Climate Change Litigation: A Global Review.* Nairobi, Kenya. p. 21.

[34]   Footnote 32, p. 7 of the unofficial translation.

[35]   *Singalanka Standard Chemicals Ltd v Thalangama Appuhamilage Sirisena and Others* C/A Application No. 85/98 (1 October 2010) and also affirmed by the Supreme Court of Sri Lanka.

order. The petitioner argued that it was operating with an environmental permit, regulated under the National Environmental Act, 1988. It argued that the act contained specific remedies that displaced the jurisdiction of the magistrate court to shut down the factory for public nuisance under the Code of Criminal Procedure.

The court dismissed the petitioner's arguments on jurisdiction. Possessing an environmental license would not in itself exonerate a licensee from liability for nuisance. The court noted that environmental permits endeavor to ensure sustainable development. Sustainable development is "an attempt to reconcile two contradictory human rights, namely the right to development and the right to environmental conservation."[36]

The court considered the community's universal rights, as well as the precautionary and polluter pays principles, given the potential for environmental harm. It declared that all members of society have a universal obligation to safeguard environmental integrity and purity. This obligation could not be constrained by agreement. The court also held that state directives within the national constitution compelled the government to "protect, preserve and improve the environment for the benefit of the community."[37] As such, where specific remedies are "inadequate, ineffective or not speedy enough then the ordinary courts . . . must have the jurisdiction to intervene to abate such nuisance."[38] Otherwise, irreversible environmental hazards might "adversely affect the present and the future generations" (footnote 38). The court concluded that magistrates' courts had the power to make orders to stop public nuisance under the Code of Criminal Procedure.

The case presents a useful, rights-based approach to reaching an equitable outcome in circumstances where the available remedy was inadequate.

2. Liability for Nuisance from a Pipeline Leak in the Philippines

The Supreme Court of the Philippines granted its first writ of *kalikasan* (nature) to stop a fossil-fuel pipeline leak in *West Tower Condominium Corp v. First Philippine Industrial Corporation et al.*[39] The respondent's pipeline system transports 60% of Metro Manila's diesel, gasoline, jet fuel, and kerosene needs. In 2010, the 117-km-long pipeline leaked. The fuel leak affected residents in two neighborhoods, as well as the West Tower condominium. The petitioners focused their arguments on the environmental damage resulting from the fuel leak.

The Court of Appeals of the Philippines awarded a writ of *kalikasan* with a temporary environmental protection order. It ordered the respondent to (i) cease operating the leaking pipeline, (ii) check the pipeline's structural integrity, and

---

[36] Footnote 35, p. 11.
[37] Footnote 35, p. 13.
[38] Footnote 35, p. 7.
[39] *West Tower Condominium Corp v. First Philippine Industrial Corporation et al.*, G.R. No. 194239, 16 June 2015.

(iii) implement measures to prevent any incidents resulting from leaks and report on the measures' effectiveness.

The Supreme Court of the Philippines affirmed this ruling. It ordered respondents to continue remediation works until the affected areas were restored. It allowed respondents to reopen the pipeline under strict conditions. The court found the respondent oil company liable for the restoration and rehabilitation costs.

However, the Supreme Court refused the petitioners' request for individual damages and the creation of a special trust fund. It held that the Philippine Rules of Procedure for Environmental Cases did not allow for personal damages or the creation of a trust fund. Separate actions for civil and criminal liability would be needed.

(See Part Two, Section III.B. Asia and the Pacific Approaches: Pipeline Emissions in the Philippines for further discussion of this case.)

III. Negligence

Plaintiffs in common law jurisdictions have also begun to use negligence claims to address the damage caused by climate change. In these cases, plaintiffs may allege that a private actor is acting negligently by engaging in behavior that contributes to climate change. Civil law jurisdictions also see claims based on negligence.

A. Global Approaches: A Duty of Care in the Netherlands

For example, the Netherlands' civil code recognizes that the government owes a duty of care to its citizens, which formed the basis of the landmark decision in *The State of the Netherlands (Ministry of Infrastructure and the Environment) v Urgenda Foundation*.[40] In Urgenda, the Hague Court of Appeal found that the government's insufficient action on climate change violated a duty of care to its citizens. The court determined that the state has a duty to take climate change mitigation measures due to the "severity of the consequences" of global warming and because of the risk of surpassing a "tipping point," which "may result in abrupt climate change, for which neither mankind nor nature can properly prepare."[41]

The decision referenced (but did not directly apply) article 21 of the Netherlands' constitution, EU emissions reduction targets, and the European Convention on Human Rights (ECHR). It also relied upon the doctrine of hazardous negligence and international norms such as the precautionary, sustainability, prevention, no harm, and fairness principles.[42]

---

[40] *The State of the Netherlands (Ministry of Infrastructure and the Environment) v Urgenda Foundation*, HA ZA 13-1396, C/09/456689, ECLI:NL:GHDHA:2018:2591, Hague Court of Appeal, 9 October 2018.

[41] Footnote 40, p. 12 of the unofficial translation from the court.

[42] For updates, see Sabin Center for Climate Change Law. *Urgenda Foundation v. State of the Netherlands* (accessed 29 April 2020).

On appeal, the Supreme Court of the Netherlands upheld the decisions of the lower courts.[43] It concluded that the government was obliged to reduce carbon emissions by 25% against 1990 levels by 2020. Without this action, climate change could have a severe impact on the lives and welfare of the residents of the Netherlands.

The government's obligation to do "its part" stemmed from its obligations under articles 2 and 8 of the ECHR.[44] Articles 2 and 8 of the ECHR impose positive obligations on the state to protect the right to life and the right to respect for private and family life.

(See Part One, Section II.A.2. The Right to Private and Family Life in the Netherlands for a full case summary of *Urgenda Foundation v The State of the Netherlands. Urgenda* is also discussed in Part One, Section III.A. Global Approaches: Violating the Law in Europe.)

Although *Urgenda* is a negligence suit against a government, not a private entity, plaintiffs have attempted to extend the Urgenda logic to a lawsuit involving a corporate emitter. In *Milieudefensie et al. v Royal Dutch Shell plc.*, plaintiffs alleged that Shell's contributions to climate change (arising from its production and promotion of fossil fuels) violated the company's duty of care under the Netherlands' law and human rights obligations (footnote 8).

According to the plaintiffs, Shell's long-standing knowledge of climate change, misleading statements about global warming, and inadequate action to reduce GHG emissions unlawfully endangered citizens and constituted hazardous negligence. The plaintiffs argued that Shell owed a duty of care under the Netherlands' civil code and the ECHR. The Netherlands' civil code authorizes tort actions against private companies. Articles 2 and 8 of the ECHR guarantee the right to life, plus rights to private life, family life, home, and correspondence. The plaintiffs sought orders directing Shell to reduce its CO_2 emissions consistent with the Paris Agreement targets—45% by 2030 based on 2010 levels and 0% by 2050. The case is still pending.

(See Part Three, Section I.A. Global Approaches: Human Rights in Nigeria and the Netherlands for further discussion of this case.)

B. Asia and the Pacific Approaches

Asia and the Pacific has not yet seen compensation claims for climate change against private actors based on negligence. Negligence suits in the region remain limited to seeking compensation for harm from environmental damage, including by fossil fuel companies.

---

[43] *The State of the Netherlands (Ministry of Economic Affairs and Climate Policy) v Urgenda Foundation*, Case No. 19/00135, ECLI:NL:HR:2019:2007, Supreme Court of the Netherlands, 20 December 2019 (unofficial translation).

[44] Footnote 43, para. 5.7.1.

1. Fisherfolk and a Pipeline in the Philippines

The Supreme Court of the Philippines explored the rights of fisherfolk to maintain their negligence suit despite deficiencies in their arguments. In *Shell Philippines Exploration B.V. v. Jalos, et al.*, fisherfolk argued that their fish catch was reduced after Shell built and operated its gas pipeline.[45] They sought compensation for impacts on their livelihood and basic needs. Shell moved for dismissal on the grounds that the case related to pollution and should be heard by the Pollution Adjudication Board. It also argued that the fisherfolk had failed to specify an actionable wrong or to contend that Shell's pipeline emitted a substance that drove away the fish.

The court agreed that the fisherfolk must first go to the Pollution Adjudication Board and dismissed the case. However, it disagreed that the fisherfolk had failed to show a cause of action.

While the complaint did not use the word pollution, it alleged that "the pipeline greatly affected biogenically hard-structured communities such as coral reefs and led [to] stress to the marine life in the Mindoro Sea." The court considered that the wording was clear. Alleging that the pipeline "greatly affected" the marine habitat fell within the defined meaning of pollution under the relevant law. The court also concluded that the fisherfolk had a valid cause of action to sue Shell. "A cause of action is the wrongful act or omission committed by the defendant in violation of the primary rights of the plaintiff." To succeed with its motion to dismiss the fisherfolk's claim, the court said that Shell should definitively

> "The construction and operation of the pipeline may, in itself, be a wrongful act that could be the basis of Jalos et al.'s cause of action. The rules do not require that the complaint establish in detail the causal link between the construction and operation of the pipeline, on the one hand, and the fish decline and loss of income, on the other hand, it being sufficient that the complaint states the ultimate facts on which it bases its claim for relief... In this case, a valid judgment for damages can be made in favor of Jalos et al., if the construction and operation of the pipeline indeed caused fish decline and eventually led to the fishermen's loss of income, as alleged in the complaint.
>
> Source: *Shell Philippines Exploration B.V. v. Jalos, et al.*, G.R. No. 179918, 8 September 2010.

---

[45]   *Shell Philippines Exploration B.V. v. Jalos, et al.* G.R. No. 179918, 8 September 2010.

show that the claim for relief did not exist. It was insufficient to argue that the fisherfolk's claim was "ambiguous, indefinite or uncertain."

2. Coal-Fired Electricity in Pakistan

Although *Ali v. Federation of Pakistan & Another* is not a suit against a private party, it alleged that the respondents are criminally negligent for seeking to expand coal-fired electricity generation.[46] The petitioner cited the Environment and Climate Change Outlook of Pakistan, 2013. It reported that Pakistan faced "cataclysmic floods and droughts."[47] Given the anticipated impacts of climate change, the petitioner argued that the respondents breached their constitutional and public trust obligations by not mitigating Pakistan's carbon emissions. The case has not yet been decided.

(See Part One, Section II.B.3.a. The Energy Sector in Pakistan for a full case summary of *Ali v. Federation of Pakistan & Another*; Part One, Section I.B.2.b. Environmental Damage and Future Generations in South Asia; Part One, Section IV.B.2. International Commitments in Pending Cases in South Asia; and Part Two, Section I.B.1.b. Constitutional Rights in Pakistan for further discussion of this case.)

A caravan at Derawar Fort in the Thar Desert, Punjab, Pakistan. The case, *Ali v. Federation of Pakistan & Another*, challenges the government's decision to exploit coal reserves in the Thar Desert (photo by Tahsin Shah).

IV. Carbon Credits

A. Global Approaches

Ensuring the validity of carbon credits is key to the functioning of carbon trading markets. To be effective, carbon credits must represent emissions reductions that (i) would not have occurred otherwise, and (ii) actually occurred and can, therefore, be verified. Double counting carbon credits undermines the validity and effectiveness of carbon trading markets. It occurs when two buyers rely on the same carbon credit to meet their emissions reductions. Carbon pricing is becoming a more popular tool for encouraging "cost-effective emissions mitigation," and courts play a critical role in ensuring the validity of carbon credits traded in the market.[48]

---

[46]   *Ali v. Federation of Pakistan*, Constitution Petition in the Supreme Court of Pakistan, 2016.
[47]   Footnote 46, p. 17, para. 13.
[48]   World Bank. 2018. *State and Trends of Carbon Pricing 2018*. Washington, DC.

1. Carbon Credit Validity in Australia and the United States

In *Australian Competition and Consumer Commission v Prime Carbon Pty Ltd*, the Australian Competition and Consumer Commission (ACCC) sued a carbon credit company. ACCC argued that Prime Carbon had falsely claimed that it was certified by the National Stock Exchange of Australia and that the National Environment Registry—through which the company supplied some of its credits—was regulated by the Government of Australia.[49] The Federal Court of Australia ruled that Prime Carbon had misrepresented its services and affiliations, violating Australian trade law (footnote 49).

For a supplier to monetize a reduction in carbon emissions as a tradable credit, the supplier must reliably calculate the emissions avoided through any given carbon credit project. Certain organizations have set standards for measuring the quantity of emissions avoided or reduced by carbon credit projects.

In *Aldabe v. Environmental Services, Inc.*, a US federal district court reviewed whether a broker company had failed its contractual obligation to provide verification services for a proposed carbon credit project.[50] The plaintiff claimed that the broker had breached its contract because it did not assess whether the plaintiff's Bolivian forest preservation project complied with the Verified Carbon Standard, which is a leading standard for certifying carbon emissions reductions. The court dismissed the case without prejudice on jurisdictional grounds. The court also suggested that the plaintiff refile in another jurisdiction.

2. Offset Purchases in Brazil and the United Kingdom

By purchasing carbon credits or "offsets," emitters can comply with regulatory emissions limits without reducing their emissions. In *São Paulo Public Prosecutor's Office v. United Airlines and Others*, the public prosecutor of São Paulo brought several cases seeking to compel airlines that make use of the region's international airport to offset their emissions—United Airlines, TAAG Linhas Aéreas de Angola, Delta Airlines, Cia. Mexicana, Emirates Airlines, Aerolíneas Argentinas, and South African Airways.[51] The offsets would be used to support reforestation in Brazil. The court rejected the suits against several of the airlines on the grounds that it lacked jurisdiction over the claims.

In *Deutsche Bank AG v Total Global Steel Ltd*, the High Court of Justice in the UK awarded damages to a multinational investment bank for breach of contract regarding offsets it had purchased.[52] The bank claimed that the offsets it had purchased from a steel company were invalid because the credits had been

---

[49] ACCC. 2010. Company Admits Misleading Consumers about Marketing Carbon Credits. Media release. 11 March.

[50] *Aldabe v. Envtl. Servs., Inc.*, No. CV 16-11067-MLW (D. Mass. Sept. 20, 2017).

[51] TRF-3, Ap. Civ. No. 000292010.2014.4.03.9999, Relator: Des. Gilberto Jordan, 29.08.2018, vol Diário Eletrônico da Justiça Federal da 3a Região [eDJF3], 13.09.2018 (Braz.).

[52] *Deutsche Bank AG v Total Global Steel Ltd* [2012] EWHC 1201 (Comm).

previously "surrendered" or used to demonstrate compliance with European emissions limitation commitments. The High Court agreed with the bank.

As carbon pricing continues to develop in the Asia and Pacific region, cases like *Deutsche Bank* could become more common.

B. Asia and the Pacific Approaches

1. Taxability of Carbon Credits in South Asia

With India being one of the biggest sellers of carbon credits, Indian tax tribunals have had several occasions to rule on the tax treatment of carbon credits. In *Dy Commissioner of Income Tax Circle 16(2), Hyderabad v. M/S My Home Power Ltd., Hyderabad,* the Hyderabad Income Tax Appellate Tribunal affirmed that the income from selling carbon credits is a capital receipt that cannot be taxed as a revenue receipt because it has no element of profit or gain.[53] Instead, carbon credit is "an entitlement" received to improve world atmosphere and environment. The assessee is granted carbon credits because it reduced its energy consumption and not because of its business.

In *Dy Commissioner of Income Tax Central Circle 2(2), Ahmedabad v. Kalpataru Power Transmission Ltd.,* the Income Tax Appellate Tribunal reversed earlier pronouncements.[54] It ruled that gains made on the sale of carbon credits should be taxed at the time a transfer for valuable consideration or a sale of the carbon credits takes place. The dispute arose because Kalpataru Power Transmission Ltd. (a power generation company) argued that carbon credit sales were nontaxable capital receipts. It maintained that the sales were tax exempt because they stemmed from (i) efforts to protect the environment by using a subsidy or grant, and (ii) contracts with countries with binding commitments under the Kyoto Protocol.

The tribunal acknowledged that reducing emissions and switching to renewable energy were integral to business. It was skeptical about the environmental or climate benefits of carbon credit sales, though. The tribunal conceded that companies must meet emission standards and conduct business in an environmentally responsible manner to generate carbon credits. But when companies obtained carbon credits, they gained an advantage incidental to conducting business in an environmentally responsible manner. As such, carbon credits were an offshoot of business and should not be glorified as an offshoot of "environmental concerns." In the tribunal's view, carbon credit transactions merely redistributed the right to emit GHG.

---

[53] *Dy Commissioner of Income Tax Circle 16(2) v. M/S My Home Power Ltd.,* I.T.A. Application Nos. 80 and 81/Hyd/2014 (Income Tax Appellate Tribunal—Hyderabad, 7 May 2014).

[54] Dy Commissioner of Income Tax Central Circle 2(2), *Ahmedabad v. Kalpataru Power Transmission Ltd.,* I.T.A. Application No. 538/Ahd/2013 (Income Tax Appellate Tribunal—Hyderabad, 18 March 2016).

The Government of India resolved this issue by amending the Income Tax Act in 2018. It now imposes a concessional tax rate of 10% on the transfer of carbon credits.[55]

2. Damages for Lost Carbon Credits in Papua New Guinea

Establishing a claim for damages due to loss of carbon credits can pose a serious challenge to landowners. This was true even after proving a defendant's liability for trespass and illegal logging in *Gramgari v Crawford & Another* when a customary landowner sued a wood products developer for entering his land and harvesting timber without authority.[56] The Papua New Guinea National Court of Justice agreed that the defendants' actions constituted a trespass causing environmental harm.

In a later hearing to assess damages, the plaintiff demanded approximately K8.8 million ($2.5 million) in general damages for loss of timber cut and exported, loss of royalties, exemplary damages, and special damages. He also sought damages for loss of biodiversity and loss of CO_2 emissions credits. The court awarded the plaintiff a notional sum of K50,000 ($14,700) for loss of royalties and dismissed all other damages claims.[57]

Evidence during the trial on assessment of damages established that the plaintiff did not own the land. The court considered that the plaintiff's estimates of damage were unrealistic. It also held that the damages claim for loss of carbon credits was "based on assumptions as to the existence of markets, which have no evidentiary basis."[58] Lastly, the plaintiff had not commenced the proceedings as a representative of his claim. Hence, his right to damages was limited to the extent of damage that he individually suffered.

The Papua New Guinea National Court rendered a similar decision in *Gau v G & S Ltd.*[59] Fugaman Gau, acting on behalf of the Songumbe-Marumbe Clan and the Boimbe Clan, successfully established the liability of G & S Ltd. for trespass, illegal logging, and other forest activities, all resulting in environmental harm. At the trial on assessment of damages, the plaintiff claimed approximately K20.2 million (about $5.9 million), representing damages for loss of timber cut and exported, environmental pollution and destruction, as well as pain and suffering. This amount was based on the area of land on which G & S was alleged to have conducted illegal logging operations, the timber harvested, and the export price of the timber. Damages for environmental pollution and destruction—loss of biodiversity and carbon emission credits—were based on assumptions about the existence of markets. The plaintiff also demanded K20,000 (about $5,880) as notional damages.

---

55 Government of India. 1961. Income Tax Act. section 115BBG. The amendments took effect on 1 April 2018.
56 *Gramgari v Crawford* [2013] PGNC 14.
57 *Gramgari v Crawford* [2018] PGNC 118.
58 Footnote 57, para. 15.
59 *Gau v G & S Ltd* [2018] PGNC 119.

During the subsequent trial, the defendant's new counsel proved that G & S had made no incursion into the plaintiff's land. Like in *Gramgari v Crawford*, the court found that the plaintiff's estimates of the value of the loss of timber cut and exported, as well as the amount of damage for environmental pollution and destruction, were based on unrealistic assumptions. It also ruled that the claim for pain and suffering had no evidentiary basis.

The court nonetheless granted a notional amount of damages equivalent to K30,000 (about $8,821) because G & S had contributed to the confusion regarding its liability for trespass and illegal logging. The court said that just because damages could not be assessed with certainty did not relieve the wrongdoer of liability.

V. Wrongful Damage to Forests

Deforestation affects the ability of forests to capture carbon and cool the air. The destruction of tropical forest cover results in an average of 4.8 gigatons of CO_2 emissions per year, "causing more emissions every year than 85 million cars would over their entire lifetime."[60] The Paris Agreement supports the use of biological sinks in climate mitigation.[61] Given the benefits of forests and the funding provided for carbon sinks, it is no wonder that tropical forests alone can provide 23% of the cost-effective climate mitigation required by 2030 (footnote 60).

Companies may be liable for destroying and damaging forests through commercial activity. Damage to forests can undermine forests' ability to provide essential ecosystem services such as capturing carbon, purifying air and water, and supporting biodiversity.

A. Global Approaches: Restoring Forests in Brazil

In some cases, courts have declared it illegal to undermine ecosystem services through damage to forests. For example, in *Public Prosecutor's Office v. H Carlos Schneider S/A Comércio e Indústria & Others*, the Superior Court of Justice in Brazil upheld a trial court's decision that a group responsible for draining and clearing a mangrove forest and putting a landfill and various structures in its place had to restore the forest.[62]

(See Part Two, Section VIII.A.1.a. Environmental Policy in Brazil for a full case summary of *Public Prosecutor's Office v. H Carlos Schneider S/A Comércio e Indústria & Others*.)

---

[60] D. Gibbs, N. Harris, and F. Seymour. 2018. By the Numbers: The Value of Tropical Forests in the Climate Change Equation. *World Resources Institute*. 4 October.

[61] Food and Agriculture Organization of the United Nations (FAO). The Clean Development Mechanism: Promoting Investment Flows from Developed to Developing Countries.

[62] S.T.J., Recurso Especial no. 650728 SC 2003 / 0221786-0, Relator: Ministro Antônio Herman Benjamin, 23 October 2007.

B. Asia and the Pacific Approaches

1. Wildfire and Illegal Logging in Indonesia

Indonesia has developed an innovative approach to deterring illegal deforestation and peatland fires, a major source of national greenhouse gas (GHG) emissions.[63] The Indonesian Ministry of Environment and Forestry has sued concession holders for illegal land clearing under tort law. As the rightful owner of all natural resources within the country, the state has a legal standing based on trusteeship. Specifically, the Ministry of Environment and Forestry has a right to sue for environmental damage under the Environmental Protection and Management Act, 2009, which imposes strict liability for inflicting serious threats to the environment.[64] The litigation seeks recovery for environmental losses like ecological damage (loss of ecosystem function), biodiversity and economic losses, and economic losses associated with carbon release.[65] The last component of the damages is particularly relevant to this report and can be used in other jurisdictions.

In *Ministry of Environment v. PT. Selatnasik Indokwarsa and PT. Simpang Pesak Indokwarsa*, the Supreme Court of Indonesia found two mining companies responsible for clearing protected forests to build a road to their mining location—and other illegal activities—resulting in serious environmental harm.[66] The court held the defendant liable based on an unlawful act—analogous to the negligence rule in the common law system—which attracts strict liability. The Ministry of Environment and Forestry argued that the illegal activities released 359 tons of carbon per hectare. Therefore, illegal activities in 208 hectares of damaged land released up to 74,672 tons of carbon. The ministry further argued that the cost of restoring released carbon was Rp90,000 per ton, for a total of Rp6.7 billion ($480,000 as of 23 May 2014).

The ministry sought compensation to cover the cost of restoring the forest's natural functions—such as watershed function, runoff and erosion control, soil formation, and nutrient recycling—and economic losses associated with environmental damage. The court ordered the defendants to jointly pay restoration costs of Rp32.3 billion ($2.3 million as of 23 May 2014).

In *Ministry of Environment v. PT. Merbau Pelalawan Lestari*, the Supreme Court of Indonesia held that the defendant illegally logged in 7,463 hectares of protected forest area.[67] The ministry argued that the illegal logging had released carbon, which should be remedied by restoring the degraded forest. It also sought

[63] D. Dunne. 2019. The Carbon Brief Profile: Indonesia. *Carbon Brief*. 27 March.

[64] A.G. Wibisana. 2019. The Many Faces of Strict Liability in Indonesia's Wildfire Litigation. *Review of European, Comparative & International Environmental Law*. 28 (2). p. 3.

[65] Footnote 64, p. 4.

[66] Supreme Court of the Republic of Indonesia, Decision No. 109 PK/Pdt/2014, *Ministry of Environment v. PT. Selatnasik Indokwarsa and PT. Simpang Pesak Indokwarsa*.

[67] Supreme Court of the Republic of Indonesia, Cessation Decision No. 460 K/Pdt/2016, *Ministry of Environment v. PT. Merbau Pelalawan Lestari*.

damages for ecological regeneration.[68] The ministry priced forest restoration at Rp32.30 per hectare, with a total cost of Rp240 billion ($17.2 million as of 10 February 2014) for 7,463 hectares.

The court accepted these arguments and ordered the company to pay compensation for illegal logging in the amount of Rp16.25 trillion ($1.2 billion as of 10 February 2014). The award included amounts for losses due to environmental damage.

The Supreme Court rendered a similar verdict in *PT. Kalista Alam v. Ministry of Environment*.[69] It found the appellant liable for intentionally draining and burning peatland to clear land for its palm oil plantation. As regulations required concessionaires to take preventive and remedial measures against fires, the appellant had committed an unlawful act. The ministry submitted expert evidence that the fires released air pollution—13,500 tons of carbon, 4,275 tons of CO_2, 49.14 tons of methane, 21.74 tons of nitrogen oxides, 60.48 tons of ammonia, 50.08 tons of ozone, 874.12 tons of carbon monoxide, and 1,050 tons of particles.[70]

The ministry sought Rp505 billion ($36 million as of 28 August 2015) in restorative damages, predominantly for ecological and economic losses and restoring the peatland. It also claimed around Rp3.11 billion ($223,000 as of 28 August 2015) for loss of biodiversity and genetic resources and approximately Rp1.64 billion ($117,000 as of 28 August 2015) for losses due to carbon release. The damages for carbon release included two components—carbon refund costs and impaired capacity to absorb carbon.

The ministry valued each ton of carbon released at Rp90,000 ($10 as of 28 August 2015). It submitted that 1,000 hectares of burned peat released 13,5000 tons of CO_2 and requested around Rp1.2 billion ($86,000 as of 28 August 2015).[71] The ministry further submitted that the peatland's reduced capacity to absorb CO_2 equated to the emission of 4,725 tons of CO_2. Accordingly, it argued that peatland restoration was required to reduce these emissions, which would cost Rp425.3 million ($30,000 as of 28 August 2015).[72]

The Supreme Court upheld earlier decisions of courts to award the ministry around Rp367 billion ($26.3 million as of 28 August 2015). The order required PT. Kalista Alam to pay Rp115 billion ($8 million as of 28 August 2015) in compensation plus almost Rp252 billion ($18 million as of 28 August 2015) for

---

[68] The claimed damages were for restoring water function, watershed management, erosion and runoff controls, biodiversity, and genetic resources.

[69] Supreme Court of the Republic of Indonesia. Decision No. 651/K/Pdt/2015, *PT. Kalista Alam v. Ministry of Environment*. For more detail regarding the plaintiff's arguments, see A.G. Wibisana. 2019. The Many Faces of Strict Liability in Indonesia's Wildfire Litigation. *Review of European, Comparative & International Environmental Law*. 28 (2). p. 5.

[70] Footnote 67, p. 22. All calculations were based on W. Seiler and P.J. Crutzen. 1980. Estimates of Gross and Net Fluxes of Carbon between the Biosphere and the Atmosphere from Biomass Burning. *Climatic Change*. 2 (3). pp. 207–247.

[71] Footnote 67, p. 26.

[72] Footnote 67, p. 27.

the restoration of the 1,000 hectares of damaged peatland. The court stated that restoration should ensure the proper refunctioning of land.

Increased wildfire litigation has arguably contributed to reduced burning in peatlands, with the number of hot spots reducing by 32.6% from 2016 to 2017.[73] While government policies and strategies are undoubtedly central to reducing carbon emissions from wildfires and illegal logging, litigation may also have an important role to play in this climate goal (footnote 73).

VI. Transparency and Business Risk

Shareholders and other stakeholders have begun to sue companies for failure to disclose climate-related risks. This recent groundswell of cases demonstrates that courts have a potential role to play in holding companies accountable to their investors and the public by assessing, disclosing, and acting on climate risk.

A. Global Approaches

1. Climate-Related Risks in the United States

Climate cases against private emitters can include allegations of fraud. For example, in *People of State of New York v. ExxonMobil Corporation*, the New York State Attorney General alleged that Exxon Mobil Corporation (Exxon)—a major oil and gas company—fraudulently deceived investors about the company's management of risks posed by climate change regulation.[74] The attorney general argued that Exxon made materially false and misleading representations about the company's "proxy costs of carbon dioxide." The case was grounded in securities law and focused on Exxon's disclosures.

The complaint asserted that Exxon had engaged in a long-standing fraudulent scheme "sanctioned at the highest levels of the company" to create the illusion that it had factored the risks of climate change regulation into its business operations.[75] The complaint alleged that Exxon made material misrepresentations and failed to disclose material facts concerning the risks to its business if the average global temperature increases by 2°C. New York State sought a broad range of orders, including an injunction, $1.6 billion in restitution for shareholders, and a detailed review of the costs associated with Exxon's failure to apply a consistent proxy cost.

---

[73] Footnote 64, p. 2.

[74] *People of the State of New York v. Exxon Mobil Corporation*, No. 452044/2018, 65 Misc. 3d 1233(A), 2019 NY slip op. 51990(U) (Sup. Ct. N.Y. Cnty. Dec. 10, 2019).

[75] Footnote 74, p. 2; and J. Benny and G. McWilliams. 2018. New York Sues Exxon For Misleading Investors On Climate Change Risk. *Reuters*. 25 October.

The Supreme Court dismissed the case in December 2019.[76] It held that the state failed to prove that Exxon "made any material misstatements or omissions about its practices and procedures that misled any reasonable investor."[77] The court clarified that its decision related to securities law solely and was, therefore, not a climate change case. "Nothing in this opinion is intended to absolve ExxonMobil from responsibility for contributing to climate change through the emission of greenhouse gases in the production of its fossil fuel products."[78]

In a related case, *Ramirez v. ExxonMobil Corp.*, a man who invested in Exxon stock filed a federal securities class action against Exxon and three Exxon officers in a US federal district court.[79] This class action suit was filed on behalf of those who bought Exxon common stock between 19 February 2016 and 27 October 2019.

The complaint alleged (i) that Exxon's public statements during 2016 and 2019 were materially false and misleading because they did not disclose that internally generated reports recognized the risks caused by climate change, (ii) that Exxon would not be able to extract existing fossil fuel reserves it claimed to have because of climate change risks, and (iii) that "Exxon had used an inaccurate price of carbon to calculate the value of certain oil and gas prospects (footnote 79)." Exxon contested those claims, but the court denied the company's motion to dismiss. The case is still pending.

2. Fiduciary Duties in Poland

Shareholders sued the Polish utility, Enea SA, in a Polish regional court in *ClientEarth v. Enea*.[80] ClientEarth, a nongovernment environmental law organization and Enea shareholder, opposed the utility's resolution to build a coal-fired power plant. ClientEarth asserted that board members breached their fiduciary duties of due diligence and failed "to act in the best interests of the company and its shareholders" given climate-related financial risks.[81] The plaintiff argued that increasing carbon prices and competition from cheaper renewable energy sources and EU energy reforms on state subsidies for coal power would make the project unprofitable, causing economic harm to shareholders (footnote 80). The plaintiffs sued under Polish commercial law.

---

[76] See Sabin Center for Climate Change Law. People of the State of New York v. Exxon Mobil Corporation (accessed 30 April 2020); and J. Schwartz. 2019. New York Loses Climate Change Fraud Case Against Exxon Mobil. *The New York Times*. 10 December.

[77] Footnote 74, p. 54.

[78] Footnote 74, p. 3.

[79] *Ramirez v. ExxonMobil Corp.*, 334 F. Supp. 3d 832 (N.D. Tex. 2018).

[80] *ClientEarth v. Enea*, judgment of the District Court of Poznań, July 31, 2019. See Sabin Center for Climate Change Law. ClientEarth v. Enea (accessed 30 April 2020).

[81] A. Garton et al. 2018. *Ostrołęka C: Energa's and Enea's Board Members' Fiduciary Duties to the Companies and Shareholders*. ClientEarth Briefing. 20 September.

In July 2019, the court annulled Enea's resolution to build the power plant on the ground that it was invalid. The decision did not consider the project's potential financial risks. ClientEarth also succeeded with separate legal action demanding that Enea disclose information regarding the plant's proposed profitability in November 2019.[82] In February 2020, Enea and its joint venture partners announced they would suspend plans to construct the power plant over economic concerns.

3. Shareholder Suits after Wildfires in the United States

Catastrophic wildfires in the state of California in 2017 and 2018 caused record death and damage. Investors and shareholders sued utility companies in California for alleged misrepresentations in connection with the wildfires. In *York County v. Rambo*, investors in bonds issued by the utility Pacific Gas and Electric Company and its parent company filed a federal securities class action in a US federal district court.[83]

Investors alleged that Pacific Gas and Electric Company had failed to take proper fire mitigation measures, and that the company's failure to do so contradicted their representations in the offering documents for bonds that investors had bought. The plaintiffs alleged that the company had stated in its offering documents that it had addressed climate change risks, including wildlife risks, but did not disclose the risks caused by company's failure to properly maintain electrical lines, nor did it mention the hundreds of fires that were already being ignited annually by the company's equipment. The case is still pending.

Similarly, in *Barnes v. Edison International*, a federal securities class action was filed in a US federal district court on behalf of parties that had acquired stock in Southern California Edison and its parent holding company.[84] The complaint alleged that the companies made false and misleading statements about their maintenance of the electric grid and wildfire risks. The complaint included an excerpt from a public statement by the company referring to increased wildfire risks due to factors including climate change and the associated financial risks to the company. The case is pending.

As extreme weather events increase in frequency due to climate change, cases like the California wildfire lawsuits may become more common.

---

[82] ClientEarth. 2020. The End of Poland's Last New Coal Plant? News release. 18 February.
[83] *York County v. Rambo*, 3:19-cv-00994 (N.D. Cal. 2019).
[84] *Barnes v. Edison International*, 2:18-cv-09690 (C.D. Cal. 2018).

VII. Enforcement Matters

Consumers and consumer protection commissions have sought to hold companies accountable for misrepresenting the environmental value of their products.

A. Global Approaches

1. Greenwashing Financial and Other Products in Australia

The Australian Competition and Consumer Commission (ACCC) is a government agency that ensures compliance with Australian competition, fair trading, and consumer protection laws. The ACCC has challenged some companies for misrepresenting the environmental benefits of their products and services.

In *Australian Competition and Consumer Commission v GM Holden Ltd*, the Federal Court of Australia declared that GM Holden—an automobile company—had violated a competition, fair trading, and consumer protection law by wrongly advertising that a certain brand of vehicle—Saab vehicles—provided "carbon neutral motoring."[85] To offset carbon emissions, GM Holden had claimed that Saab would plant 17 native trees for every Saab vehicle purchased. It had not, however, shown any change in the way it manufactured Saab vehicles, and its carbon offset claim was misleading and contravened the law.

In accordance with consent orders, GM Holden undertook to advise its marketing staff to avoid "misleading and deceptive" marketing tactics and to plant 12,500 native trees to offset all the carbon emissions that would occur by Saab vehicles sold during the marketing campaign.

The ACCC similarly challenged corporations in the Federal Court of Australia for false green advertising in *Australian Competition and Consumer Commission v De Longhi Australia Pty Ltd*,[86] *Australian Competition and Consumer Commission v V8 Supercars Australia Pty Ltd*,[87] *Australian Competition and Consumer Commission v Goodyear Tyres*,[88] and *Australian Competition and Consumer Commission v Prime Carbon Pty Ltd* (footnote 49).

(See Part Three, Section IV.A.1. Carbon Credit Validity in Australia and the United States for a full case summary of *Australian Competition and Consumer Commission v Prime Carbon Pty Ltd*.)

---

[85] *Australian Competition & Consumer Commission v GM Holden Ltd* [2008] FCA 1428.

[86] Australian Competition and Consumer Commission (ACCC). 2008. De Longhi Alters "Environmentally Friendly" Claims. Media release. 30 April.

[87] ACCC. 2008. V8 Supercars Corrects Carbon Emissions Claims. Media release. 18 September.

[88] ACCC. 2008. Goodyear Tyres Apologises, Offers Compensation for Unsubstantiated Environmental Claims. Media release. 26 June.

In all these cases, the companies were required to adjust their marketing practices and/or undergo compliance training.

2. Class Action Suit Alleging Misrepresentation in the United States

Consumers may also challenge companies for claiming that their products are environmentally friendly in ways they are not. For example, in *Smith v. Keurig Green Mountain, Inc.*,[89] a California resident filed a class action suit in state court against a company that makes single-serve "coffee pods." The complaint alleged that the company falsely represented the ability to recycle the coffee pods. The class action suit pointed to the negative effects of plastic waste, including how degrading plastic released large amounts of methane, a powerful GHG. The complaint alleged a breach of an express warranty, as well as violations of California consumer protection law and unfair competition law. The case is still pending.

---

[89] *Smith v. Keurig Green Mountain, Inc.*, RG18922722 (Cal. Super. Ct. 2018).

Photo by Gerhard Jörén/ADB.

Women fetching water during a very dry season in Myanmar. Climate change will affect water security, with up to 3.4 billion people in Asia living in water-stressed areas by 2050. Adaptation measures are needed to improve water resource management (photo by Myo Thame/ADB).

PART FOUR

ADAPTATION

Adaptation litigation in Asia and the Pacific remains relatively novel and limited in scope. Litigants have focused on asserting that the government has failed to undertake any or sufficient adaptation measures. Adaptation litigation will likely to grow, considering the intensity of impacts facing the region.

Although cases considering adaptation to climate change impacts have existed for more than a decade, they have begun to move in novel directions in recent years. Climate adaptation cases can take several forms. First, some of these cases challenge governments and corporations for failing to take the necessary actions to adapt to climate change impacts. Many of these cases were only recently filed and remained pending. Second, some cases concern environmental review and requirements to consider how climate change may impact a proposed project or exacerbate how a project affects the environment. Third, developers and other petitioners have challenged governments for taking actions or making decisions to adapt to climate change impacts. For example, developers have sued local government entities for restricting or prohibiting development in the floodplain.

Some cases included in this section have already been introduced in Part One, which focuses on mitigation-related lawsuits. This section focuses on the importance of cases from an adaptation perspective by highlighting emerging litigation about climate change adaptation in EIAs and cases that challenge government adaptation action.

I.   Failure to Adapt

A.   Global Approaches

To prepare for the many impacts of climate change, corporations and governments at all jurisdictional levels from the local to the international will need to take various actions. Petitioners have sued different levels of government, seeking to determine and establish legal obligations to take climate action.

1.   A Violation of Human Rights in Australia and France

Some petitioners seek to clarify a body of human rights obligations for national governments to prepare for climate change. For example, in *Notre Affaire à Tous and Others v. France*, several NGOs sued the French government in the Administrative Court of Paris, alleging that the "government's failure to implement proper measures to effectively address climate change violated a statutory duty to act."[1] The plaintiffs asked the court to order the government to take the necessary measures to adapt the national territory to the effects of climate change and to protect citizens' lives and health from the risks of climate change. The case remains pending.

(See Part One, Section III.A. Global Approaches: Violating the Law in Europe for a full case summary of *Notre Affaire à Tous and Others v. France*; and Part Four, Section IV.A.2. Reducing Emissions in Canada and France for further discussion of this case.)

Eight Torres Strait Islanders lodged a petition to the United Nations Human Rights Committee in 2019, alleging that Australia is violating their human rights due to climate inaction.[2] Situated off the northern tip of Queensland, Australia, the Torres Strait Islands are low-lying and vulnerable to sea level rise and ocean acidification. Culturally distinct from mainland indigenous Australians, Torres Strait Islanders have a unique and ancient island culture.[3] The complaint is the first time that peoples of low-lying islands have filed legal action with a UN body against a national government for inaction on climate change. It is also the first human rights-based climate litigation in Australia (footnote 2).

The petitioners argue that Australia's inadequate mitigation planning and failure to fund coastal defense measures on their islands constitute human rights violations under the International Covenant on Civil and Political Rights.[4] Specifically, the inaction impacts their right to culture; their right to be free from arbitrary interference with privacy, family, and home; and their right to life. Although this case remains pending, the litigation has produced a win for the community—the Australian government has promised A$25 million (about $17 million) in funding for coastal defense.[5]

(See Part Five, Section IV.A. Global Approaches: Climate Change in Australia and Black Carbon in Canada for further discussion of this case.)

2. Government Liability in the United States

In many cases focused on adaptation, climate change features in the background rather than in the main text. Petitioners do not necessarily identify climate change as an issue for deliberation. Instead, issues focus on the mechanisms

---

1   Letter of Formal Notice to Officials, *Notre Affaire à Tous and Others v. France* (filed Dec. 17, 2018).
2   ClientEarth. Torres Strait FAQ; and Sabin Center for Climate Change Law. Petition of Torres Strait Islanders to the United Nations Human Rights Committee Alleging Violations Stemming from Australia's Inaction on Climate Change (accessed 30 April 2020).
3   ClientEarth. Torres Strait FAQ.
4   ClientEarth. 2019. Human Rights and Climate Change: World-First Case to Protect Indigenous Australians. News release. 12 May. See also *International Covenant on Civil and Political Rights*, New York, 16 December 1966, *United Nations Treaty Series*, Vol. 999, No. 14668, p. 171.
5   ClientEarth. 2020. Torres Strait Islanders Win Key Ask After Climate Complaint. News release. 19 February.

or adaptations needed to respond to the uncertainties brought about by climate change, like shifting shorelines or more intense storms.[6] Negligence and condemnation cases brought against the government following a disaster can sometimes fit this model.

In the US, the concept of sovereign immunity determines the extent to which local, state, and national governments will have liability for a failure to adapt to climate change,[7] particularly in cases concerning failure to take specific actions. The destruction following Hurricane Katrina gave rise to two cases brought in 2005 that illustrate this point. These cases concerned the role of the Mississippi River Gulf Outlet (MRGO) shipping channel in worsening flooding in the city of New Orleans.

Since the US Army Corps of Engineers finished excavating MRGO in 1968, it has widened from 500 feet to nearly 2,000 feet due to natural wave action, storms, and the wakes of large ships. By 2005 the shipping channel's banks sat close to levees built to protect neighborhoods from flooding.

In two cases, plaintiffs sought damages for the effects of the Katrina storm surge spread via MRGO into New Orleans. *In re Katrina Canal Breaches Litigation*, plaintiffs alleged that the negligent action of the Army Corps of Engineers had exacerbated flood damage after Hurricane Katrina.[8] A US federal appellate court rejected the negligence claim.

In *St. Bernard Parish Government v. United States*, a US federal appellate court found that the federal government was not liable for flood-related damage caused by Hurricane Katrina and other hurricanes in St. Bernard Parish and New Orleans.[9] The court concluded that the government could not be liable "on a takings theory for inaction" and that the government's construction and operation of MRGO "was not shown to have been the cause of the flooding."[10] The court reasoned that the plaintiffs and the US Court of Federal Claims applied the wrong legal standard when analyzing causation. They failed to "account for government flood control projects that reduced the risk of flooding" (footnote 10).

Consequently, the plaintiffs failed to "present evidence comparing the flood damage that actually occurred to the flood damage that would have occurred if there had been no government action at all."[11] They also neglected to take into account the government-sponsored Lake Pontchartrain and Vicinity Hurricane

---

[6]   UN Environment Programme. 2017. *The Status of Climate Change Litigation: A Global Review.* Nairobi. p. 22.

[7]   J. Klein. 2015. *Potential Liability of Governments for Failure to Prepare for Climate Change.* Sabin Center for Climate Change Law, Columbia Law School. New York. August.

[8]   *In re Katrina Canal Breaches Litigation*, 696 F.3d 436, 441 (5th Cir. 2012) (en banc).

[9]   *St. Bernard Par. Gov't v. United States*, 887 F.3d 1354 (Fed. Cir. 2018), *cert. denied sub nom. St. Bernard Par. v. United States*, 139 S. Ct. 796, 202 L. Ed. 2d 571 (2019).

[10] Footnote 9, p. 3.

[11] Footnote 9, p. 14.

Protection Project—a system of levees and floodwalls—that mitigated the MRGO impact.

(See Part Five, Section II.A.2. Hurricanes on the Mainland United States for further discussion of this case.)

3. Action Against Local Government in the United States

"Failure to act" cases have also been brought in local courts against local governments. Various efforts to prepare for climate change will be the responsibility of local governments. Adaptation requirements may shift the scope of local governments' legal obligations. For example, Staten Island homeowners sued New York City for negligence in *Wohl v. City of New York* over its alleged failure to inspect and maintain sewers after they overflowed and damaged residents' cars and homes.[12]

The New York Supreme Court in Staten Island held that the city was not negligent. After referring to climatological reports from the National Climatic Data Center, the court observed that New York City had experienced "inordinate rainfall" during two storms in August 2011.[13] On the evidence, the court was satisfied that the "Staten Island sewer system had not been designed to accommodate the volume of rain that fell during the storms" (footnote 13). Hence, it concluded that "the sole proximate cause of the flooding was the volume of precipitation, not the City's inspection and maintenance failures" (footnote 13).

4. Corporate Failures in Disasters in the United States

Pre- and post-disaster cases can also seek to establish corporate liability or allege a legal violation based on a company's failure to prepare its facilities for climate change impacts and risks. Under this theory, a pair of suits in the US were filed by an environmental group against the fossil fuel companies ExxonMobil (*Conservation Law Foundation v. ExxonMobil Corp*) and Shell (*Conservation Law Foundation, Inc. v. Shell Oil Products*).[14] Both suits concern pre-disaster preparations.

The allegations in these cases concerned the companies' failures to prepare their coastal petroleum product storage terminals for the effects of climate change, including "sea level rise, increased precipitation, increased magnitude

---

[12] *Wohl v. City of New York* 2014 NY Slip Op 51618(U), Decided on October 22, 2014, Supreme Court, Richmond County.

[13] Sabin Center for Climate Change Law. Wohl v. City of New York (accessed 1 May 2020).

[14] *Amended Complaint, Conservation Law Found., Inc. v. Shell Oil Products US*, No. 1:17-cv-00396 (D.R.I. Oct. 25, 2017) (alleging 20 violations of the Clean Water Act (CWA) and one violation of Resource Conservation & Recovery Act (RCRA)). On 4 October 2018, the Conservation Law Foundation filed a motion for leave to file a second amended complaint, which alleges an additional RCRA violation; Amended Complaint, *Conservation Law Found. v. ExxonMobil Corp.*, No. 1:16-cv11950 (D. Ma. Oct. 20, 2017) (alleging 14 violations of the CWA and 1 violation of RCRA).

and frequency of storm events, and increased magnitude and frequency of storm surges."[15] The plaintiffs argued that even though ExxonMobil had "long been aware of climate change and the related risks," it failed to address them, which violated multiple environmental statutes.[16]

The Massachusetts Federal Court stayed *Conservation Law Foundation v. ExxonMobil Corp* in March 2020, deferring to the primary jurisdiction of the US Environmental Protection Agency (EPA).[17] The agency is currently renewing Exxon's permit for the storage terminal. The court reasoned that the agency is better equipped to consider scientific and policy issues, and the terms of the renewed permit may render this case moot. The parties may report to the court on the permit status for consideration of whether to lift the stay.

In *Conservation Law Foundation, Inc. v. Shell Oil Products*, the environmental group was able to demonstrate standing by establishing that harms were imminent rather than far out in the future. This suit remains pending.

(See Part One, Section I. Standing for a full discussion of judicial approaches to standing issues.)

Other post-disaster suits have raised claims against corporate actors under state-level air and water codes and tort law. In 2017, Hurricane Harvey flooded the Arkema Crosby chemical plant in Harris County, Texas, leaking chemicals into surrounding waters and causing explosions which exposed nearby residents and first responders to toxic fumes. In *Harris County, Texas et al. v. Arkema Inc.*, Harris County and the State of Texas sued the chemical plant for violations of the Texas Air and Water Codes even though the plant experienced an unprecedented level of flooding.[18]

As climate change makes unprecedented levels of flooding increasingly foreseeable, these suits could multiply. This suit is still pending, as are several additional suits against the chemical plant in relation to this incident.

(See Part Five, Section II.A.2. Hurricanes on the Mainland United States for a full case summary of *Harris County, Texas et al. v. Arkema Inc.*)

B. Asia and the Pacific Approaches

Suits assailing government failure to implement national laws or policies on climate change adaptation are not common in Asia. The authors found no examples of such litigation in the Pacific. More commonly, parties sue

---

15 *Complaint, Conservation Law Foundation, Inc. v. Shell Oil Products US*, No. 1:16-cv-11950 (D. Ma. Sept. 29, 2016). pp. 17 and 58

16 Footnote 15, p. 31, para 97.

17 *Conservation Law Foundation v. ExxonMobil Corp.*, No. 1:16-cv-11950 (D. Mass. Mar. 31. 2020); Sabin Center for Climate Change Law. Conservation Law Foundation v. ExxonMobil Corp. (accessed 4 May 2020).

18 *Petition from Harris County, Texas v. Arkema Inc.*, No. 2017-76961-7 (Tex. Dist. Ct. Nov. 16, 2017).

governments over specific obligations to safeguard an aspect of ecosystem integrity like coastal or mangrove forest resilience. Litigants ground such suits on their constitutional right to life, environment, water, or equality before the law. Concern for ecosystem integrity frequently drives this litigation, with little explicit mention of climate change adaptation. Nevertheless, the cause benefits, with court orders furthering adaptation action.

1. National Government's Failure to Act Violates Constitutional Rights

Environmental litigation based on constitutional rights is prevalent in South Asia. Such claims frequently assert that the government's failure to act assails their right to life. Courts have started applying the constitutional right to life in cases relating to adaptive action.

a) Climate and Water Justice in Pakistan

Leghari v. Federation of Pakistan marks a watershed moment, incorporating "climate justice" into Asian climate change adaptation jurisprudence.[19] Leghari claimed that the government's failure to implement adaptation policy and plans undermined his constitutional right to life. He argued that climate change existentially threatened Pakistan. Further, climate change affected water, food, and energy security, directly impacting him as a farmer. Leghari asserted that dealing with climate change was not optional; it was an emergency. Therefore, any further inaction or delay in implementing the National Climate Change Policy 2012 would result in disastrous consequences for him and the country.

Leghari included the provincial government in his suit, arguing it was equally responsible for responding to climate change's adverse impacts. Hence, it should also prepare a water conservation strategy.

> " Climate Justice covers agriculture, health, food, building approvals, industrial licenses, technology, infrastructural work, human resource, human and climate trafficking, disaster preparedness, health, etc.
>
> Source: *Leghari v. Federation of Pakistan*, PLD 2018 Lahore 364, para. 22.

The court treated climate change as a defining challenge of our time, demanding immediate and effective action. Faced with such urgent challenges, the court believed that environmental jurisprudence must shift to "climate justice."[20]

While mitigation might be addressed with environmental justice, the court reasoned that "adaptation can only be addressed through climate justice."[21] Climate justice, said the court, required a multifaceted approach. New stakeholders must be involved in the environmental dialogue.

---

[19] *Leghari v. Federation of Pakistan*, PLD 2018 Lahore 364.
[20] Footnote 19, para. 20.
[21] Footnote 19, para. 22.

Adaptation approaches should embrace new dimensions like health security, food security, water security, human displacement, human trafficking, and disaster management (footnote 21). Working toward climate justice meant understanding the climate impacts of and on agriculture, health, food, building approvals, industrial licenses, technology, infrastructural work, human resources, human and climate trafficking, and disaster preparedness (footnote 21).

Water justice, a sub-concept of climate justice, was also defined. Water justice, said the court, referred to the ability of individuals and communities to access clean water for physical, cultural, and spiritual survival, and for recreation. It considered that the impacts of climate change made water resource management—an essential adaptive activity—a crisis of governance and justice. Therefore, when adjudicating water cases, the court urged judges to consider the necessary and inseparable connection of water with the environment, land, and other ecosystems. The court stressed that climate and water justice were interconnected and rooted in the fundamental rights to life, environment, and human dignity.

The court also discussed tools available to judges in responding to climate change. For example, reading foundational constitutional rights—the rights to life, human dignity, property, information—with constitutional values—political, economic, and social justice—provided a judicial tool kit to address the government's response to climate change.

> Right to life and [r]ight to human dignity under Articles 9 and 14 of the Constitution protect and realise human rights in general, and the human right to water and sanitation in particular. In adjudicating water and water-related cases, we have to be mindful of the essential and inseparable connection of water with the environment, land and other ecosystems. Climate Justice and Water Justice go hand in hand and are rooted in Articles 9 and 14 of our Constitution and stand firmly on our [preambular] constitutional values of social and economic justice.[22]

As the government had not undertaken substantial work to implement the climate change policy, the court constituted the Climate Change Commission, which was required to report progress to the court.

(See Part One, Section II.B.2.a. Climate Justice in the Philippines and Pakistan for a full case summary of *Leghari v. Federation of Pakistan*; and Part Two, Section VII.B.3. Water Justice is Climate Justice in Pakistan for further discussion of this case.)

b) Adaptation Plans in South Asia

Litigants in India have likewise pushed governments to implement climate change action plans. In *Gaurav Kumar Bansal v. Union of India & Ors*, Bansal argued that the national and state governments had failed to implement India's

---

[22] Footnote 19, para. 23.

National Action Plan on Climate Change, 2008–2017, which included adaptation action.[23] He asked the National Green Tribunal (NGT) for orders to (i) direct the national government to place on record all relevant material evidencing its implementation of the plan, and (ii) restrain the state governments from acting in violation of the plan. The Ministry of Environment and Forests argued that the plan was in effect and that it had directed the state governments to implement and act consistently with the plan.

Evidence during the trial showed that while some states had submitted their action plans on climate change to the Ministry of Environment and Forests, others had not. The NGT ordered the state governments to comply with the ministry's directions by preparing their draft state action plans on climate change and submitting them to the ministry for approval.

(See Part One, Section III.B.1. Climate Change Commitments in South Asia for further discussion of this case.)

2. Specific Obligations of Governments' Failure to Act

Various Asian cases recognize that protecting glaciers, rivers, flood zones, lakes, forests, coastal areas, and agricultural land is imperative for enhancing adaptive capacity to climate change and protecting fundamental rights.

a) Protecting Mangroves in India

Healthy mangrove forests support coastal aquatic ecosystems and promote water security. Water security is not limited to ensuring that there is enough water for people and economic activities. "It is also about having healthy aquatic ecosystems and protecting us against water-related disasters."[24] Box 4.1 explains the crucial role mangroves play in strengthening climate resilience and carbon capture in coastal areas.

In 2017, Asia and the Pacific produced up to 80% of the world's farmed shrimp.[25] In the Bay of Bengal, litigants have challenged shrimp farming due to concerns about its impacts on mangroves and coastal ecology.

In *S. Jagannathan v. Union of India*, the petitioner challenged the government's decision to allow shrimp farming in ecologically sensitive coastal areas.[26] The petitioner argued that an EIA should be required for shrimp farms. The court agreed. After discussing the "depressing" socioeconomic losses and environmental

---

[23] *Gaurav Kumar Bansal v. Union of India & Ors.*, Original Application No. 498 of 2014 (National Green Tribunal, 23 July 2015). The National Action Plan on Climate Change also covered mitigation.

[24] ADB. 2016. *Asian Water Development Outlook 2016: Strengthening Water Security in Asia and the Pacific*. Manila, p. xiv.

[25] FAO. 2018. *Farmed Shrimp Output Increased by about 6 Percent in 2017*. 29 May.

[26] *S. Jagannathan v. Union of India*, (1997) 2 SCC 87.

degradation associated with the industry, the court ordered the government to require strict environmental testing and EIAs for shrimp farming.[27] It also ordered the government to (i) constitute an authority under the Environment Protection Act, 1986 for the protection of coastal areas; and (ii) deal especially with the shrimp culture industry in the coastal states.

Box 4.1: Protecting Mangroves and Coastal Areas

Of the world's mangrove ecosystems, 46% are in South Asia, Southeast Asia, and the Pacific.[a] Southeast Asia is home to "51 of the world's known 73 species" and 35.6% of the world's mangrove population.[b] Mangroves forests support biodiversity, provide important ecosystem services, and protect coastlines against storm surges. A recent study showed that a 2-meter-wide strip of mangroves along the shore could reduce wave height by 90%.[c] This protective capacity makes mangroves important for boosting resilience in coastal regions and protecting them from water-related disasters.[d]

Mangrove forests, tidal marshes, and seagrass meadows are also carbon capture warriors. They are the most carbon-rich forests in the tropics, trapping carbon dioxide and other greenhouse gases in flooded soils for hundreds to thousands of years.[e] Protecting mangroves boosts not only coastal resilience but also carbon capture, and stops the release of carbon emissions when mangroves are destroyed.

Mangrove forests' enormous potential to fight climate change seems poorly understood or undervalued. The International Union for Conservation of Nature (IUCN) estimates that a growing list of countries have cleared 50%–80% of their mangroves in the last 20 years.[f] Before that, more than 35% of the world's mangrove habitats were cleared between 1980 and 2000.[g] Mangrove loss hot spots include Myanmar and the Philippines, followed by Cambodia, Indonesia, and Malaysia (footnote a).

Aquaculture has been the leading cause of mangrove clearing for the last 20 years.[h] Land conversion for rice agriculture and palm oil plantations, pollution, timber harvesting, and—to a lesser extent—natural disasters have also driven mangrove clearing (footnote b).

---

[a] S. Gandhi and T. Gareth Jones. 2019. Identifying Mangrove Deforestation Hotspots in South Asia, Southeast Asia and Asia-Pacific. *Remote Sensing*. 11 (6). p. 728.

[b] Footnote a, p. 3.

[c] S. Chapman. 2018. Mangroves Protect Coastlines, Store Carbon—and Are Expanding with Climate Change. *The Conversation*. 9 February; C. Doughty et al. 2017. Impacts of Mangrove Encroachment and Mosquito Impoundment Management on Coastal Protection Services. *Hydrobiologia*. 803 (1). pp. 105–120.

[d] Other studies showed that mangrove forests helped reduce shoreline damage during Tropical Storm Wilma. See E. Granek and B. Ruttenberg. 2007. Protective capacity of mangroves during tropical storms: a case study from 'Wilma' and 'Gamma' in Belize. *Mar Ecol Prog Ser*. 343. pp. 101–105.

[e] D. Donato et al. 2011. Mangroves among the Most Carbon-Rich Forests in the Tropics. *Nature Geoscience*. 4. pp. 293–297; D. Herr. 2017. Mangroves and Marshes Key in the Climate Change Battle. International Union for Conservation of Nature (IUCN).

[f] IUCN. Pacific Mangroves Initiative.

[g] S. Chapman. 2018. Mangroves Protect Coastlines, Store Carbon—and Are Expanding with Climate Change. *The Conversation*. 9 February.

[h] D. Rochmyaningsih. 2017. Aquaculture Is Main Driver of Mangrove Losses. *SciDev.Net*. 22 June.

Source: Authors.

---

27 Footnote 26, p. 136, para. 33 and pp. 147–150, para. 52.

b) Protecting Mangroves in Bangladesh

The Bangladesh Environmental Lawyers Association (BELA) also challenged the government's alleged failure to regulate shrimp farming in Bangladesh in *BELA Vs. Bangladesh*.[28] BELA argued that 8,506.67 hectares of mangrove forest in the Sunderbans had been cleared since the government allowed commercial shrimp farming. Consequently, shrimp cultivation occupied 217,000 hectares in the fiscal year 2006–2007. BELA argued that modern saline water shrimp cultivation caused shrinkages to agricultural lands, increased soil salinity, contaminated drinking water, and decreased biodiversity. BELA asserted that the shrimp farming had polluted land and water bodies and caused salinity intrusion to more than 60% of the cultivable land in three districts by the Bay of Bengal.

The court agreed with the Indian Supreme Court's approach in *S. Jagannathan v. Union of India*. It ordered that there must be an EIA for all shrimp farming, which must consider the principle of intergenerational equity. It also banned the conversion of agricultural lands, salt pan lands, mangroves, wetlands, forestlands, and village common land into shrimp farms.

While climate change did not feature as an issue in these decisions, requiring strict environmental monitoring of shrimp farming is important for protecting mangroves—a useful biological ally in the fight against climate change.

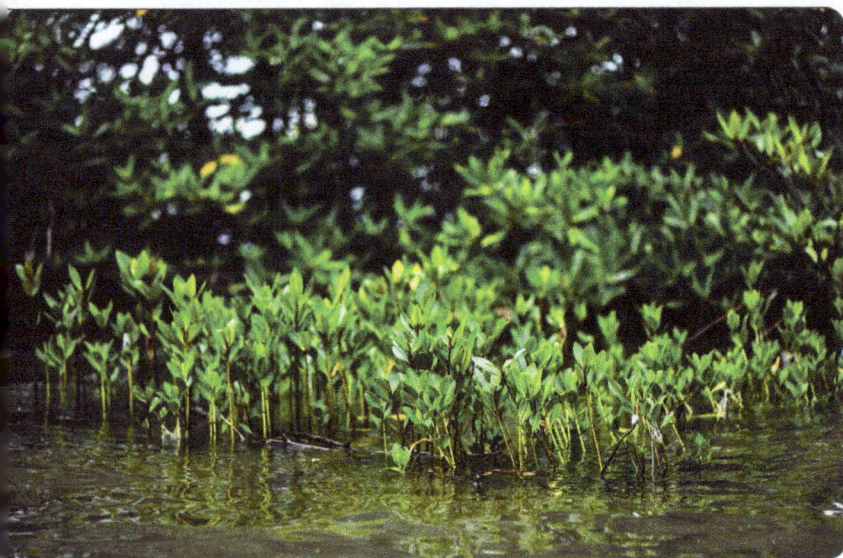

Young mangrove trees along the shores of East Tanjung Pinang, Indonesia. Mangrove forests are biodiverse and protect coastal communities from storm surges, flooding, and erosion. They have significant potential to sequester carbon, making them vital for climate adaptation and mitigation responses (photo by Eric Sales/ADB).

(See Part Five, Section V.B. Impacts of Resource Scarcity and Disaster on Women in South Asia for further discussion of *BELA Vs. Bangladesh*.)

Coastal resilience to disaster was central to the decision in *BELA Vs. Bangladesh*.[29] Petitioners sought to stop deforestation and environmental destruction within the coastal greenbelt of Sonaichhari. The government had leased land to four respondents, who cut down coastal trees to set up their shipbreaking operation.

The court directed the government to protect and afforest coastal lands immediately. It noted that this era of extreme climatic events had resulted in cyclones, floods, and erosion, leaving Bangladesh highly vulnerable to climate-related disasters. The court considered coastal afforestation crucial for protecting coastal people's lives, safety, and property. It also suggested the government-appointed mobile courts to monitor and protect the coastal belt from environmentally destructive activities.

---

[28] *BELA Vs. Bangladesh*, WP No. 57 of 2010, D-/01-02-2012.
[29] *BELA Vs. Bangladesh*, WP No. 1207 of 2009.

Finding that the leases were against the public interest and without lawful authority, the court declared that they had no legal effect. The court observed that the state was the trustee of all natural resources. The government must not arbitrarily allow these resources to be converted into private ownership at the peril of the general public.

c) Protecting Adaptive Capacity of Inland Water Bodies

Courts across Asia have moved to protect the capacity of lakes, rivers, and glaciers to supply fresh water. They have also protected flood plains and natural drainage systems.

Rivers in South Asia. In *Environmental and Ecological Protection Samithy v. The Executive Engineer,* the Kerala High Court recognized the importance of bamboo to protecting rivers.[30] Petitioners challenged the state government's decision to grant permits for the cutting and removal of bamboo along the banks of the Siruvani River in a national park in the Indian state of Kerala.

The court noted that deforestation affected climatic systems and depleted water resources, the life blood of the ecosystem.[31] It considered the quality and quantity of freshwater sources critical to ecosystems, with diminished water resources increasing the environmental costs of production (footnote 31). The court discussed the vulnerability of water supply systems to climatic change, noting that the Intergovernmental Panel on Climate Change (IPCC) estimated that there would be a 40% shortfall in drinking water within the next 50 years.

The court further recognized forests' role as a carbon sink, acting as a "global thermostat."[32] The court held that the bamboo and vegetation were essential for sustaining the life of a perennial river. It directed the respondents to stop cutting and removing the bamboo clusters and other vegetation.

Reservations in Sri Lanka. Litigants in Sri Lanka disputed the government's decision to allow construction on "special area" land within the Mahaweli Development Programme in *Environmental Foundation Ltd. and Others v Mahawali of Sri Lanka and Others.*[33] Founded in the 1960s, the program artificially created a reservation area in the mountains of Kandy for the water management of hydroelectric power generation, irrigation development, flood control, and community settlements.[34] Within the reservation area are three reservoirs as well as the Victoria Randenigala Rantambe Sanctuary, Sri Lanka's largest nature park.

---

[30] *Environmental and Ecological Protection Samithy v. The Executive Engineer,* (1991) 2 KLJ 571.

[31] Footnote 30, para. 5.

[32] Footnote 30, para. 6.

[33] *Environmental Foundation Ltd. and Others v Mahawali of Sri Lanka and Others* 2010 1 Sri LR 1.

[34] The Mahaweli Authority manages the land under the Mahaweli Authority Act No. 23 of 1979. The government established the reservation under the Fauna and Flora Protection Ordinance (Cap. 469), as amended by Act No. 44 of 1964 and Act No. 1 of 1970.

The Environment Foundation Limited argued that the approved construction site was less than 100 meters from the Victoria Reservoir and within the Victoria Randenigala Rantambe Sanctuary. Therefore, it fell under the National Environmental Act, No. 47 of 1980, which prescribed stringent requirements for construction approval, including the prerequisite to prepare an EIA or initial environmental examination.

The court noted that the directive principles within the Sri Lankan constitution were not enforceable and did not confer legal rights or obligations. Nevertheless, it considered that the principles (i) equated to the public trust doctrine, and (ii) guided state functionaries in the excise of their powers.[35] The first to fourth respondents were, therefore, obliged to ensure that land use within the reservation realized the goals of the Mahaweli Development Programme. The respondents' decisions to alienate the lands from the reservation and permit construction on them were unauthorized and violated the petitioners' right to equality and equal protection before the law under the constitution.

The significance of this case lies in its treatment of the directive principles under the constitution. By equating them to the public trust doctrine, the court incorporated that principle into Sri Lankan law and found that the government must act in accordance with the principle of public trust.

Flooding in South Asia. In the following cases, litigants and courts have stressed the need to protect the natural capacity of floodplains and natural drainage systems to absorb water and divert flooding. While these cases may not make climate adaptation a central theme of the decision, they deal with issues that are critical to protecting Asia's adaptive capacity to flooding. By 2025, up to 341 million people will be at risk of flooding in inland areas across Asia.[36] Bangkok, Dhaka, and Ho Chi Minh face a high risk of flooding (footnote 36). As such, decisions protecting natural drainage systems could be significant contributions to climate change adaptation action.

In *K.S. Ali v. State of Kerala*, the court stressed the importance of protecting Kerala's lakes.[37] The High Court of Kerala directed the government to investigate and take action regarding illegal intrusions on Lake Vembanad. The court considered biodiversity conservation fundamental for responding to climate change and protecting key ecosystem services. It noted that lotic ecosystems—flowing water ecosystems such as rivers and streams—provided water and flood control.[38] It also observed that the world's sinks—mangroves, woodlands, and wetlands—absorbed pollution, decimated heat and wave energy, and maintained sufficient oxygenation.

---

[35] The court cited *Sugathapala Mendis v Chandrika Kumaratunga and Others* and *Wattegedara Wijebanda v Conservator General of Forests and Others* as authority for this interpretation.

[36] ADB. 2015. *Climate Change Resilience in Asia's Cities.* Infographic. Manila. 6 May.

[37] *K.S. Ali v. State of Kerala*, 2017 (3) KHC 395; 2017 (3) KLJ 278.

[38] L.G. Leff. 2019. Freshwater Habitats. In T.M. Schmidt, ed. *Encyclopedia of Microbiology (Fourth Edition)*. Cambridge, Massachusetts: Academic Press. pp. 300–314.

The court concluded that as public authorities had constitutional and statutory duties, they must play a key role in biodiversity conservation. Against this backdrop, the court held that it was time to deal firmly with transgressions and the government's failure to implement laws.

Courts in Bangladesh have issued some decisions to protect Dhaka's flood zones, which shield the city from flooding. In *Metro Makers and Developers Limited Vs. BELA*, BELA challenged a residential development.[39] BELA alleged that Metro Makers and Developers Limited (Metro Makers) was building on land designated as a sub-flood flow zone under Dhaka's master plan. The plan identified sub-flood flow zones as "areas either temporally or seasonally flooded (flood lands)."[40] BELA contended that the land was critical for protecting Dhaka's environment. Metro Makers argued that it undertook the residential development legally and that it had sold lots to bona fide third parties, whose purchases should be protected.

The Supreme Court of Bangladesh halted the development. The master plan, observed the court, sought to protect sub-flood flow zones to ensure their continued functioning, reducing negative impacts on waterways. Allowing parties to fill up Dhaka's natural drainage systems would impair their capacity to handle rain and flooding.

The court held that the constitutional right to life—incorporating the right to protection and improvement of environment and ecology—trumped all other claims and legal rights, including the rights of the third party purchasers. Even without a law protecting flood zones, citizens were entitled to preserve and protect health, environment, and ecology within the metropolitan area. Hence, citizens were entitled to protect their city's flood zones.

This decision followed a 2011 Supreme Court decision in *BELA Vs. Bangladesh*.[41] In that case, the court also found that illegal housing projects that filled in Dhaka's natural drainage systems had caused serious damage to the city's environment and affected residents' right to life.

In *President, Bangladesh Garment Manufacturers and Exporters Association Vs. Bangladesh*, the Supreme Court of Bangladesh upheld a decision directing the BGMEA to demolish its illegally constructed building.[42] Bangladesh Garment

> "The Public Trust Doctrine, taken together with the Constitutional Directives of Article 27, reveal that all state actors are so principally obliged to act in furtherance of the trust of the People that they must follow this duty even when a furtherance of this trust necessarily renders inadequate an act or omission that would otherwise legally suffice.
>
> Source: *Sugathapala Mendis v Chandrika Kumaratunga and Others* 2008 Sri LR 339, p. 14.

---

[39] *Metro Makers and Developers Limited Vs. BELA*, 2012 65 DLR (AD) 181.
[40] Footnote 39, per Syed Mahmud Hossain, J.
[41] *BELA Vs. Bangladesh*, Writ Petition No. 6072 of 2010, 8 June 2011.
[42] *President, Bangladesh Garment Manufacturers and Exporters Association (BGMEA) Vs. Bangladesh*, 9 SCOB [2017] AD.

Manufacturers and Exporters Association built a 15-story commercial complex covering part of Begunbari Khal and Hatirjheel Lake, two natural water bodies in Dhaka City. The court observed that the water bodies played a pivotal role in keeping Dhaka safe from waterlogging and flooding during the heavy rains of the monsoon season. Hence, the government had classified them as water bodies under the Master Plan of Dhaka City. The court found that the organization had never acquired legal title to Begunbari Khal and Hatirjheel Lake as they were protected water bodies, making the commercial construction unlawful.

In *Sugathapala Mendis v Chandrika Kumaratunga and Others*, the Supreme Court of Sri Lanka intervened in the government's decision to allow a golf course development within ecologically sensitive wetlands.[43] The court noted the wetland's significance as a breeding place and home to nine threatened species, as well as its capacity for flood retention. The court linked the directive principles under the Sri Lankan constitution with the public trust doctrine. It considered that both created a duty to act in furtherance of the citizens' trust.

(See Part One, Section I.B.2.c. Violations of Public Trust in Sri Lanka for a full case summary of *Sugathapala Mendis v Chandrika Kumaratunga and Others*.)

Glacier Resilience in South Asia. Glaciers play an important part in ensuring water security in South Asia. Box 4.2 briefly discusses the climate change impacts of melting glaciers, including energy insecurity and increased vulnerability to intense flooding and seawater rise.

Box 4.2: Protecting Glaciers

Melting glaciers make Asia more vulnerable to intense flooding. Accelerated glacier meltwater will combine with heavier rains and superstorms, causing intense flooding.[a] Glaciers have also accounted for 25%–30% of recorded sea level rise since 1961, impacting countries across Asia and the Pacific. After glacier melt peaks and glaciers shrink, they will supply less meltwater to Asia's rivers. Water levels in rivers will lessen and be less reliable sources of water in dry seasons, stressing food production.[b] By 2090, Asia could see noticeably decreased glacier runoff feeding its rivers, meaning lower water levels and reduced water security, particularly during drought. Decreased water supply also threatens hydropower generation.

---

[a] J.G. Cogley. 2017. The Future of Asia's Glaciers. *Nature: International Journal of Science.* 549 (7671). pp. 166–167; Agence France-Presse. 2017. Asia's Glaciers to Shrink by a Third by 2100, Threatening Water Supply of Millions. *The Guardian.* 14 September.

[b] W. Buytaert. Glacier melt and water security. *Grantham Institute—Climate Change and the Environment.*

Source: Authors.

---

[43] *Sugathapala Mendis v Chandrika Kumaratunga and Others* 2008 Sri LR 339.

The High Court of Uttarakhand demonstrated a keen awareness of the importance of glaciers to India's water security in *Tara Singh Rajput v. State of Uttarakhand*.[44] Petitioners sued the state to prevent indiscriminate tree cutting and unauthorized constructions near the Bhimtal Lake area in Uttarakhand state. They argued that these activities threatened the lake's fragile ecology and environment. Glacier protection featured heavily in this decision.

> 10. The Court also takes judicial notice of the fact that there is a large scale degradation of environment/ ecology in the Himalayas. The glaciers are rapidly depleting/receding. The colour of glaciers has also turned to black. Glaciers are the source of mighty rivers including Ganges and Yamuna. The rapid depletion of glaciers may lead to drying up of rivers causing immense miseries to the people in Uttarakhand and other States. It is the duty of all of us to protect the glaciers and to restore them to their pristine glory. The human activities around glaciers, the haphazard constructions and de- forestation has played havoc with the environment and ecology of the area.
>
> 11. Out of three percent fresh water available on earth, 67 percent of water is stored in glaciers and ice-caps. Himalayan Glaciers alone contribute/supply 30-40 percent of water. Millions of lives are dependent on these rivers . . . Gangotri Glacier itself is more than 30 kilometers long and covers an area of about 148 square meters.
>
> 12. Gangotri Glacier is the source of river Ganga and Yamnotri Glacier is the source of river Yamuna. Yamnotri Glacier is situated at a height of 6387 meters from the sea level. Furthermore, there is less amount of snow due to climatic change. Melting of glaciers has outpaced the snowfall. There is also a rise in the average temperature of the earth.
>
> Source: *Tara Singh Rajput v. State of Uttarakhand*, 2017 (7) FLT 216; 2016 SCC OnLine Utt 1730, paras. 10–12.

The court was extremely concerned that Himalayan glaciers were retreating and blackening. Global warming, it said, was causing glacier melt to outpace snowfall. The court noted that only around 3% of the world's water was fresh, making Himalayan glaciers critical for water supply. The court commented that Himalayan glaciers supplied around "30%–40%" of the world's water supply and fed Asia's mighty rivers, including the Ganges and Yamuna Rivers.[45]

---

[44] *Tara Singh Rajput v. State of Uttarakhand*, 2017 (7) FLT 216; 2016 SCC OnLine Utt 1730.
[45] Footnote 44, para. 11.

Concerned by the gravity of large-scale environmental degradation in the Himalayas, the court ordered a statewide response intended to protect and preserve the environment and ecology of Uttarakhand. The court ordered authorities to remove illegal constructions from the fragile glacier areas. It banned (i) new constructions and buildings within a 25-km radius of all glaciers, and (ii) the burning of fossil fuels within 10 km from the edges of Uttarakhand's glaciers.[46] The court banned tree cutting and new constructions near the Bhimtal, Nainital, Khurpatal, Sattal, and Naukuchiatal lakes. It ordered the government to require assessments of bearing capacity for any new constructions within a 2 km radius of the lakes.

(See Part One, Section II.B.3.c. Glacier Protection in South Asia for further discussion of this case.)

3. Protecting Biodiversity in South Asia

Limited or no statutory protection ought not to render courts powerless to protect ecological balance. *In re: Construction of Park at Noida Near Okhla Bird Sanctuary*, residents in the state of Uttar Pradesh challenged a large government-driven recreational park project adjacent to the Okhla Bird Sanctuary.[47] To make way for the park's commemorative plaza, national memorial, and pedestrian pathways, contractors cut down 6,186 trees and moved another 179 trees.

Applicants argued that the government had failed to obtain environmental clearance and that the project was harming the bird sanctuary's sensitive ecological balance. They also asserted that the project had disregarded the Supreme Court's previous directions on maintaining buffer zones around national parks. The government argued a project EIA was unnecessary because the land was not zoned as forestland.

As the land was not classified as forestland, the court found there was no legal requirement for a project EIA. Further, although the project impacted the sanctuary's sensitive and fragile ecological balance, there was no legislation to prohibit these impacts. While the court had previously issued directions on the need for buffer zones around sanctuaries and national parks, the government had not implemented those directions.

In recognizing that this case warranted judicial intervention, the court explained:

> But the absence of a statute will not preclude this Court from examining the project's effects on the environment with particular reference to the Okhla Bird Sanctuary. For, in the jurisprudence

---

[46] In paragraph 14 of the decision, the court directed the state government to provide liquefied petroleum gas and kerosene oil as a replacement fuel, which are both fossil fuels. It is unknown if the parties sought clarification regarding the implementation of this contradictory order. Footnote 44, para. 14.

[47] *In re: Construction of Park at Noida Near Okhla Bird Sanctuary*, (2011) 1 SCC 744.

developed by this Court Environment is not merely a statutory issue. Environment is one of the facets of the right to life guaranteed under article 21 of the Constitution. Environment is, therefore, a matter directly under the Constitution and if the Court perceives any project or activity as harmful or injurious to the environment it would feel obliged to step in.[48]

The court permitted the project to proceed subject to conditions recommended by three expert bodies. This decision is not a climate case. The parties did not raise climate change arguments, and the court did not discuss the issue. However, the case demonstrates the willingness of the court to consider the impact that environmental damage can have on the fundamental right to life.

Climate change law is fairly new. There are many facets of climate change that remain unregulated. Like this case, disputes may arise over actions that are not outlawed, but which cause undeniable climate injury. Such injury can undermine the basic right to live. In such cases, an equitable outcome might rely on focusing on the primary rights of citizens to ensure sustainable development.

4. Protecting Agricultural Land and Ensuring Sustainable Development

a) Farming Land in South Asia

In *Karnataka Industrial Areas Development Board v. Sri C. Kenchappa & Ors.*, local farmers disputed the government's decision to allot land for a research and development facility in a southern state in India.[49] Once established, the facility would employ around 500 scientists, 150 staff members, and 250 technical people. The local farmers argued that if all of their gomal (cattle grazing) land was acquired and converted into an industrial park, they and their cattle would suffer grave hardship. They claimed that depriving them of their land violated their constitutional rights to life and equality before the law.

In its decision, the Supreme Court of India stressed the dire and urgent need for sustainable development in the face of environmental degradation and climate change. Courts, it said, had played an important role in preserving and protecting "ecology and environment in consonance with the provisions of the Constitution" over the last 40 years.[50] The precautionary principle, the polluter pays principle, and public trust doctrine should also guide sustainable development. The court made the following directions:

(i)   All future land acquisition for development must take into account the impacts on the ecology and environment.

---

[48]   Footnote 47, para. 74.

[49]   *Karnataka Industrial Areas Development Board v. Sri C. Kenchappa & Ors.*, (2006) 6 SCC 371.

[50]   Footnote 49, para. 101.

(ii)   The state development board must require recipients of land allotments to obtain a clearance from the state pollution control board for the proposed development.

b)   Food Security in South Asia

There are instances of farmers objecting to government decisions to allow industrial development on agricultural land. Farmers have raised the need to protect agricultural land for future food production, which will likely become stressed in the era of climate change.

In *M. Farooque Vs. Government of Bangladesh*, the court stressed the importance of regenerative land use:

> The writers of history have seldom noted the importance of land use. They seem not to have recognized that the destinies of most of man's empires and civilizations were determined largely by the way the land was used. While recognizing the influence of environment on history, they fail to note that man usually changed or despoiled his environment.
> . . .
> How did civilized man despoil his favorable environment? He did it mainly by depleting or destroying the natural resources. . . . Then his civilization declined amidst the despoilation [*sic*] of his own creation or he moved to new land. There have been from ten to thirty different civilizations that have followed this road to ruin (the number depending on who classifies the civilizations).[51]

In India, in *Manu Anand v. State of Kerala & Others*, the petitioner opposed a government order empowering a district collector to grant designated agricultural land for use in a quarry.[52] Under the Kerala Government Land Assignment Act, 1960 the government was permitted to grant public agricultural land for use in personal cultivation and house sites, and for the beneficial enjoyment of adjoining land. In addition to the permitted purposes, the government had the discretion to assign the land for any purpose, including industrial purposes like quarrying, provided it was in the public interest.

The court held that the government could not lawfully delegate power to the district collector to assign land for purposes that were not explicitly permitted under the act. As such, the district collector had no power to grant the public land for use as a quarry. Only the government retained discretion to make such a grant. However, the court cautioned the government that it should not determine public interest merely by reference to market conditions. The Kyoto Protocol and the

---

51   V. Carter and T. Dale. 1955. Topsoil and Civilization. Revised ed. Norman: University of Oklahoma Press, cited by the court in *M. Farooque Vs. Government of Bangladesh* 17 BLD (AD) 1 (1997), p. 32.
52   *Manu Anand v. State of Kerala & Others*, 2016 (3) KHC 164; 2016 (2) KLT 529.

UN Framework Convention on Climate Change (UNFCCC) "reminds the nation to strive for the policies and measures to minimise adverse effects on climate change and to promote sustainable forms of agriculture in the light of climate change conditions."[53]

The court also observed that any measure or action ignoring intergenerational equity was against the public interest. It highlighted the need to retain agricultural land for food production. Referring to the report of the 64th UN General Assembly, the court reminded the government that by 2050

> the world need[s] to double food production to satisfy the need of the entire world population. The soaring heatwaves due to climatic variation is [a] pointer to the erosion of agricultural landscapes from the State. The food security and afforestation programmes cannot be ignored while evolving policy on public interest for assignment of Government Land (footnote 52).

This case demonstrates the capacity of courts to connect land grant disputes with climate change adaptation, particularly the need to protect food security.

5. Corporate Failure in Disasters in Viet Nam

The authors found no civil litigation over corporate failure to act, either post- or pre-disaster. However, a flooding incident at the Hố Hô hydropower plant in Viet Nam provides an Asian example of liability flowing from the failure to act to ensure infrastructure could withstand torrential wet season rains.

From 14 to 15 October 2016, the Hố Hô hydropower plant in Ky Anh district suddenly released 192 cubic meters of water per second from its dam following torrential rains from a tropical depression.[54] Combined with heavy rain, the discharge caused flooding, killing 21 people and inundating over 24,000 houses downstream.[55] The power plant released the water without notifying downstream communities.[56] Before the 2016 wet season, the power plant had failed to inspect its facilities, making it difficult for the company to predict possible hazards (footnote 54). It also failed to maintain an annual regulation water plan or a notification and reporting regime.[57]

---

[53] Footnote 52, para. 17.
[54] *Vietnamnet*. 2016. Ministry Publishes Violations of Ho Ho Hydropower Plant. 2 November; *Viet Nam News*. 2016. MoIT Publishes Violations of Hố Hô Hydropower Plant. 1 November.
[55] D. Hung. 2016. Stranded Flood Victims in Ha Tinh on Verge of Running Out Food. *VnExpress*. 17 October.
[56] *VnExpress*. 2016. Deadly Floods Blamed on Hydropower Power Plants in Central Vietnam. 16 October.
[57] *Viet Nam News*. 2016. Hố Hô Hydropower Plant Fined Over VNĐ115 Million for Violations in Water Resource Management. 18 November.

The Ministry of Natural Resources and Environment fined the power plant for regulatory noncompliance. The ministry also announced that it would revoke the power plant's operation license if repeated violations occur (footnote 57). The company also paid D448 million ($20,000) in compensation to local communities.[58]

There is no information to suggest that the government, community, or power plant attributed the incident to climate change or to the failure to adapt to changing weather patterns due to climate change. However, this tragic incident is a cautionary tale of how the failure to adapt infrastructure can result in loss of life and legal risks such as compensation claims and regulatory fines. As climate change impacts worsen, so will the magnitude of rainstorms. Such events will move from being unexpected to foreseeable events. Ensuring regulatory compliance and regular safety inspections will be critical to companies for minimizing their risk exposure.

II. Reverse Environmental Impact Assessments

A. Global Approaches

Typically, environmental review cases concern a project's or policy's impact on the environment. Sometimes, however, they seek to improve or require what has been called reverse environmental impact assessment (REIA). REIA examines how the environment will affect a project to understand how the project will, in turn, impact the environment. Below are examples from the US and Australia of REIAs in environmental review and planning suits.

(See Part Two, Section II.A.2. Environmental Impact Statements Cases and Part Two, Section III.A.3. Environmental Impact Statements in the United States for a discussion of mitigation-related EIA cases.)

1. Climate Change Impacts on Projects in Australia

In Australia, a suite of cases has considered climate change impacts on proposed projects. Most often, these cases concern coastal residential development. For example, in *Myers v South Gippsland Shire Council,* the Victorian Civil and Administrative Tribunal (VCAT) heard a case concerning an application to split coastal land into two residential lots.[59] A citizen filed suit, claiming that the vulnerability to impacts of climate change had not been properly considered in the application and that the subdivision would be contrary to the character of the

---

58 Thuy Mi. 2016. Ha Tinh Hydropower Plant Compensates for Flood Discharge. RFI. 20 November.
59 *Myers v South Gippsland Shire Council (No 1)* [2009] VCAT 1022 and *Myers v South Gippsland Shire Council (No 2)* [2009] VCAT 2414.

bay where the coastal land was located. In an interim decision, the VCAT ordered the applicant to submit a coastal hazard vulnerability assessment of the impacts of climate change on the proposed lots before it could decide on the subdivision.

The vulnerability assessment revealed that the proposed coastal residential lot would be inundated by flooding and storm surges by 2100. In its final decision, the VCAT applied the precautionary principle in line with the government's current policy platform. The VCAT refused approval for the subdivision given the lack of specific local policy or planning scheme to address the predicted impacts of climate change, including sea level rise and increased storm surge (footnote 59). The VCAT could not "support a subdivision in the knowledge that without mitigation works, there will be no dune, no road, no access to the site and the site is likely to be inundated with sea water" because "to grant a permit in these circumstances would consent to a poor planning outcome that will unnecessarily burden future generations."[60]

An example of an Australian REIA case that does not concern residential development is *Alanvale Pty Ltd v Southern Rural Water Authority*.[61] In this case, a company challenged the Southern Rural Water Authority's decision to deny them licenses for groundwater extraction. The VCAT held that the Southern Rural Water Authority's claim that there was a risk in over-allocating the groundwater supply was substantiated by the possibility of rainfall being scarce as a result of climate change. The tribunal justified their decision based on the precautionary principle.

(See Part Two, Section VII.A.1. Water Management in Australia for further discussion of this case.)

2. Climate Change Impacts on Projects in the United States

In the US, case law has established certain responsibilities under the federal environmental review process to consider how climate change will affect the project or decision being reviewed. Relatedly, an environmental review must assess the cumulative combined effects on the environment of climate change and the proposed project or decision.

In *AquAlliance v. US Bureau of Reclamation,* a California federal court found that environmental review under the National Environmental Policy Act (NEPA) required a federal agency to conduct further analysis of how climate change would impact a water transfer project in California.[62] Although the final environmental impact statement or report stated that climate change would cause declines in snowpack and streamflow, it failed to address why these declines would not impact the project significantly (footnote 62).

---

[60] *Myers v South Gippsland Shire Council (No 2)* [2009] VCAT 2414, paras. 31, 33–34.

[61] *Alanvale Pty Ltd v Southern Rural Water Authority* [2010] VCAT 480.

[62] *AquAlliance v. US Bureau of Reclamation*, 287 F. Supp. 3d 969 (E.D. Cal. 2018) (appealed Sept. 19, 2018).

In another US case, *Norwalk Harbor Keeper v. US Department of Transportation*, a local conservation organization filed a lawsuit in the federal district court in Connecticut challenging an environmental review.[63] The review was for the Norwalk River Railroad Bridge replacement project in Norwalk, Connecticut pursuant to the NEPA. The complaint argued that in selecting a bridge design, the defendant agencies "failed to consider the reasonable alternative of a fixed bridge at the level of the existing swing bridge."[64] The organization argued that the agencies should have considered designs that would be resilient to climate change and severe weather events, especially heatwaves. The complaint stressed that heatwaves "could cause rail tracks to expand and buckle," making track alignment problematic on a moveable bridge, necessitating track repairs and speed restrictions.[65]

The organization further claimed that although the project environmental assessment identified resilience to climate change and severe weather events as a critical parameter for evaluating design alternatives, it failed "to follow through with an adequate resiliency analysis."[66] The federal district court for the District of Connecticut found in favor of the defendant agencies.[67] It concluded that the defendant agencies did not have an obligation to consider a low-level fixed bridge option due to resilience considerations. As such, the defendants had acted reasonably in deciding not to move forward with the fixed bridge options.

While case law can incrementally refine a body of requirements for how climate change impacts on a project must be considered during the environmental review, legislatures can also establish legal requirements directly. Several countries have amended their laws concerning environmental review to require analysis of climate change effects, including the EU, Kiribati, and Vanuatu.[68] Agencies can further issue guidance to clarify and codify these practices, enhancing opportunities for decision-makers "to modify design features, develop alternatives, or adopt other measures to mitigate climate-related risks."[69]

The Sabin Center for Climate Change Law has published model protocols for assessing the impact of climate change on the built environment and natural resource-related projects under environmental review statutes.[70]

---

[63] *Norwalk Harbor Keeper v. US Department of Transportation*, Complaint, No. 3:2018cv00091 (D. Conn filed Jan. 17, 2018).

[64] Footnote 63, p. 2, para. 7.

[65] Footnote 63, p. 19, para. 90 and p. 13, para. 68.

[66] Footnote 63, p. 13, para. 66.

[67] *Norwalk Harbor Keeper v. US Department of Transportation*, No. 3:18-cv-00091 (D. Conn Jul. 8, 2019).

[68] J. Wentz. 2015. *Assessing the Impacts of Climate Change on the Built Environment under NEPA and State EIA Laws: A Survey of Current Practices and Recommendations for Model Protocols*. Sabin Center for Climate Change Law, Columbia Law School. New York. August.

[69] Footnote 68, p. i.

[70] Footnote 68, p. 49–56; and J. Wentz. 2016. *Considering the Effects of Climate Change on Natural Resources in Environmental Review and Planning Documents: Guidance for Agencies and Practitioners*. New York: Sabin Center for Climate Change Law, Columbia Law School. pp A-1–A-12.

B.   Asia and the Pacific Approaches: Failing to Assess Cumulative Impacts in South Asia

Decisions requiring an REIA are rare in Asia. The authors could not find any REIA decisions from the Pacific.

The Supreme Court of India discussed the need for cumulative EIAs in *Alaknanda Hydro Power Company Ltd. v. Anuj Joshi and Ors.*[71] The court was concerned about the government's failure to assess the cumulative impacts of multiple hydropower projects in the Alaknanda and Bhagirathi river basins of the northern Indian state of Uttar Pradesh. It noted that each of the hydro projects had required the construction of dams, tunnels, and powerhouses. Construction also relied on blasting and caused deforestation.

The court found that there had been no scientific assessment of the cumulative impacts of these activities on the local environment. The court directed the government to stop granting environmental permits for hydropower projects in Uttar Pradesh until further order.

The court also expressed concern about the relationship between large numbers of hydropower projects and catastrophic flooding in Uttarakhand in June 2013. Around 5,700 people died in floods and landslides following a multiday cloudburst.[72] The court ordered the government to establish an expert body to assess whether hydroelectric power projects in Uttarakhand had (i) contributed to the environmental degradation within the state and, if so, to what extent; (ii) contributed to the 2013 flooding; and (iii) impacted biodiversity in the Alaknanda and Bhagirathi river basins.[73]

(See Part Two, Section IV.B.1. Hydropower in South Asia for a full case summary of *Alaknanda Hydro Power Company Ltd. v. Anuj Joshi and Ors.*)

Understanding the extent of large-scale infrastructure impacts on the surrounding ecology's adaptive capacity will become necessary. Studies have linked the 2013 Indian flooding event to global warming, stating that future catastrophic flooding events are expected as climate change impacts intensify.[74] Assuming that Asia and the Pacific will mirror litigation trends in the US, courts can expect more litigants to sue over government failure to take adaptive capacity into account.

---

[71]   *Alaknanda Hydro Power Company Ltd. v. Anuj Joshi and Ors.*, (2014) 1 SCC 769.
[72]   BBC. 2013. India Floods: More Than 5,700 People 'Presumed Dead.' 15 July.
[73]   Footnote 71, p. 809, para. 52.
[74]   D. Grossman. 2015. Unnatural Disaster: How Climate Helped Cause India's Big Flood. *Yale Environment 360*. 23 June; World Bank. 2013. *India: Climate Change Impacts*. 19 June.

III. Suits Against Taking Adaptation Actions

As government entities make decisions and take adaptation actions to prepare for climate change, they are sometimes sued by developers or property owners negatively affected by these actions. These suits may allege statutory, constitutional, and/or other violations. In the US, many of these cases are heard in state or administrative courts because they concern state or local permitting decisions.

A.   Global Approaches

1.   Zoning Laws and Planning Policy in the United States

In some instances, these cases concern changes to zoning laws. In *Murphy v. Zoning Board of City of Stamford,* a Connecticut state court rejected an argument that the City of Stamford Zoning Board failed to provide sufficient reasons for changing the definition of building height in its zoning regulations, which affected the plaintiffs.[75] The court referred to a staff report that described a clear necessity for regulating "the elevation of residential buildings in order to protect against coastal flooding."[76] A letter from the planning board explained that the amended definition was an "appropriate and measured response to climate change and expected increases in coastal flooding."[77] As such, the court held that the purpose of the amendment was "reasonably and rationally related to one of the principal purposes of zoning" (footnote 77).

In *Argos Properties II, LLC v. City Council for Virginia Beach,* a Virginia state court dismissed a developer's challenge to a city council's denial of a rezoning application in a flood-prone area.[78] The Virginia Beach City Council denied the developer's application to rezone a 20-hectare property for residential development because it failed to assess the impact of a 45.72-cm sea level rise and heavier storms on stormwater system performance. The developer argued that the council's actions were arbitrary, capricious, and ultra vires (beyond the council's authority). The developer also claimed the denial violated its constitutional rights to equal protection (equal treatment under the laws). All claims were dismissed by the trial court, which also ruled that defendants' actions were not beyond their authority. Other times these cases may challenge a government's planning policy. For example, in *Olympic Stewardship Foundation v. State of Washington Environmental and Land Use Hearings Office,* a US state appellate court upheld Jefferson County's 2014 Shoreline Master Program.[79] The program controlled shoreline

---

[75]   *Murphy v. Zoning Board of City of Stamford,* No. FSTCV145014294S (Conn. Super. Ct. Nov. 16, 2016).

[76]   Footnote 75, p. 9.

[77]   Footnote 75, p. 10.

[78]   *Argos Properties II, LLC v. City Council for Virginia Beach,* No. CL18002289-00 (Va. Cir. Ct. filed May 17, 2018).

[79]   *Olympic Stewardship Foundation v. State of Washington Environmental and Land Use Hearings Office,* 199 Wash. App. 668, 399 P.3d 562 (2017), *cert. denied sub nom. Olympic Stewardship Found. v. State of Washington Envtl. & Land Use Hearings Office,* 139 S. Ct. 81, 202 L. Ed. 2d 25 (2018).

use and development with planning policies and development regulations. One petitioner argued that a provision in the Master Program goals section addressing climate change and sea level rise was unconstitutionally vague.

The court upheld the program, finding there was sufficient clarity regarding the implementation of the goal for shoreline use. The Master Program guidelines, observed the court, clarified that the "policy goals might not be achievable and . . . should be pursued only via development regulations where such regulations do not unconstitutionally infringe upon private property rights."[80] Hence, the goal provision was not vague, and the petitioner's "assertions that the Master Program will be administered arbitrarily or capriciously are speculative" (footnote 79).

2. Planning Permits Denied in Australia and the United Kingdom

Courts in Australia have also heard challenges from developers that were denied permits on a climate change-related basis. A developer contested a council's decision to reject an application to develop a 39-lot subdivision on flood-prone land in *Pridel Investments Pty Ltd v Coffs Harbour City Council*.[81] Climate change featured in the council's arguments at trial, particularly that the development proposal (i) presented an unacceptably high risk of flooding; (ii) failed to manage flood risks under climate change in accordance with normal practice; and (iii) failed to account for various climate change impacts in accordance with state coastal policy, which requires ecologically sustainable developments.

The Land and Environment Court of New South Wales refused the development application. It noted that the development plan presumed a 100-year life but did not take into account the risks posed by dune erosion and denuded vegetation due to coastal processes and climate change. Dune and vegetation loss exposed the development to the prospect of coastal inundation—episodic flooding—at any time. In such circumstances, the development did not meet the principles of "ecological sustainable development" within the state coastal policy or ensure that the development would be safe from coastal hazards for 100 years.[82]

The development's isolated and disconnected location also meant that it was "urban sprawl along the coast," impermissible under coastal development guidelines. Further, insufficient emergency access to the development, which was essential given the site's flood-prone nature and inherent bushfire risks, created a "fatal flaw" in the application.[83]

Claimants in the UK challenged the decision refusing their permit application for mixed-use redevelopment in *Castletown Estates Ltd and Carmarthenshire County*

---

[80] Footnote 79, p. 34.
[81] *Pridel Investments Pty Ltd v Coffs Harbour City Council* [2017] NSWLEC 1042.
[82] Footnote 81, para. 159.
[83] Footnote 81, para. 59.

Council v Welsh Ministers.[84] The claimants argued that the minister relied upon inaccurate flood maps, which had shown that the site was at risk of flooding. They also disputed the minister's precautionary approach, which evaluated additional criteria to assess the impact of climate change on future flooding. Specifically, he considered the rate of rise of floodwaters, the maximum speed of inundation, and the maximum velocity of floodwaters.

The Queen's Bench Division of the High Court of Justice found that the minister was entitled to adopt a robust approach by considering additional criteria for assessing flood risk. The application for appeal was dismissed.

3. Government "Taking" of Property in the United States

The US constitution provides that the government cannot "take" private property without providing just compensation. In other countries, this type of action—in which the government takes private property ostensibly for a public good—is sometimes referred to as an "expropriation." US takings cases in the climate change adaptation context may prove relevant for other jurisdictions.

State governments in the US have successfully defended condemning private property for climate adaptation purposes and compensating the property owner through the process of "eminent domain." For example, in *State of New Jersey v. North Beach 1003, LLC*, the New Jersey Appellate Division ruled that the New Jersey Department of Environmental Protection had authority to condemn private property to take perpetual easements for shore protection purposes and that the easements could allow public access to, and use of, the areas covered by the easements.[85]

The court held that the New Jersey Department of Environmental Protection had acted within its statutory authority when it acquired property interests to construct a dune and berm system along Long Beach Island and along 22.5 km of coastline in northern Ocean County after Superstorm Sandy. The court found that there was specific statutory authorization under "beach protection powers" for this type of eminent domain.[86] Further, the court determined that the state could obtain a lesser property interest such as an easement (rather than fee simple ownership of the property).

In other instances, the plaintiffs may accuse the government of a "regulatory taking" if a new climate-related policy deprives the owner of the economically beneficial use of the property.

In *Columbia Venture, LLC v. Richland County*, a state court found that floodway restrictions imposed on a development were not a regulatory taking.[87] The

[84] *Castletown Estates Ltd and Carmarthenshire County Council v Welsh Ministers* [2013] EWHC 3293 (Admin).

[85] *State of New Jersey v. North Beach* 1003, LLC, 451 N.J. Super. 214, 166 A.3d 239 (App. Div. 2017).

[86] Footnote 85, p. 24.

[87] *Columbia Venture, LLC v. Richland County*, 413 S.C. 423, 776 S.E.2d 900 (2015).

South Carolina Supreme Court dismissed a developer's argument that prohibiting constructions in floodways caused economic loss, constituting an unconstitutional taking. Columbia Venture bought land with intent to develop it, but knowing that the Federal Emergency Management Agency was designating the land as a regulatory floodway.

The federal agency requires communities to prohibit encroachments in regulatory floodways. The county's restrictions on encroachments in a regulatory floodway were more stringent and forward-looking than those set by the federal agency.[88] A former county planning director testified that federal flood maps "rely on historical flood records" and do not "project the potential of increased flooding in the future from urbanization or from the possibility of more intense storms due to climate change" (footnote 87).

The court concluded that no taking occurred. It considered that the developer's "lack of reasonable investment-backed expectations coupled with the legitimate and substantial health and safety-related bases for the county's floodplain development restrictions outweighed" the developer's economic injury.[89]

B.   Asia and the Pacific Approaches: Protecting Coastal Properties in Samoa

The authors are not aware of cases challenging governmental adaptation action in South Asia, Southeast Asia, or the Pacific. However, a private citizen in Samoa sued his neighbors (and relatives) to stop them from placing any rock, fill, or material within the foreshore and coastal waters next to his land. He further objected to their plans to reclaim land to protect their coastal property from cyclones.

In *Keil v Minister of Natural Resources and Environment*, the Minister of Natural Resources and Environment consented to an application from Kyle and Adele Keil (second defendants) to reclaim part of the foreshore adjacent to their land.[90] Their house had been damaged in a cyclone, and they wanted to prevent further damage. The plaintiff argued that the environmental protection act was meant to protect the environment and that the minister had failed to consider the impact on the environment.

The court upheld the minister's decision to allow the Keils to reclaim land and conduct works to make their land more resilient to future cyclones. The court concluded that the defendant did not have an obligation to give reasons for the decision. Neither did the court find the decision to be illegal, unreasonable, or irrational, and that the first defendant had access to environmental information when making the decision.

---

[88]   Footnote 87, p. 4.
[89]   Footnote 87, p. 25.
[90]   *Keil v Minister of Natural Resources and Environment* [2003] WSSC 54.

Bhutanese woman harvesting rice crops from the field. Climate change disproportionately impacts women, children, older adults, indigenous peoples, the poor, and coastal and agrarian societies (photo by Eric Sales/ADB).

PART FIVE

PEOPLE WHO ARE VULNERABLE TO CLIMATE CHANGE

> **"**
>
> **People** who are socially, economically, culturally, politically, institutionally, or otherwise marginalized are especially vulnerable to climate change and also to some adaptation and mitigation responses. . . This heightened vulnerability is rarely due to a single cause. Rather, it is the product of intersecting social processes that result in inequalities in socioeconomic status and income, as well as in exposure. Such social processes include, for example, discrimination on the basis of gender, class, ethnicity, age and (dis)ability.
>
> Source: IPCC. 2014. Summary for Policymakers. In C.B. Field et al., eds. *Climate Change 2014: Impacts, Adaptation, and Vulnerability.* Cambridge and New York: Cambridge University Press. p. 6.

Litigation remains an important tool for protecting the rights of people made vulnerable by the adverse impacts of climate change. The IPCC reports that disadvantaged and vulnerable populations—including indigenous peoples and communities dependent on agricultural or coastal livelihoods—face disproportionately higher risks of adverse consequences of global warming.[1] Keeping global warming to 1.5°C (compared with 2°C) will reduce the number of people harmed by climate-related risks and poverty by "up to several hundred million by 2050" (footnote 1). Rising average global temperature will increase poverty and disadvantage (footnote 1).

Within this context, climate migrants, disaster-affected and indigenous people, and citizens advocating for greater public participation have all brought claims against governments and private actors, seeking protection from climate-related harms. In adjudicating these claims, courts around the world have relied on relevant

---

[1] IPCC. 2018. Summary for Policymakers. In V. Masson-Delmotte et al., eds. *Special Report: Global Warming of 1.5°C.* In press. p.32.

international law and domestic law. States, according to the Office of the UN High Commissioner for Human Rights, are "legally bound to address [climate-related] vulnerabilities in accordance with the principle of equality and non-discrimination."[2]

This nondiscrimination principle requires states to "identify marginalized or vulnerable individuals and groups; address specific needs through 'targeted and differentiated interventions'; and tackle underlying power imbalances and structural cases of 'differential vulnerability' within and between households while building the ecological resilience necessary to reduce vulnerability and achieve threshold needs."[3]

I. Migration

Climate-induced migration is a growing challenge, yet climate migrants enjoy a limited legal status in international law. There is no standard definition of a climate migrant. Furthermore, the Convention Relating to the Status of Refugees (the 1951 Refugee Convention), which governs refugee law, does not extend protection to climate migrants.

During 2000–2015, Pacific Islanders argued in more than 20 administrative and judicial cases in Australia and New Zealand that they should receive protection under refugee law because of climate change—all of the cases failed.[4] Courts have reasoned that climate migrants seeking protection under refugee law do not qualify because they do not meet the requirements set out by the 1951 Refugee Convention.

A. Global Approaches

1. Climate Migration in New Zealand

New Zealand courts have developed the most robust jurisprudence on climate migration to date. Unfortunately, courts have been reluctant to extend the protection of refugee law to climate migrants.

In *Teitiota v The Chief Executive of the Ministry of Business, Innovation and Employment*, the New Zealand Supreme Court found that an i-Kiribati, Teitiota, did not qualify as a refugee under international law.[5]

---

[2]   Office of the UN High Commissioner for Human Rights. 2009. *Report of the Office of the United Nations High Commissioner for Human Rights on the Relationship between Climate Change and Human Rights.* A/HRC/10/61, p. 15, para. 42.

[3]   A.D. Fisher. 2014. *A Human Rights-Based Approach to the Environment and Climate Change: A GI-ESCR Practitioner's Guide.* Geneva: The Global Initiative for Economic, Social and Cultural Rights. p. 5.

[4]   J. McAdam. 2017. Building International Approaches to Climate Change, Disasters, and Displacement. *Windsor Yearbook of Access to Justice.* 33. pp. 1–14.

[5]   *Teitiota v Chief Executive of the Ministry of Business, Innovation and Employment,* [2014] NZCA 173 (New Zealand).

Teitiota sought refugee status in New Zealand because of the effects of sea level rise and environmental degradation on his home island, Kiribati. The court reasoned that Teitiota's case did not meet the required elements for refugee status under the Refugee Convention because "while Kiribati undoubtedly faces challenges, Teitiota does not, if returned, face 'serious harm' and there is no evidence that the Government of Kiribati is failing to take steps to protect its citizens from the effects of environmental degradation to the extent that it can."[6]

The Refugee Convention extends protection only to petitioners with a well-founded fear of persecution because of "race, religion, nationality, political opinion, or membership of a particular social group."[7] The petitioners must also be unable to gain protection from their home country (footnote 5). The court noted, however, that the court's decision did not mean "that environmental degradation resulting from climate change or other natural disasters could never create a pathway into the Refugee Convention or protected person jurisdiction."[8]

(See Part One, Section I.A.3. for further discussion of this case.)

Similarly, the New Zealand Refugee Status Appeals Authority affirmed the denial of a Tuvaluan family's application for refugee status in New Zealand in *Refugee Appeal No. 72189/2000*.[9] The family argued that they suffered both environmental and economic hardship, including the erosion of the Tuvaluan coastline and the submersion of their family property during high tides.

The authority reasoned that refugee status was not appropriate because the family was not "differentially at risk of harm amounting to persecution due to any one of" the five grounds of protection under the Refugee Convention.[10] It further said that "all citizens face the same environmental problems and economic difficulties" and were "unfortunate victims . . . of the forces of nature."[11] The family did not receive refugee status in New Zealand.

However, New Zealand's Immigration and Protection Tribunal did grant a resident visa to a family from Tuvalu based on "exceptional circumstances."[12] In *re: AD (Tuvalu)*, a family from Tuvalu sought resident visas in New Zealand and argued that they would suffer if they were deported to Tuvalu because of climate change impacts.

The Immigration and Protection Tribunal found that the family had established "exceptional circumstances of a humanitarian nature, which would make it unjust or unduly harsh for the appellants to be removed from New Zealand" pursuant

---

6   Footnote 5, para 12.
7   Footnote 5, p. 4.
8   Footnote 5, para 13.
9   Refugee Appeal Nos. 72189-72195/2000, RSAA (17 August 2000) (Tuvalu).
10   Footnote 9, para 4.
11   Footnote 9, para 13.
12   In *re: AD (Tuvalu)* [2014] NZIPT 501370–371.

to the Immigration Act 2009.[13] The tribunal grounded its finding on factors other than climate change. The tribunal considered it significant that the appellants were "well-loved and integral members of a family which has, effectively, migrated to New Zealand in its entirety."[14] Deporting the family would, therefore, impose an "unusually significant disruption to a dense network of family relationships spanning three generations in New Zealand." (footnote 14).

While the tribunal declined to reach the question of whether climate change provided a basis for granting resident visas in this case, it did acknowledge that climate change impacts may undermine the enjoyment of human rights.

2.   Climate Migration in Australia

Like New Zealand judiciaries, Australian courts and tribunals have, for the most part, rejected arguments that climate migrants should be protected under refugee law. In *RRT Case Number 0907346*, for example, the Australian Refugee Review Tribunal denied an i-Kiribati's appeal of the rejection of their application for refugee status in Australia.[15] The appellant pointed to environmental and economic difficulty, including climate change impacts like saltwater intrusion, food insecurity, and sea level rise. The tribunal determined that the applicant did not face persecution based on any of the five grounds established in the Refugee Convention. Further, no persecutor could be identified.

Although the tribunal noted that other jurisdictions have laws that allow people to seek protection based on natural disasters and environmental degradation, Australia was not among them. The tribunal was bound to apply Australian law as it currently stood. Therefore, while the tribunal acknowledged the grave circumstances which the applicant faced, it concluded that "they are not matters against which . . . the Refugee Convention as it applies in Australia is able to provide protection."[16]

Despite the limited application of refugee law to climate migrants, in cases where climate change interacts with recognized grounds for protection—such as conflict—the Refugee Convention will likely apply.[17] Furthermore, some jurisdictions do offer protection to people displaced by natural disasters and environmental degradation.

For example, the 1969 Organization of African Unity Convention extends refugee protection to persons fleeing because of "events seriously disturbing public

---

13   Footnote 12, p. 8, para 30.
14   Footnote 12, p. 8, para 31.
15   *RRT Case No. 0907346* [2009] RRTA 1168.
16   Footnote 15, para 54.
17   W. Kälin. 2010. Conceptualising Climate-Induced Displacement. In J. McAdam, ed. *Climate Change and Displacement: Multidisciplinary Perspectives*. Oxford: Hart Publishing. pp. 81–103.

order," including natural hazards.[18] Cases where climate migrants seek refugee protection have not yet been tried in jurisdictions besides New Zealand and Australia. However, as the number of climate migrants grows, climate migration-related claims may also increase.

3. Climate Migration in International Tribunals

After being deported to Kiribati, Teitiota petitioned the UN Human Rights Committee in 2015 for a violation of his human rights. Teitiota argued that New Zealand had infringed his right to life under article 6 of the International Covenant on Civil and Political Rights.[19] He claimed that climate change made habitable land in Kiribati scarce, causing a housing crisis and deadly land disputes. Sea level rise had contaminated sources of fresh water, degrading his health and damaging crops. Teitiota and his wife feared that their children would drown during a storm surge or tidal event.

In January 2020, the committee ruled against Teitiota.[20] It was not satisfied that there was a violation of his right to life under the International Covenant on Civil and Political Rights. To succeed, the committee concluded that Teitiota must demonstrate that he suffered a personal risk of arbitrary deprivation of life as opposed to a risk derived from the general conditions shared by all i-Kiribati. The committee reasoned that there was still 10–15 years for the Government of Kiribati to adapt to climate change. Therefore, Teitiota's complaint could not succeed.

However, the committee warned that "environmental degradation, climate change and unsustainable development constitute some of the most pressing and serious threats to the ability of present and future generations to enjoy the right to life."[21] Unless there is robust international action, extreme outcomes may result. Vulnerable countries may become "submerged under water," making living conditions "incompatible with the right to life with dignity before the risk is realized."[22] Such an outcome would violate the affected peoples' right to life, and it would be unlawful for states to refuse entry to such climate migrants (footnote 22).

Two committee members dissented from the majority opinion. One dissent concluded that New Zealand's decision to deport Teitiota was arbitrary because the state did not show that Teitiota had access to safe drinking water. The second dissent found that New Zealand had imposed an unreasonable burden of proof on Teitiota to show that there was a real risk of arbitrary deprivation of life. The

---

[18] UN High Commissioner for Refugees. 1969. *OAU Convention Governing Specific Aspects of Refugee Problems in Africa.* Article 2.

[19] *International Covenant on Civil and Political Rights,* New York, 16 December 1966, *United Nations Treaty Series,* Vol. 999, No. 14668, p. 171.

[20] UN Human Rights Committee. 2020. *Views Adopted by the Committee under Article 5 (4) of the Optional Protocol, Concerning Communication No. 2728/2016.* CCPR/C/127/D/2728/2016. 7 January 2020.

[21] Footnote 20, p. 12, para. 9.4.

[22] Footnote 20, p. 15, para. 9.11.

committee member considered that climate change had made living conditions in Kiribati significantly grave.

In consequence, Teitiota faced "a real, personal and reasonably foreseeable risk of a threat to his right to life."[23] Although Kiribati's efforts to adapt to climate change were laudable, the committee member thought that living conditions robbed Teitiota of a right to life and dignity within the meaning of the International Covenant on Civil and Political Rights. New Zealand's decision to return Teitiota to Kiribati was, therefore, "more like forcing a drowning person back into a sinking vessel, with the 'justification' that after all there are other voyagers on board."[24]

The committee's decision to hear Teitiota's communication acknowledged the need to give climate migrants a forum for justice, advancing climate migration jurisprudence. Indeed, it heard the petition because it accepted that climate change was degrading living conditions in Kiribati. Further, the committee cautioned states about the legality of rejecting climate migrants in the future.

However, commentators have observed two pitfalls with the decision.[25] First, the committee held that Teitiota did not meet the threshold of risk required to demonstrate arbitrary detention of life. He did not prove that tidal events or storm surges were "occurring with such regularity as to raise the prospect of death occurring to the author or his family members to a level rising beyond conjecture and surmise, let alone a risk that could be characterized as an arbitrary deprivation of life" (footnote 20). As commentators said, "the committee's interpretation of the threshold of risk creates a perverse outcome, where climate impacts must result in death more regularly before the committee can find a violation of the right to life" (footnote 25).

Second, the committee's conclusion that Teitiota did not experience a personal risk infers that only the most vulnerable can demonstrate a right to protect their right to life under international law (footnote 25). It also downplays the widespread impacts of climate change on societies, especially Pacific states. It could result in outcomes where some people can legally migrate, splitting up communities, and leaving others to cope with what remains.

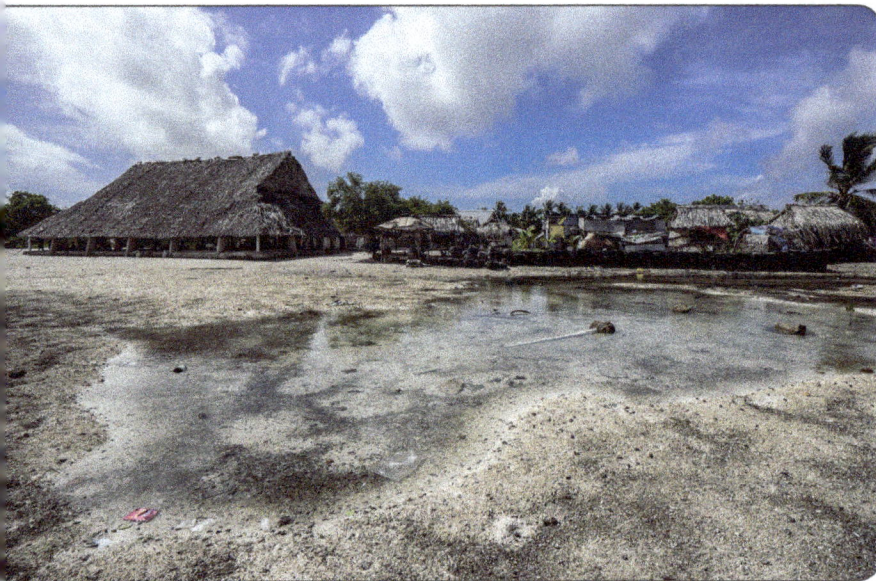

Washed out seawall in Tarawa, Kiribati. Kiribati faces becoming uninhabitable from sea level rise and rising ocean temperatures (photo by Eric Sales/ADB).

---

23   Footnote 20, Annex 2, p. 20, paras. 1 and 5.
24   Footnote 20, Annex 2, p. 21, para. 6.
25   H. Aidun and A. Francis. 2020. UN Human Rights Committee Issues Landmark Climate Migration Decision. *Sabin Center for Climate Change Law: Climate Law Blog.* 21 January.

B. Asia and the Pacific Approaches: Migration with Dignity in Kiribati

> "We are a country of low-lying coral atolls with most islands rising no more than two metres above sea level. Coastal protection through seawall construction is the main adaptation measure currently undertaken by Government but this is limited to the protection of public infrastructure. We simply do not have the resources to extend the protection to private properties. Adaptation measures of moving inland and to higher ground [are] impractical for us. We cannot move further inland due to the narrowness of our islands nor are there higher grounds to which we could escape from the rising seas.
>
> Source: A. Tong. 2008. *Statement by His Excellency Anote Tong: President of the Republic of Kiribati.* Presented during the General Debate of the 63rd Session of the UN General Assembly. New York. 25 September.

During 2003–2006, the Government of Kiribati innovated its "Migration with Dignity" policy as part of its Kiribati Adaptation Program.[26] Migration with dignity focuses on relocating i-Kiribati if mitigation and adaptation fail (footnote 26). The government later embedded the objectives of migration with dignity in the Kiribati National Labour Migration Policy of 2015, which promotes decent overseas work opportunities for i-Kiribati.[27]

There has since been much interest in the concept. Some suggest that it would help migrants maintain their cultural integrity while accessing education, employment, and health care.[28] It might also be a useful starting point for adaptation, especially for low-lying atoll islands. Many constitutions protect human dignity, as does international law.

The UN highlighted the importance of working together to enable communities and individuals to "live in safety and dignity" in the Global Compact for Safe,

---

[26] C. McMichael, C. Farbotko, and K.E. McNamara. 2019. Climate-Migration Responses in the Pacific Region. In C. Menjívar, M. Ruiz, and I. Ness, eds. *The Oxford Handbook of Migration Crises.* Oxford: Oxford University Press. p. 305; Government of Kiribati. Climate Change: Kiribati Adaptation Program.

[27] Government of Kiribati, Ministry of Labour and Human Resource Development. 2015. *Kiribati National Labour Migration Policy.* Tarawa.

[28] Environmental Law Institute. 2019. Seminar on Migration with Dignity: Lessons from Pacific Islanders in the United States. Washington, DC. 12 March.

Orderly and Regular Migration.[29] Objective 2 of the Global Compact for Migration commits to minimizing "the adverse drivers and structural factors that compel people to leave their country of origin," including climate change.

But what does it mean in a litigation context? Climate migration litigation to date has focused on cross border litigation, with parties basing their claims on the 1951 Refugee Convention. As shown in the climate migrant cases in Australia and New Zealand, that litigation has failed. Moreover, the issues raised in those cases may also not apply to the domestic context.

Many countries will probably have to respond first to internal displacement from climate impacts. In 2018 alone, for instance, flooding in Bangladesh, India, and Nepal displaced millions.[30]

Meanwhile, the Pacific grapples with displacement from increasingly intense cyclones and sea level rise. In 2015, Cyclone Pam displaced 65,000 people, more than 20% of Vanuatu's population.[31] Widespread crop destruction during the storm affected the livelihood of at least 80% of Vanuatu's rural population (footnote 31).

In 2019, the IPCC released its special report on the ocean and cryosphere.[32] It conceded that the only viable response for some communities facing sea level rise and warming oceans would be migration away from their homeland.[33] Domestic legal frameworks and courts will need to respond to disputes arising from disaster, displacement, and relocation.

How might dignity be relevant when dealing with post-disaster or resettlement lawsuits? Dignity connotes treating people with worth, honor, and esteem. Valuing people means respecting their ideas and giving them choices—and opportunities—for migration or resettlement. When people face life without safety, livelihood, and dignity, they will likely move.[34]

A court's ability to protect dignity lies in its power to protect the rights of people facing disaster and displacement. It lies in a court's power to protect people's right

---

[29] General Assembly Resolution 74/244. *Global Compact for Safe, Orderly and Regular Migration*, A/RES/72/244 (24 December 2017), art. 13.

[30] D. Eckstein, M. Hutfils, and M. Winges. 2018. *Global Climate Risk Index 2019: Who Suffers Most from Extreme Weather Events? Weather-Related Loss Events in 2017 and 1998 to 2017.* Briefing Paper. Bonn: Germanwatch e.V. p. 7.

[31] Government of Vanuatu. 2015. *Vanuatu Post-Disaster Needs Assessment: Tropical Cyclone Pam, March 2015.* Port Vila.

[32] H.O. Pörtner et al. 2019. Summary for Policymakers. In *IPCC Special Report on the Ocean and Cryosphere in a Changing Climate.* Geneva: IPCC.

[33] N. Abram et al. 2019. Chapter 1: Framing and Context of the Report. In *IPCC Special Report on the Ocean and Cryosphere in a Changing Climate.* Geneva: IPCC. pp 1–51.

[34] J. McAdam. 2016. Climate Change Displacement. Discussion given during Addressing Climate Displacement Globally and Locally—A Panel Discussion. Harvard Law School, Cambridge. 21 October.

to take part in discussions shaping their future lives, especially vulnerable groups. This part also discusses post-disaster lawsuits and participatory rights.

II. Post-Disaster Lawsuits

A. Global Approaches

The devastation that natural disasters cause has given rise to various legal claims. In the US (mainland and territories), evacuees, property owners, as well as local and national governments have sued public and private defendants. The legal claims have been for injury sustained because of defendants' behavior, such as their response—or failure to respond—after natural disasters.

1. Hurricane Maria in Puerto Rico

After Puerto Rico was devastated by Hurricane Maria in September 2017, both private and public plaintiffs sought redress by claiming federal aid benefits and timely payouts from private insurers. Courts have demonstrated varying levels of sympathy for these claims.

In *Santos v. Federal Emergency Management Agency*, a federal district court in the US mainland denied Hurricane Maria evacuees' request for a preliminary injunction.[35] The Hurricane Maria evacuees, who were staying in hotels through a federal disaster recovery program, sought to halt evictions of hundreds of evacuees in a class action suit. The plaintiffs had received housing assistance under the US federal disaster recovery agency's transitional shelter assistance program when Hurricane Maria displaced them. They argued that the federal disaster agency should extend the housing assistance program. The disaster agency's response after Hurricane Maria, they further argued, fell short in comparison with the aid that was provided after other hurricanes—namely Katrina, Harvey, and Irma. The evacuees alleged that their equal protection and due process rights had been violated.

The federal court determined that the plaintiffs' constitutional rights had not been violated because they did not have a property interest in the housing benefits evacuees received. Furthermore, the plaintiffs had not established that they were similarly situated to victims of hurricanes Harvey and Irma, such that their equal protection rights were violated. Although the court denied the preliminary injunction, the court acknowledged that the plaintiffs had suffered irreparable harm and did not have any other place to go once the housing assistance program ended.

In *Michael Pierluisi, as Secretary of the Department of Consumer Affairs et al. v. MAPFRE PRAICO Ins. Co et al.*, the Government of Puerto Rico sued some

---

35   *Santos v. Fed. Emergency Mgmt. Agency*, 327 F. Supp. 3d 328 (D. Mass. 2018).

insurance companies for their failure to respond promptly to insurance claims after Hurricane Maria.[36] The lawsuit was an attempt to prevent insurance companies from dropping residential property damage claims that had not been litigated within 1 year of the date of loss, pursuant to the "Suit Against Us" provisions in their policies. After the case was filed, the Puerto Rican legislature enacted a law that established that people with potential insurance claims would not have to file lawsuits within a year to preserve their unresolved claims. The Trial Court in San Juan then dismissed the suit for mootness.

2. Hurricanes on the Mainland United States

Private companies may be liable for damage that results during a hurricane because of inadequate upkeep of their facilities. In *Harris County v. Arkema, Inc.*, a Texas county sued a chemical manufacturer for unauthorized air and water emissions following Hurricane Harvey.[37] Arkema, Inc.'s facility flooded during the hurricane, cutting its primary and backup power. Harris County argued that the power loss meant that certain organic peroxides manufactured at the facility increased in temperature and decomposed, which led to fires and unauthorized air emissions under the Texas Clean Air Act. The flooding also resulted in industrial wastewater overflow, violating the Texas Water Code. Harris County further alleged that Arkema, Inc. failed to obtain permits under the county's floodplain regulations for structures sitting beneath the base flood level—the level of a 100-year flood.

This case is still pending, and the county seeks civil penalties, response costs, and a permanent injunction. The county also asks the court to direct Arkema, Inc. to arrange an independent third-party environmental audit of the facility and its disaster preparedness, which contains recommendations for implementation measures.

(See Part Four, Section I.A.4. Corporate Failures in Disasters in the United States for further discussion of this case.)

Property owners in St. Bernard Parish and Lower Ninth Ward in a southern US city sued the government for temporary taking of property after flooding during and after Hurricane Katrina damaged their property. In *St. Bernard Parish Government v. United States*, the plaintiffs alleged that the government negligently failed to properly maintain or modify the Mississippi River–Gulf Outlet channel, which worsened flooding.[38] The plaintiffs were ultimately unsuccessful because they could not demonstrate that the government's action or inaction contributed to the flooding.

(See Part Four, Section I.A.2. Government Liability in the United States for a full case summary of *St. Bernard Parish Government v. United States*.)

---

[36] *Michael Pierluisi, as Secretary of the Department of Consumer Affairs et al. v. MAPFRE PRAICO Ins. Co et al.*, SJ2018CV07570 (Tribunal de Primera Instancia Centro Judicial de San Juan 2018).

[37] *Harris County v. Arekma, Inc.*, 2017-76961 (D. Ct. Harris Cty. 2017).

[38] *St. Bernard Par. Gov't v. United States*, 887 F.3d 1354 (Fed. Cir. 2018), *cert. denied sub nom. St.Bernard Par. v. United States*, 139 S. Ct. 796, 202 L. Ed. 2d 571 (2019).

B.   Asia and the Pacific Approaches

Asia and the Pacific is arguably more affected by climate change disaster than any other region. The Germanwatch Global Climate Risk Index 2019 listed five Asian countries in its top 10 countries most affected by climate change in 2017.[39] For 1998–2017, Germanwatch reports that Myanmar (third), the Philippines (fifth), Bangladesh (seventh), Pakistan (eighth), and Viet Nam (ninth) are in the 10 countries most affected by climate change.[40]

The Germanwatch Global Climate Risk Index is not a comprehensive assessment of climate vulnerability. It does not assess slow onset impacts from sea level rise, saltwater incursion, ocean acidification, or melting glaciers—impacts that threaten the Pacific.[41] As such, low-lying Pacific atolls do not factor in this index. And yet, Pacific atolls already grapple with monster storms, sea level rise, and saltwater inundation. Notwithstanding these impacts, there are no reported cases about these impacts from the Pacific.

1.   Disaster Relief for People in South Asia

Despite the high number of climate-induced disasters, post-disaster litigation in Asia and the Pacific remains novel. Nevertheless, litigants in Bangladesh and India have argued for government relief following damaging storms.

BELA Vs. Bangladesh & Ors. deals with post-disaster relief following Cyclone Aila.[42] The cyclone tore through the Khulna and Satkhira districts in Bangladesh on 25 May 2009, killing around 190 people.[43] Strong tidal surges destroyed approximately 1,000 km of embankments, flooded significant parts of the districts, and left hundreds of thousands homeless and distressed.[44] According to the petitioners, the cyclone destroyed more than 83,000 houses in Satkhira. By December 2009, thousands of people still lived in temporary shelters, and embankments remained damaged.

The petitioners argued that the Bangladesh constitution and laws entitled them to the necessities of life. They maintained that Cyclone Aila had demonstrated that Bangladesh was unprepared to deal with the magnitude of natural disasters anticipated with climate change. The petitioners sought directions ordering the repair and maintenance of damaged embankments in coastal zones and the

---

[39]   D. Eckstein, M. Hutfils, and M. Winges. 2018. *Global Climate Risk Index 2019: Who Suffers Most from Extreme Weather Events? Weather-Related Loss Events in 2017 and 1998 to 2017.* Briefing Paper. Bonn: Germanwatch e.V. Table 1. Germanwatch reports that the Climate Risk Index indicates a level of exposure and vulnerability to extreme events.

[40]   Footnote 39, Table 2. p. 8.

[41]   Footnote 39, p. 3.

[42]   *BELA Vs. Bangladesh & Ors,* Writ Petition No. 8483 of 2009.

[43]   Islamic Relief. 2014. *Still Feeling the Toll of Cyclone Aila.* 5 June.

[44]   Emergency Capacity Building Project. 2009. Bangladesh: Hundreds of Thousands Still Homeless Three Months after Cyclone Aila. London. Reliefweb. 24 August.

construction of shelters in cyclone-vulnerable coastal districts. The petitioners also sought adequate food, health care services, and sanitation for residents remaining in shelters.

The Supreme Court of Bangladesh granted interim orders. It directed the government to declare the disaster-affected areas, repair damaged embankments, and provide support to affected residents until they were able to return to their homes and work. Otherwise, this case remains pending.

Early access to crop insurance for farmers devastated by storms arose in *Subhash C. Pandey v. Union of India.*[45] Severe rain and hailstorms hit the Indian state of Madhya Pradesh in early 2014 just before the harvest, leaving crops unfit for harvest. The applicant alleged that farmers had suffered hardship and burned their crops to remove crop residue, causing severe environmental pollution. The farmers needed humanitarian relief. The applicant told the National Green Tribunal (NGT) that the National Agricultural Insurance Scheme had not yet paid farmers, with some desperate farmers committing suicide.

Primarily concerned by the crop burning, the NGT constituted a committee to recommend environmentally sustainable options for managing crop residue. Following the committee's recommendations, the state government announced it would distribute straw reapers to farmers to help them to collect and use crop residue rather than burning it. The NGT asked the government and the government insurance scheme to consider measures that would enable payment of interim relief to affected farmers. It noted that such measures might prevent suicides, protecting dependent families from further trauma. The NGT also suggested that the government revise the scheme rules for declaring a disaster—a prerequisite to payment of compensation.

Gaurav Kumar Bansal v. Union of India and Ors concerned disaster response in India.[46] Two writ petitions asked the Supreme Court of India to direct the national and state governments to properly prepare for disasters and implement the Disaster Management Act, 2005. The petitioners sought the development of national and state disaster management plans. The litigation followed the deadly and unprecedented flood and landslide disaster in the state of Uttarakhand in 2013. The court observed that if the state government had effectively implemented the disaster management law and adequately prepared, "the disaster could have been mitigated."[47]

During the hearing, the union government directed all state governments to prepare minimum standards and guidelines for disasters. The guidelines should cover the provision of food, water, sanitation, and medical cover to disaster

---

[45]   *Subhash C. Pandey v. Union of India*, Original Appeal No. 107/2014 (CZ) (National Green Tribunal, 2 December 2014).

[46]   *Gaurav Kumar Bansal v. Union of India and Others,* Civil Appeal No. 444 of 2013 (Supreme Court, 8 May 2017).

[47]   Footnote 46, para. 1.

victims, with special provisions for widows and orphans. The union government prepared and approved the national plan for disaster management, and each state constituted a state disaster management authority. When the court issued a judgment, all states except two had prepared a state disaster management plan. More than 600 districts had completed their district disaster management plans, with preparation underway for those districts without a plan.

The Supreme Court entered judgment in 2017, being satisfied that there had been sufficient compliance with the law. However, the court stressed the need for vigilance at all levels of government. It encouraged the National Disaster Management Authority to regularly publish its annual report for the benefit of concerned stakeholders and to update plans based on experience.

(See Part Five, Section V.B. Impacts of Resource Scarcity and Disaster on Women in South Asia for further discussion of this case.)

2. Disaster Relief for Ecosystems in South Asia

Post-disaster litigation can also extend to ecosystem relief and protection. Forest fires in Uttarakhand prompted the High Court of Uttarakhand to direct the central government to create a national forest policy in *Protection of Forest Environment v. Union of India*.[48] A 2015 forest survey revealed that half of India's national forest and tree cover (around 25% of the country's geographical area) was fire prone. Further evidence demonstrated that forest officers lacked the training and resources to control forest fires. The court devoted much attention to wildlife impacted by the fires. Forests, the court said, minimized pollution, absorbed CO_2, and regulated the climate.

The court concluded there was a legal and moral obligation to protect forests. In addition to ordering a national forest policy, the court directed governments to strengthen disaster management plans. Among other things, it also instructed state governments to (i) provide funding to control forest fires, (ii) repair early warning alert systems, and (iii) require developers to maintain at least 20% greenery in housing development projects. It concluded, "Let us save forest to save ourselves."[49]

3. Suing Private Entities in the Philippines

The Philippines has been home to a vanguard human rights inquiry into alleged violations by the world's "carbon majors." In 2015, a collective of petitioners—including survivors of Super Typhoon Haiyan and fisherfolk from Alabat, Philippines—filed a complaint against carbon majors at the Philippine Commission on Human Rights (CHR).[50] Central to the case was the impact of

---

[48] *Protection of Forest Environment v. Union of India*, 2016 SCC OnLine Utt 2073.
[49] Footnote 48, p. 47.
[50] Case No. CHR-NI-2016-0001, Commission on Human Rights Philippines. The carbon major are 47 investor-owned producers of oil, natural gas, coal, and cement.

Typhoon Haiyan (Yolanda) damage and rehabilitation. Myrna Ecija and her family lost their house in Barangay 67. Her family decided to stay and rebuild their house from the debris where their house formerly stood (photo by Ariel Javellana/ADB).

disasters on vulnerable communities in the Philippines. The petitioners argued that the carbon majors had contributed to climate change, which was impacting their human rights. Further, the petitioners asserted that the carbon majors should bear responsibility for these impacts.

In formally opening the investigation, the chair of the CHR stated:

> We can no longer ignore the impact of significant changes in global temperatures and the rising sea levels on people's lives. We have been witness ourselves in this country to a spate of natural disasters and super typhoons such as Ondoy, Sendong, Pablo, and of course Yolanda, with grave consequences. Some of the survivors and victims of these disasters who have directly suffered from them are here with us today.[51]

In December 2019, Commissioner Cadiz discussed the commission's findings during the United Nation's annual climate summit.[52] The carbon majors, said Commissioner Cadiz, have contributed to dangerous climate change—a climate emergency that is impacting human rights (footnote 52). People must have the right to access justice and remedies for these impacts. Therefore, the carbon majors may be held legally and morally liable for the impacts of climate change.

---

[51] J.L.M.C. Gascon. 2018. First day of hearing in Case No. CHR-NI-2016-0001. Manila. Quoted in *Greenpeace International*. 2018. Landmark Human Rights Hearings against Fossil Fuel Companies Begin in the Philippines. 27 March.

[52] J. Paris. 2019. CHR: Big Oil, Cement Firms Legally, Morally Liable for Climate Change Effects. *Rappler*. 11 December; and T. Challe. 2020. Philippines Human Rights Commission Found Carbon Majors Can Be Liable for Climate Impacts. *Sabin Center for Climate Change Law: Climate Law Blog*. 10 January.

The commission concluded that it could not impose legal liability under international human rights law for climate damage resulting from fossil fuel extraction and trading. Instead, the commission stated that national courts might hold fossil fuel companies accountable under domestic laws. When determining liability for climate-related harm, national courts could reference international human rights law as a standard.

Commissioner Cadiz cautioned fossil fuel companies against continuing their businesses as usual (footnote 52). He stressed that moral liability could transform into legal liability as corporate regulatory frameworks evolve over this century. Further, in the commission's opinion, the carbon majors were exposed to both civil and criminal liability, especially for fraud, willful obfuscation, and obstruction. In short, where climate denial or other actions amount to criminal behavior, corporate executives may be exposed to criminal prosecution.[53] The commission has yet to publish its decision at the time of writing.

(See Part Three, Section I.B.1. Human Rights and Climate Change in the Philippines for further discussion of this case.)

III. Participatory Rights

Participatory rights help ensure that those affected by environmental decision-making, including the most vulnerable, can shape the outcomes that impact their lives. Recognizing this, the UN Framework Convention on Climate Change (UNFCCC) encourages states "to promote and facilitate public participation in addressing climate change and its effects and developing adequate responses."[54] It is not always clear what constitutes "effective" or "adequate" public participation. Yet at a minimum, meaningful public participation requires (i) assessment and disclosure of environmental impacts; (ii) effective communication of those impacts, e.g., in a language and venue that are accessible to the persons who will be affected; and (iii) an opportunity for affected persons to "voice their concerns."[55]

This section discusses challenges to government-led public participation processes made by environmental organizations and community groups. In assessing whether participatory rights have been violated, courts have relied on applicable international, national, and constitutional law.

---

[53]   Center for International Environmental Law. 2019. Groundbreaking Inquiry in Philippines Links Carbon Majors to Human Rights Impacts of Climate Change, Calls for Greater Accountability. News release. 9 December.

[54]   *United Nations Framework Convention on Climate Change*, New York, 9 May 1992, *United Nations Treaty Series*, Vol. 1771, No. 30822, p. 107, art. 6.

[55]   United Nations. 2012. *Report of the United Nations Conference on Sustainable Development.* UN Doc. A/CONF.216/6. p. 2.

A.   Global Approaches

1.   Nuclear Policy in the United Kingdom

Multilateral conventions may set legally enforceable standards for public participation in environmental matters. In *Greenpeace v Secretary of State for Trade and Industry*, for example, the High Court of Justice in the UK upheld a challenge to a government-backed consultation process based on EU law.[56] The challenge, led by the environmental NGO Greenpeace, concerned the UK government's nuclear policy.

The secretary of state for trade and industry had announced a 12-month consultation process in 2005 around the government's review of its nuclear power station policy. Despite many submissions against nuclear energy, the secretary of state published a report announcing that the government would support the construction of new nuclear plants in the country. The plaintiffs claimed that the consultation had been flawed, and the court agreed.

The court reminded the secretary of state that the government had signed and ratified the Aarhus Convention on Access to Information, Public Participation in Decision-Making and Access to Justice in Environmental Matters (footnote 56). The government was thus bound by international law to provide full public consultation. The court highlighted, among other shortfalls, that insufficient information was given to consultees, that the consultation document was seriously misleading, and that the consultation period was insufficient. Nevertheless, the court held that the better outcome in the case was to grant declaratory relief, rather than a quashing order as asked by the plaintiffs.

2.   Coal Mine Extraction in Australia

In *River SOS Inc v Minister of Planning*, the New South Wales Land and Environment Court upheld a government official's approval process for the expansion of a coal mine.[57] A community group challenged the New South Wales planning minister's mining approval process, claiming that the process did not meet public participation standards. The minister approved a $50 million expansion of a coal mine in June 2009. Later in the assessment process, the minister approved a substantially revised version of the project without providing any further opportunities for public participation.

The body responsible for conducting a public hearing on the proposed mine expansion, the Independent Planning Commission, held a public hearing on the earlier version of the mine plan but not the revised version. The community group claimed that the commission's failure to conduct a public hearing on the revised mine plan violated a statutory duty under state law—in particular, the Environmental Planning and Assessment Act, 1979.

---

[56]   *Greenpeace v Secretary of State for Trade and Industry* [2007] EWHC 311 (Admin).
[57]   *River SOS Inc v Minister of Planning* [2009] NSWELC 213.

The court determined that the commission had no statutory duty to conduct public hearings. The act only required the commission to conduct a public hearing if the planning minister requested it. In this case, the minister had asked that the commission conduct a hearing. The commission did hold a hearing in relation to the earlier version of the mine approval plan. Therefore, the court reasoned that the commission had fulfilled its duty and upheld the minister's approval of the coal mine expansion.

3. Cap and Trade in Canada

In *Greenpeace Canada v Minister of the Environment, Conservation (Ontario)*, environmental groups filed suit against the provincial government of Ontario in Canada.[58] The plaintiffs claimed that the government failed to meet legal requirements for public consultation on regulations that would end Ontario's cap-and-trade program, and for a proposed bill to combat climate change. The plaintiffs also claimed that the proposed bill would undermine the province's legislative regime for fighting climate change by repealing the Climate Change Mitigation and Low-Carbon Economy Act, 2016. The act included targets to reduce GHG emissions.

The plaintiffs argued that the government's failure to hold a notice and comment period on the regulations and the proposed bill violated the Environmental Bill of Rights, which gave Ontario citizens the statutory right to participate in environmental decision-making in Ontario. For example, the bill requires the government to undertake a notice and comment process on decisions that have a significant environmental impact. A Canadian divisional court dismissed the case.

B. Asia and the Pacific Approaches

Vulnerable groups are disproportionately affected by climate change impacts. Some vulnerable groups—such as children, the elderly, and women—suffer more during natural disasters due to their smaller size or mobility issues. Competing for food, water, or the resources to seek help can be difficult. Other vulnerable groups—such as indigenous peoples—face "political and economic marginalization, loss of land and resources, human rights violations, discrimination and unemployment," and climate change will exacerbate these challenges.[59] Furthermore, indigenous peoples and poor minorities are frequently excluded from disaster responses.

Asia is also home to around two-thirds of the world's indigenous peoples.[60] Ensuring the right of vulnerable groups in the region to participate meaningfully in policy, planning, and implementation of climate change-related initiatives and

---

[58] *Greenpeace Canada v Minister of the Environment (Ontario)*, (2018) Case no. 575/18 (Can.).
[59] United Nations. Climate Change and Indigenous Peoples: Backgrounder.
[60] S. Errico. 2017. *The Rights of Indigenous Peoples in Asia: Executive Summary*. Geneva: International Labour Organization.

projects, including energy projects, can secure a more equitable result for all. Courts can protect the right to participate.

1.   Failure to Consult in South Asia

Courts in Asia have considered the right of public consultation for expressways. *Imrana Tiwana v. Province of Punjab* concerned the failure of the Lahore Development Authority (LDA) to consult with the public about a 7-km expressway in the Pakistani city of Lahore.[61] Litigants challenged the expressway's EIA along with the approval granted by the Environmental Protection Agency (EPA). The petitioners stressed that the LDA (i) failed to seek public comment on the expressway when preparing the EIA, and (ii) commenced construction before obtaining project approval from the EPA. Rather than conducting a merits review, the High Court of Lahore focused on the constitutional dimensions of the case, in particular the essential nature of environmental justice to fundamental rights.

The court observed that the global community designed EIAs to function as a sustainable development tool. Thus, EIAs integrated "environmental considerations into socio-economic development and decision-making processes."[62] The court stressed that public participation, "akin to environmental democracy, . . . is an integral part of EIA and affirms that public is the direct beneficiary of the environment and must be heard."[63] Therefore, public consultation required project proponents to seek the views of the public as well as other concerned stakeholders, including government agencies.

The court held that the LDA's failure to seek public comment or to await the protection agency's approval before commencing construction was a fatal flaw. It set aside the EIA for the construction phase.

> " Public participation, which is akin to environmental democracy, and as provided above, is an integral part of EIA and affirms that public is the direct beneficiary of the environment and must be heard.
>
> Source: *Imrana Tiwana v. Province of Punjab*, PLD 2015 Lahore 522, para. 41, p. 53.

(See Part Two, Section V.B.2.a. More Highways, More Emissions in Pakistan for a full case summary of *Imrana Tiwana v. Province of Punjab*; and Part Two, Section I.B.1.b. Constitutional Rights in Pakistan for further discussion of this case.)

In *Heather Therese Mundy v Central Environmental Authority* in Sri Lanka, the appellant argued that she was denied an opportunity to be heard in relation to the proposed Colombo–Matara Expressway.[64] The Road Development Authority (RDA) submitted an EIA report for the expressway based on an identified route, which

---

[61]   *Imrana Tiwana v. Province of Punjab*, PLD 2015 Lahore 522.
[62]   Footnote 61, para. 35, p. 47.
[63]   Footnote 61, para. 41, p. 53.
[64]   *Heather Therese Mundy v Central Environmental Authority*, SC Appeal 58/2003.

the Central Environmental Agency approved conditionally. After modifying the route to the "final trace," the RDA sought to compulsorily acquire the appellant's land, which sat along the final trace. The RDA did not seek further approval from the environmental agency for the modified route or consult with the appellant. The plaintiff argued that the RDA had violated her constitutional right to equality before the law because it failed to give her notice or consult with her.

The Supreme Court of Sri Lanka concluded that the final trace constituted an alteration to the project. Therefore, the RDA ought to seek environmental agency approval for the alteration after complying with applicable EIA procedures and affording the appellants natural justice. As the project impacted the appellant, she was entitled to natural justice and had a right to comment on the final trace.

The court allowed the project to proceed to avoid further delay and public expense. However, it ordered the RDA to compensate the appellant for the breach of natural justice and infringement of her constitutional right to equality before the law.

In *Hanuman Laxman Aroskar v. Union of India*, the Supreme Court of India held that "responsive, inclusive, participatory and representative decision making are key ingredients to the rule of law."[65] The appellants challenged the environmental clearance granted to a greenfield international airport in the state of Goa. They argued that the project proponent's EIA had disclosed neither the need to cut down 54,676 trees nor the impacts on ecologically sensitive zones in the neighboring state of Maharashtra.

Around 1,500 people had participated in public consultations, with 70 people speaking and 1,150 comments made. While stakeholders had expressed various environmental concerns about impacts on water and nearby cashew plantations, the project proponent omitted these concerns from the materials provided to the Expert Appraisal Committee. Appellants argued that the government's decision-making process in granting environmental clearance was flawed.

Considering the purpose of India's EIA procedure, the court reasoned that the procedural requirements contained in the 2006 notification embodied a meaningful link to the union government's quest to pursue the Sustainable Development Goals (SDGs). It emphasized that the development goals seek to "protect, restore and promote sustainable use of terrestrial ecosystems, sustainably."[66] It concluded that ecosystem protection was, therefore, crucial to combating climate change.

The court also described a broadened notion of sustainable development. Sustainable development should move from "a need-based standard to a standard based on freedoms."[67] A freedom-based approach to sustainable

---

[65] *Hanuman Laxman Aroskar v. Union of India*, 2019 SCC OnLine SC 441. pp. 87–88, para. 140.
[66] SDG 15. The court stated that SDG 16 "emphasises the need to protect, restore and promote sustainable use" (footnote 65, p. 86, para. 137); however, that was a reference to SDG 15.
[67] Footnote 65, p. 81, para. 129.

development meant that environmental preservation enabled current generations to enjoy expanded freedoms without compromising the capability of future generations to have similar privileges.

> "
> Maintenance of eco systems [*sic*] is hence crucial to efforts to combat climate change, mitigate and reduce the risks of natural disasters including floods and landslides. In this backdrop, promoting environmental justice and ensuring strong institutions is quintessential to promoting peaceful and inclusive societies for sustainable development.
>
> Source: *Hanuman Laxman Aroskar v. Union of India*, 2019 SCC OnLine SC 441, p. 86, para. 137.

Within the environmental governance framework, the court considered that the processes of making the decision "are as crucial as the ultimate decision."[68] For that reason, the EIA regulatory process had prescribed a process of "disclosures, studies, gathering data, consultation and appraisal … that would secure decision making which is transparent, responsive and inclusive" (footnote 68). These findings imply that stakeholders have the freedom to participate.

The Supreme Court held that there had been an "abject failure" of due process commencing with the project proponent's nondisclosure of vital project information.[69] It directed the Expert Appraisal Committee to revisit its recommendations.

(See Part Two, Section V.B.3. Airports and a Failure of Due Process in South Asia for a full case summary of *Hanuman Laxman Aroskar v. Union of India*.)

In January 2020, the Supreme Court determined that the airport project could proceed.[70] It was satisfied that the project proponent had sought to remedy its failures by considering additional information and that the environmental clearance and previous court orders imposed mitigatory conditions. The court, therefore, deemed it appropriate to appoint the National Environmental Engineering Research Institute to oversee compliance with the court's directions.

IV. Indigenous Rights

The UN Declaration on the Rights of Indigenous Peoples recognizes that "Indigenous peoples have the collective right to live in freedom, peace and security" and a corresponding right "not to be subjected to forced assimilation or destruction of their culture."[71]

---

[68] Footnote 65, p. 88, para. 141.

[69] Footnote 65, p. 43, para. 67.

[70] *Hanuman Laxman Aroskar v. Union of India*, MA No. 965 of 2019 (Supreme Court of India, 16 January 2020).

[71] General Assembly Resolution 61/295, *United Nations Declaration on the Rights of Indigenous Peoples*, A/RES/61/295 (13 September 2007), articles 7 & 8.

Climate change will likely destroy or damage many ecosystems that indigenous people rely on for their livelihoods and cultural identity. Resource scarcity resulting from damaged ecosystems has the potential to drive indigenous peoples permanently or temporarily from their land. Displacement can undermine indigenous peoples' physical, emotional, spiritual, or economic attachment to their land, making them especially vulnerable to climate change impacts. These impacts mean that climate change possibly violates the principle laid out in the declaration. Indeed, the Inter-American Court of Human Rights has decided several cases on the obligation to protect indigenous rights in the context of projects that affect their lands and resources.[72]

Men of the Huli from Mount Hagen, Papua New Guinea. Nearly two-thirds of the world's indigenous peoples live in Asia and the Pacific. Climate change threatens their territories, culture, and lives (photo by Trevor Cole).

A. Global Approaches: Climate Change in Australia and Black Carbon in Canada

Some undecided cases have also spoken more directly to the issue of indigenous rights and climate change. The plaintiffs in the *Petition of Torres Strait Islanders to the United Nations Human Rights Committee Alleging Violations Stemming from Australia's Inaction on Climate Change* submitted a petition against the Australian government to the UN Human Rights Committee. They alleged that the government's failure to address climate change violated their fundamental human rights under the International Covenant on Civil and Political Rights.[73] That petition is pending.

(See Part Four, Section I.A.1. A Violation of Human Rights in Australia and France for a full case summary of the Petition of Torres Strait Islanders to the *United Nations Human Rights Committee Alleging Violations Stemming from Australia's Inaction on Climate Change*.)

In the *Petition to the Inter-American Commission on Human Rights Seeking Relief from Violations of the Rights of Arctic Athabaskan Peoples Resulting from Rapid Arctic Warming and Melting Caused by Emissions of Black Carbon by Canada*, the Arctic Athabaskan Council claimed that Canada's fragmentary and loose regulations of

---

[72] See, e.g., *Saramaka People v. Surin*, 2007 Inter-Am. Ct. H.R. (ser. C) No. 172, para. 95 (Nov. 28, 2007); *Indigenous Cmty. Yakye Axa v. Para.*, Inter-Am. Ct. H.R. (ser. C), No. 146, para. 143 (June 17, 2005); *Maya Indigenous Cmty. Of the Toledo Dist. v. Belize*, Case 12.053, Inter-Am. Ct. H.R., Response No. 40/04, OEA/SEr.L/V/II.122 doc. 5 rev., para. 113 (2004); *Indigenous Community of Awas Tingni v. Nicaragua*, Inter-Am. Ct. H.R. (Ser. C) No. 79, para. 148 (Aug. 31, 2001).

[73] *Petition of Torres Strait Islanders to the United Nations Human Rights Committee Alleging Violations Stemming from Australia's Inaction on Climate Change* (UN H.R. Comm. filed 2019).

black carbon emissions threatened the Athabaskan people's human rights.[74] The indigenous petitioners claimed a violation of their rights to property, preservation of health, the benefits of their culture, and their means of subsistence as established by the American Declaration of the Rights and Duties of Man.

The petition described high rates of warming in the Arctic and the impacts of that warming on the Athabaskan people. For example, ecological disruptions made hunting and fishing more difficult and undermined the Athabaskan people's ability to maintain cultural traditions. The petitioners attempted to establish a causal chain between the government's lack of regulation of black carbon, Arctic warming, and the harm they were suffering. The petitioners also claimed that Canada was violating its duties to avoid transboundary harm and protect the environment as required by the precautionary principle. The case has not yet been decided.

A similar petition, *Petition to the Inter-American Commission on Human Rights Seeking Relief from Violations Resulting from Global Warming Caused by Acts and Omissions of the United States*, was filed with the Inter-American Commission on Human Rights.[75] The commission declined to exercise jurisdiction over the matter.[76]

B.   Asia and the Pacific Approaches

Around 260 million indigenous peoples live in Asia—roughly two-thirds of the world's indigenous peoples (footnote 60). Indigenous peoples have profound spiritual, cultural, and physical ties with their land. They traditionally live subsistence lifestyles, farming, herding, fishing, and hunting.[77] Their close relationship with their land and its resources means that indigenous peoples are among the first to face the effects of climate change. Such effects magnify the "political and economic marginalization, loss of land and resources, human rights violations, discrimination and unemployment" that indigenous peoples currently face (footnote 59).

Courts in Asia and the Pacific have not seen climate-specific litigation from indigenous peoples. But that is not because indigenous communities are not affected by climate change. Sea level rise, ocean acidification, droughts, and cyclones threaten indigenous communities in the Pacific.[78] Across Asia and the Pacific, indigenous peoples face displacement from extreme weather events,

---

[74] *Petition to the Inter-American Commission on Human Rights Seeking Relief from Violations of the Rights of Arctic Athabaskan Peoples Resulting from Rapid Arctic Warming and Melting Caused by Emissions of Black Carbon by Canada* (Inter-Am. Comm'n H.R. filed 2013).

[75] *Petition to the Inter-American Commission on Human Rights Seeking Relief from Violations Resulting from Global Warming Caused by Acts and Omissions of the United States* (Inter-Am. Comm'n H.R. filed 2005).

[76] *Sheila Watt-Cloutier, et al.*, Petition N° P-1413-05 United States (Nov. 16, 2006).

[77] M. Cherrington. 2008. Indigenous Peoples and Climate Change. *Cultural Survival Quarterly Magazine.* 32 (2).

[78] Pan American Health Organization and World Health Organization. 2014. *Recommendations for Engaging Indigenous Peoples in Disaster Risk Reduction.* p. 11.

infrastructure projects, and predatory land acquisition connected with biofuels. Each of these happenings has a climate dimension. Where the infrastructure project is for renewable energy or farmland is needed for biofuel, the issues are connected with climate change.

This discussion aims to highlight some of the issues that judges may wish to consider when responding to litigation involving indigenous peoples in this era of climate change. Indeed, rights-based approaches may be warranted to ensure justice in the Anthropocene.[79]

1. Land Acquisition for Hydropower in Malaysia

Three indigenous men (respondents) argued that a hydropower dam in Malaysia would impact the environment, impairing their livelihood in *Ketua Pengarah Jabatan Alam Sekitar & Anor v Kajing Tubek & Ors & Other Appeals*.[80] The project proposed to resettle 10,000 indigenous peoples from their land in Sarawak, Malaysia. The respondents did not represent the other impacted indigenous peoples, nor did they dispute the resettlement or compensation. Instead, they claimed that the project proponent denied them procedural fairness—it failed to give them a copy of the project EIA.

Respondents argued that the project proponent had, therefore, failed to comply with the Malaysian EIA law. Finding that the respondents had no cause of action, the court dismissed the matter. A state ordinance applied to the project and not the national EIA law. As such, the respondents had no right to receive or comment on the project EIA.

Despite dismissing the case, the court acknowledged the harm caused by depriving indigenous people of their culture. It stated that divestment of one's livelihood or one's way of life—in this case of one's culture—amounted to a deprivation of the constitutional right to life. However, because the government was taking life in accordance with existing and valid law, it was a legal deprivation of life. Therefore, the respondents had not suffered an injury that could be remedied under Malaysian law.

2. Excess Waste and Impacts on Indigenous Peoples in Fiji

Where indigenous peoples suffer current or future environmental impacts, courts and tribunals can include consideration of fundamental rights in decision-making processes. Such an approach will be useful when adjudicating climate change and sustainable development.

---

[79] Scientists have defined the Anthropocene as a new geological epoch on Earth that has been profoundly influenced by human action. See D. Carrington. 2016. The Anthropocene Epoch: Scientists Declare Dawn of Human-Influenced Age. *The Guardian.* 29 August; Subcommission on Quaternary Stratigraphy. 2019. *Results of binding vote by AWG.* 21 May.

[80] *Ketua Pengarah Jabatan Alam Sekitar & Anor v Kajing Tubek & Ors & Other Appeals* [1997] 4 CLJ 253.

In *re Irava Bottle Shop,* a licensing authority refused an application for a fifth liquor store within the 2,000-person indigenous community in Fiji.[81] The health inspector had objected to the application because of concerns regarding excess waste from beer bottles. He described beer bottle retaining walls behind residents' houses. The beer bottles could not be recycled on Rotuma Island and created a risk of mosquito-borne diseases.

The authority considered there was a need to protect residents from excess hazardous waste and alcohol abuse. It noted that such a finding was consistent with Fiji's Environmental Management Act 2005, which seeks to protect Fiji's environment from waste and pollution.

The authority also reviewed international norms, including those within the UN Declaration on the Rights of Indigenous Peoples.[82] The declaration, it said, obliged states to prevent the storage of hazardous waste in indigenous communities without their free, prior, and informed consent (FPIC). Rather than calling for a site visit, the authority considered the history of Rotuma's cession into Fiji. Rotuma's tribal chiefs had agreed to cede their territory, wishing for the "peace and security" of the Rotuman people. Protecting the island from excessive waste was consistent with peace and order, in the authority's opinion.

Furthermore, states should protect families—society's natural and fundamental group unit—and improve the environment for present and future generations.[83] In the circumstances, the authority considered it "our business to protect [the] environment for future generations as we do not own this soil or this world; but we borrowed it from our future generations."[84]

3. Steel Mill in Pakistan Causing Pollution

The Peshawar High Court also adopted a rights-based approach to protect tribal land against pollution in Peshawar, Pakistan.

In *Ali Steel Industry v. Government of Khyber Pakhtunkhwa,* a steel manufacturer challenged an order ceasing its steel mill operation.[85] The environmental protection authority found that the mill operators had not (i) obtained the required environmental clearances, or (ii) installed a pollution control system. The inspection revealed that the mill was in a densely populated area, close to schools and a children's medical center, and was releasing dangerous air pollution.

Ali Steel Industry argued that its mill was within the Provincially Administered Tribal Area, an area unregulated by the state environmental law. Hence, the

81 In *re Irava Bottle Shop* [2013] FJLLAE 1.
82 General Assembly Resolution 61/295, *United Nations Declaration on the Rights of Indigenous Peoples,* A/RES/61/295 (13 September 2007), articles 7 & 8.
83 Footnote 81, paras. 32–24.
84 Footnote 81, paras. 31.
85 *Ali Steel Industry v. Government of Khyber Pakhtunkhwa,* 2016 CLD 569.

environmental protection authority lacked jurisdiction to issue a closure order under the Environmental Protection Act, 2014.

The court dismissed the case. It could not ignore air pollution that was dangerous to human health. The court reasoned that the non-extension of environmental laws to the community did not "grant any license to any person to threaten the health or life of the locales by one's actions/activities."[86] The right question was whether air pollution was hazardous to human life and the surrounding environment. The court held that the right to an environment that did not harm health or well-being and that protected present and future generations was essential to political and social justice in Pakistan. Such a right was integral to the constitutional rights to life and dignity.

The *Ali Steel* case highlights that courts and tribunals can make decisions to protect the environment and interests of indigenous peoples simply by adjudicating the issue before them. Constitutional rights and universal principles of sustainable development, intergenerational equity, and public trust provide effective judicial tools for adjudicating environmental and climate change disputes involving indigenous peoples.

4. Palm Oil in Asia

Its capacity for lowering emissions made palm oil biofuel a popular option for fighting climate change.[87] But its spike in popularity has harmed indigenous peoples across Asia. In 2008, the chairperson of the UN Permanent Forum on Indigenous Issues warned that continued expansion of biofuel plantations could rob up to 60 million indigenous people of their land and livelihoods.[88] Unscrupulous biofuel producers resorted to intimidation, violence, and land grabbing to acquire land for palm oil plantations (footnote 88).

The Kapa indigenous community of Western Sumatra has been embroiled in a land dispute with Wilmar International—the world's largest palm oil company—for over 5 years. In 2017, the Roundtable on Sustainable Palm Oil ruled that Wilmar International had violated the Kapa's rights.[89] In 2005, Wilma International paid compensation to the Kapa under a "peace agreement" (footnote 89).

Subsequently, the local government granted Wilmar International interim permits to establish a palm oil plantation in the Kapa's land. However, the Kapa asserted that they never granted their FPIC to a land use rights permit over their land.

---

[86] Footnote 85, para. 8.

[87] Biofuels are liquid or gas fuels made from corn, palm oil, sugarcane, soya, and wheat. Bioenergy covers approximately 10% of the total world energy supply. *GreenFacts*. 2020. Liquid Biofuels for Transport Prospects, Risks and Opportunities; and S.S. Abdul Ghani. 2019. Could the EU's Ban on Palm Oil in Biofuels Do More Harm Than Good? *World Economic Forum*. 8 October.

[88] Survival. 2008. *Biofuels Threaten Lands of 60 Million Tribal People*. 30 April.

[89] R. Diaz-Bastin. 2017. *Wilmar Appeals RSPO Ruling that It Grabbed Indigenous Lands in Sumatra*. Mongabay. 17 May.

Community members complained that Wilmar International's operations deprived them of accessing and controlling customary lands. The Roundtable on Sustainable Palm Oil rules require member companies to obtain FPIC from indigenous communities. Hence, it ruled in favor of the Kapa. Although Wilma International requested a merits review of their decision in 2017, the matter remained unresolved.[90]

This dispute highlights the challenges for indigenous communities and companies in working with each other. Projects within indigenous communities' lands can result in physical, economic, or spiritual displacement. Despite the passage of the UN Declaration on the Rights of Indigenous Peoples in 2007, not all countries recognize the rights of indigenous peoples to exercise FPIC or share the profits of resource exploitation in their territories (footnote 82).

FPIC is mandatory in the Philippines under Republic Act No. 8371 (the Indigenous Peoples' Rights Act of 1997). In *Orissa Mining Corporation Ltd. v. Ministry of Environment & Forest & Others*, the Supreme Court of India imposed FPIC as a precondition to final government approval for a bauxite mining project impacting traditional lands.[91] It was irrelevant that the community did not live on the affected lands.

Even if not required by law, many financiers demand borrowers to adhere to the Equator Principles, which obliges companies to seek FPIC from indigenous peoples.[92] However, the process of obtaining FPIC from indigenous communities can be challenging for everyone involved and differs across countries. The 2013 Equator Principles acknowledged there was "no universally accepted definition of FPIC" (footnote 92).

In 2017, the Equator Principles Association broadcasted its intent to update the principles, noting that updates were needed to clarify FPIC procedures and in a post-Paris Agreement climate.[93]

FPIC could also arise in national resettlement projects, pursued as an adaptation measure.

Disputes before courts and tribunals involving FPIC are likely to focus on whether the community granted consent. Rights-based approaches may be useful for courts in resolving issues like whether indigenous communities (i) had meaningful participation in an FPIC consultation process, and (ii) achieved consensus regarding a proposal. Protecting procedural rights will likely be key in such disputes.

---

[90] *Wilmar*. 2017. Update: Wilmar's Appeal on Land Conflict in West Sumatra Granted by the RSPO Complaints Panel. News release. 26 April; and P. Anderson. 2019. Report Shows Widespread Human Rights Violations in Wilmar's Palm Oil Operations in West Sumatra. Forest Peoples Programme. Press release. 4 November.

[91] *Orissa Mining Corporation Ltd. v. Ministry of Environment & Forest & Others*, Writ Petition (Civil) No. 180 of 2011 (Supreme Court of India, 18.04.2013).

[92] Equator Principles Association. 2013. *The Equator Principles: June 2013*. Principle 5: Stakeholder Engagement. pp. 7–8.

[93] Equator Principles Association. 2017. EP Association Annual Meeting 2017 Outcomes. News release. 2 November.

V. Women and Climate Change in Asia

Gender-based climate litigation is rare in Asia, and the authors found no cases in the Pacific. However, this lack of litigation does not mean that climate change is not impacting women. Indeed, "climate change is not neutral," especially in Asia and the Pacific.[94]

Women are disproportionately affected in climate-induced disasters and by resource scarcity in agrarian economies.[95] In developing countries, women constitute 43% of the agricultural workforce and yet grow 60%–80% of the food.[96] As climate change threatens food security across Asia and the Pacific, it will be crucial to ensure that women can access resources to enable them to continue producing food.

Protecting women's right to legally hold land is an effective way of safeguarding their capacity to grow food. While the issue of women's land rights may not seem connected with climate change, this section explores some of the connections between women and climate change.

A. Impacts on Women from Alleged Climate Inaction

In Pakistan, a coalition of women sued the government, seeking more aggressive climate mitigation action on the grounds that climate change disproportionately affects them as women.

In *Maria Khan et al. v. Federation of Pakistan et al.*, five women claimed that the government's climate "inaction" breaches commitments under the Paris Agreement and violated their fundamental rights as women.[97] The claim hinged on the government's alleged failure to support or approve renewable energy projects or to release an updated renewable energy policy. The petitioners asserted that the government's "deliberate inaction" was unconstitutional and unduly affected them as women, a class of citizens who were disproportionately disadvantaged by climate change.[98]

The petitioners contended that women suffer more from the effects of climate change because they "face social constraints, have less access to education and

---

[94] P. Hawken, ed. 2017. *Drawdown: The Most Comprehensive Plan Ever Proposed to Reverse Global Warming.* New York: Penguin Books.

[95] For example, after two tropical cyclones hit Tafea Province in Vanuatu in 2011, there was a 300% increase in new domestic violence cases. See D. Kilsby and H. Rosenbaum. 2012. *Scoping of Key Issues in Gender, Climate Change, and Disaster Risk Management.* Internal Briefing Document for UN Women. New York.

[96] FAO. 2011. *The State of Food and Agriculture 2010–2011.* Rome. p. 5.

[97] *Maria Khan et al. v. Pakistan et al.*, Writ Petition No. 8960 of 2019, High Court of Lahore. p. 4, para. 6.

[98] Footnote 97, p. 11, para. 24.

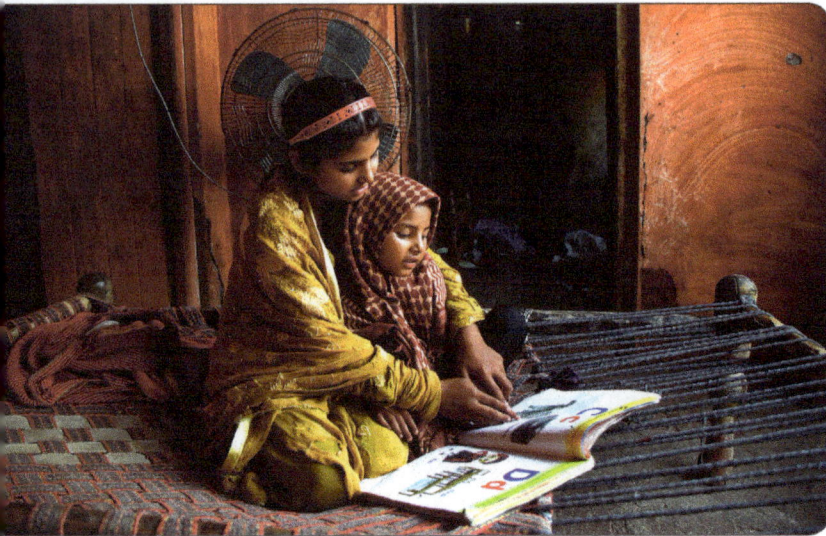

A young girl teachers her sister to read in Punjab, Pakistan. A case in Pakistan argues that women and girls suffer more from the effects of climate change because they face social constraints, lack educational opportunities, and are left out of political and household decision-making (photo by Sara Farid/ADB).

opportunities than men and are usually excluded from political and household decision-making processes."[99] During disasters, women are more likely to suffer due to their limited access to financial, natural, institutional, or social resources. Limited mobility—stemming from restrictive dress codes imposed on women—also renders women more vulnerable to disasters. Further, women's productive and reproductive activities make them disproportionately susceptible to changes in biodiversity, cropping patterns, and vector-borne diseases (footnote 99).

Given the disproportionate impacts of climate change on women, petitioners argued that the government must take more action in renewable energy development in Pakistan. This case remains pending before the High Court of Lahore.

(See Part One, Section II.B.3.a. The Energy Sector in Pakistan for a full case summary of *Maria Khan et al. v. Federation of Pakistan et al.*; Part One, Section III.B.1. Climate Change Commitments in South Asia; and Part One, Section IV.B.2. International Commitments in Pending Cases in South Asia for further discussion of this case.)

B.   Impacts of Resource Scarcity and Disaster on Women in South Asia

Courts in Asia have also recognized the impacts of climate change and resource scarcity on women. In *BELA Vs. Bangladesh*, BELA disputed the government's decision to allow shrimp cultivation in Chakaria (within the Sunderbans).[100] BELA argued that shrimp farms had cleared around 8,500 hectares of mangrove forest, polluted land and water bodies, and caused salinity intrusion to more than 60% of the cultivable land in three districts by the Bay of Bengal. BELA sought orders to protect and afforest coastal lands.

The Supreme Court of Bangladesh agreed with BELA's arguments. It reasoned that coastal afforestation provides important protection to coastal people's lives, safety, and property in this era of "extreme climatic events." The court expressed concerns over the impacts on women of resource scarcity caused by the salinity intrusion. It said, "In view of declining supply of eggs and milk from household poultry and fish and water from the ponds, women not only have to walk miles to collect drinking water for their families, but are also compelled to engage in shrimp fry/seed collection for extra earning to meet the family demands."[101]

---

[99]   Footnote 97, p. 12, para. 25.
[100]   *BELA Vs. Bangladesh*, WP No. 57 of 2010, D-/01-02-2012.
[101]   Footnote 100, p. 205.

(See Part Four, Section I.B.2.b. Protecting Mangroves in Bangladesh for a full case summary of *BELA Vs. Bangladesh.*)

The case of *Gaurav Kumar Bansal v. Union of India and Ors* resulted in national guidelines for disasters with special provisions for widows and orphans (footnote 46). In 2013, unprecedented heavy monsoon rains caused disastrous flooding and landslides in Uttarakhand.[102] The petitioners sued, wanting the national and state governments to develop disaster management plans. The court agreed and held multiple hearings to manage the matter.

Throughout the case, the union government reported that it had instructed all state governments to prepare minimum standards and guidelines for disasters. It also directed the state governments to ensure that the disaster guidelines took into account the needs of widows and orphans in post-disaster situations.

(See Part Five, Section II.B.1. Disaster Relief for People in South Asia for a full case summary of *Gaurav Kumar Bansal v. Union of India.*)

Knowledge about the impacts of resource scarcity and disaster on women is a useful tool in litigation. It equips courts with the capacity to direct or encourage government agencies to adopt gender-sensitive climate change planning and responses.

C. Female Landownership and Climate Change

Enabling women to own or hold legal tenure to land is effective climate change action.[103] Project Drawdown estimates that providing resources, financing, and training to women smallholder farmers around the world could reduce CO_2 emissions by 2.06 gigatons by 2050, ranking women smallholders as the 62nd most effective climate change solution.[104] That figure is around 5.5% of the total fossil fuel emissions in 2017.[105]

As discussed in the introduction to this section, women grow up to 80% of the food in developing economies (footnote 96). The Food and Agriculture Organization of the UN reports that rural women could boost their farm yields by 20%–30% if given the same access to productive resources as men (footnote 96). Such productive resources include land, technology, financial services, education, and markets. These increased farm yields could translate into reducing the number of hungry people globally by 12%–17% (footnote 96).

---

[102] *BBC News*. 2013. India Floods: More Than 5,700 People 'Presumed Dead'. 15 July.

[103] Footnote 94. Project Drawdown ranks women smallholders as the 62nd most effective climate change solution.

[104] Project Drawdown. Solutions. Project Drawdown is a research organization dedicated to reviewing, analyzing, and identifying the "most viable global climate solutions." See Project Drawdown. About Project Drawdown.

[105] Fossil fuels emitted 36.2 gigatons of CO_2 in 2017. *World Resources Institute*. 2018. New Global CO_2 Emissions Numbers Are In. They're Not Good. News release. 5 December.

Accessing finance and resources for farming is difficult for women because they frequently do not own or hold legal tenure over their farmland. Fewer than 20% of the world's landowners are women.[106] Female rates of landownership are lower in Asia, where women own around 10% of land.[107] In Pakistan, only 2% of women own land.[108] Women frequently face legal and customary barriers to acquiring or inheriting land, including when widowed.

Not having legal ownership of land also affects women's income capacity and ability to provide for their families. It diminishes their status in the community or household, limiting their capacity to participate in decision-making and making them vulnerable to displacement.[109] Displacement then exposes women to forced migration and trafficking.

Courts have the power to protect women's ability to hold or inherit land, which has flow-on benefits for climate action. In *Jance Faransina Mooy-Ndun v. Junus Ndoy et al.*, the Supreme Court of Indonesia invalidated a customary rule that the inheritance rights of women were not equal with those of men.[110] The court held that the customary law violated the principles of equality before the law and nondiscrimination under the Constitution of Indonesia.

In *Daw San Lwin v. Daw Than (aka) Daw Than Than*, the Supreme Court of Myanmar recognized a widow's right to inherit from her late husband's inherited property even though she had since remarried.[111] The court found that the widow inherited the rights of primogeniture upon the death of her father-in-law, which are perpetual and not extinguished by remarriage.

These cases and this topic may seem unrelated to climate change. However, when seen through the climate change lens, protecting the ability of women to own land has benefits for sustainable development and emissions reductions.

---

[106] M. Villa. 2017. Women Own Less Than 20% of the World's Land. It's Time to Give Them Equal Property Rights. *World Economic Forum*. 11 January.

[107] N. Rao. 2011. Women's Access to Land: An Asian Perspective. Paper prepared for the Expert Group Meeting on Enabling Rural Women's Economic Empowerment: Institutions, Opportunities and Participation. Accra, Ghana. 20–23 September. p. 12; and C. Liamzon, A. Arevalo, and M.J. Naungayan. 2015. Women's Land Rights in Asia. *Land Watch Asia Issue Brief*. Manila: ANGOC. p. 2.

[108] C. Liamzon et al. 2015. Women's Land Rights in Asia. *Land Watch Asia Issue Brief*. Manila: ANGOC. p. 2.

[109] Footnote 94, p. 76.

[110] Supreme Court of Indonesia, Decision No. 1048/K/Pdt/2012, *Jance Faransina Mooy-Ndun v. Junus Ndoy et al.* (2012).

[111] *Daw San Lwin v. Daw Than (aka) Daw Than Than*, Case No. 19/2007, Special Civil Appeal Case, Supreme Court, Myanmar Law Report 2007. pp. 29–42.

VI. Children and Climate Change in Asia

Without climate action, future generations will potentially "inherit nothing but parched earth incapable of sustaining life."[112] Children's small size and reliance on caregivers make them extremely exposed to disasters, especially if separated from their parents or guardians. They cannot compete with adults in a fight for food or water, and they do not have the same capacity to seek help. Children are also more susceptible to being trafficked, abused, or exploited.[113]

Climate change impacts children's health, nutrition, and education. The United Nations Children's Fund (UNICEF) reports that climate change "disproportionately heightens the risk of diseases affecting children, including malaria, dengue fever, Zika and Japanese encephalitis."[114] Around 88% of climate change-related disease affects children aged 5 or less.[115] Climate change increases the frequency of extreme weather events, amplifying inequities for children and undermining their life prospects.[116] Children from poorer families are more likely to experience flooding, to attend flood-prone schools (impacting their education), and to live in farming families.[117]

A. Children and Deforestation

In 1993, the Supreme Court of the Philippines recognized the right of children to demand environmental and climate change action. In *Oposa v. Factoran*, the court recognized that children could demand the end to mass deforestation and that they had a right to inherit a balanced environment (footnote 112). As well as stressing the environmental impacts of mass deforestation, the petitioners argued that deforestation diminished global absorption of carbon dioxide.

Although the plaintiffs had constitutional rights to a clean and healthful ecology, the court stressed that the petition's success need not rest on that right. The right to a balanced and healthy environment "concerns nothing less than self-preservation and self-perpetuation" (footnote 112). These rights, said the court, "predate all governments and constitutions" and "are assumed to exist from the inception of humankind" (footnote 112).

Oposa v. Factoran reminds us of the presence of natural rights that do not necessarily require expression under a law to seek their protection. (See Part One, Section I.B.1.a. Class Actions and Future Generations in the Philippines for a full

---

[112] *Oposa v. Factoran*, G.R. No. 101083, 30 July 1993, per Davide, JR., J.
[113] N. Rees and D. Anthony, eds. 2015. *Unless We Act Now. The Impact of Climate Change on Children*. New York: United Nations Children's Fund (UNICEF). p. 30.
[114] J. Bornstein Ortega and C. Klauth. 2017. *Climate Landscape Analysis for Children in the Philippines: How Climate, Environment and Energy Issues Affect Filipino Children*. Manila: UNICEF. p. 20.
[115] Y. Zhang, P. Bi, and J.E. Hiller. 2007. Climate Change and Disability-Adjusted Life Years. *J Environ Health*. 70 (3). pp. 32–36.
[116] Footnote 114, p. 54.
[117] Footnote 114, p. 36.

case summary of *Oposa v. Factoran. Oposa* is also discussed in Part One, Section II.B.1.b. Quality of Life in Southeast Asia; Part One, Section II.B.2.a. Climate Justice in the Philippines and Pakistan; Part Two, Section VIII.B.1. Timber Licenses in the Philippines; and Part Five, Section VI.A. Children and Deforestation.)

B.   Children and Disproportionate Impacts of Climate on Their Future

In *Pandey v. Union of India and Another*, the petitioner specifically argued the need for greater climate action in India, as it would disproportionately impact children and future generations.[118] Ridhima Pandey argued that children were more vulnerable to pollution, heat waves, drought, floods, and other disasters. Further, impacts would progressively worsen over their lives.

Citing estimates from the World Health Organization, she said that children suffer more than 80% of illnesses and mortality attributable to climate change. Pandey also highlighted data from UNICEF, which estimated that children under 5 carry more than 88% of the global burden of disease due to climate change. She argued that children faced health impacts, displacement, conflict, and destruction of family and community structures.

She contended that children and their caregivers have no meaningful way of protecting themselves from the dangers of climate change, given the nature of the threat. She also argued that only states could reverse climate change, just as only states could initiate national emissions reductions and protect sinks to reduce global atmospheric CO_2 levels to below 350 parts per million (ppm) by 2100. And yet, children were excluded from the decision-making processes concerning responses to climate change, a phenomenon that children did not create. Therefore, it was incumbent on the government to take appropriate and effective science-based measures to ensure that climate change would not disproportionately impact her, children, and future generations.

The National Green Tribunal (NGT) disposed of the claim in January 2019.

(See Part One, Section II.B.2.b. Existential Threat and Intergenerational Equity in South Asia for a full case summary of *Ridhima Pandey v. Union of India & Another* and information regarding the 350-ppm threshold. *Ridhima Pandey* is also discussed in Part One, Section III.B.1. Climate Change Commitments in South Asia; and Part One, Section IV.B.1. International Commitments in Settled Cases in South Asia for further discussion of this case.)

---

[118] *Ridhima Pandey v. Union of India & Another*, Original Application No. 187 of 2017 (National Green Tribunal, 15 January 2019).

C. Climate Complaint to the United Nations Committee on the Rights of the Child

On 23 September 2019, 16 young people filed a complaint to the UN Committee on the Rights of the Child.[119] Five of the petitioners come from Asia and the Pacific. Ridhima Pandey is from India; Carlos Manuel is from Palau; and David Ackley III, Ranton Anjain, and Litokne Kabua hail from the Marshall Islands. Greta Thunberg is also a petitioner. The petition, submitted under the Third Optional Protocol to the Convention on the Rights of the Child, protested the lack of action by the governments of Argentina, Brazil, France, Germany, and Turkey.

The petitioners argued that each of the respondents was knowingly causing and perpetuating the climate crisis.[120] They asked the committee to find that the "climate crisis is a children's rights crisis."[121] While they acknowledged that children and adults share the same human rights, the petition focused on the specific impacts of climate change on children. The 16 young people argued that the Convention on the Rights of the Child compels countries to "respect, protect, and fulfill children's inalienable right to life."[122] As climate change threatens to undermine this right, climate action is, therefore, a human rights priority (footnote 122).

The petitioners asked the committee to recommend that the respondents "amend their national and subnational laws and policies to ensure that mitigation and adaptation efforts are being accelerated to the maximum extent of available resources and on the basis of the best available scientific evidence."[123] The petitioners also sought committee recommendations that the respondents lead "cooperative international action" and promote the involvement of children in climate mitigation and adaptation action.[124] The petition is ongoing at the time of writing.

---

[119] *Chiara Sacchi et al. v. Argentina et al.* Communication to the Committee on the Rights of the Child, submitted on 23 September 2019.

[120] *Convention on the Rights of the Child*, New York, 20 November 1989, *United Nations Treaty Series*, Vol. 1577, No. 27531, p. 3. The convention is the world's most widely ratified human rights instrument. Except for the United States, all UN members are party to the convention.

[121] Footnote 119, p. 95, para. 325.

[122] Footnote 119, p. 3, para. 13.

[123] Footnote 119, p. 95, para. 328.

[124] Footnote 119, p. 95, para. 329.

Aerial shot of Tuvalu. Given their extreme vulnerability to climate change, Pacific island countries have actively pushed to limit global warming to 1.5°C above preindustrial temperatures and have also questioned the climate obligations of states with higher emissions (photo by Eric Sales/ADB).

PART SIX

TRANSBOUNDARY LITIGATION

I. Global Approaches: Transboundary Harm in South America

States have an obligation to address transboundary environmental harms based, among others, on customary international law. Given that greenhouse gas (GHG) emissions cause transboundary harm, states may have a duty to address climate impacts outside their jurisdiction.

The International Court of Justice (ICJ) has stated that it is "every State's obligation not to allow knowingly its territory to be used for acts contrary to the rights of other States."[1] This is because the "principle of prevention" requires a state to "use all the means at its disposal in order to avoid activities which take place in its territory, or in any area under its jurisdiction, causing significant damage to the environment of another State."[2] The ICJ's position is consistent with the "no harm" principle (or the principle of *sic utere*).[3] States should assess how activities within their jurisdiction will adversely affect the climate and provide adequate notice to the international community.

In *Pulp Mills on the River Uruguay (Argentina v. Uruguay)*, the ICJ held that countries have an obligation to other states to conduct environmental assessments when there is a risk of transboundary harm.[4] Argentina filed suit against Uruguay, claiming that Uruguay had violated a treaty signed by both countries in relation to the River Uruguay. The joint treaty included provisions for preventing pollution of the river, as well as protecting and preserving the aquatic environment.

---

[1]   *Pulp Mills on the River Uruguay (Argentina v. Uruguay), Judgment, ICJ Reports 2010*, pp. 55–56 (citing *Corfu Channel (United Kingdom v. Albania), Merits, Judgment, ICJ Reports 1949*, p. 22); see also *Trail Smelter (United States v. Canada)*, 3 RIAA 1938, 1963 (Mar. 11, 1941) ("No state has the right to use or permit the use of its territory in such a manner as to cause injury . . . in or to the territory of another or of the properties or persons therein, when the case is of serious consequence and the injury is established by clear and convincing evidence."); and see *Matthew Lukose & Others v. Kerala State Pollution Control Board & Others* (1990) 2 KLJ 717. p. 724.

[2]   *Pulp Mills on the River Uruguay (Argentina v. Uruguay), Judgment, ICJ Reports 2010*, p. 56 (citing *Legality of the Threat or Use of Nuclear Weapons, Advisory Opinion*, ICJ Reports 1996 (I), p. 242, para. 29).

[3]   M. Jervan. 2014. The Prohibition of Transboundary Environmental Harm. An Analysis of the Contribution of the International Court of Justice to the Development of the No-Harm Rule. *PluriCourts Research Paper* No. 14-17.

[4]   *Pulp Mills on the River Uruguay (Argentina v. Uruguay), Judgment, ICJ Reports 2010*, p. 83.

Argentina claimed, however, that Uruguay had violated the treaty by authorizing, building, and commissioning two pulp mills on the River Uruguay. These pulp mills had allegedly undermined the water quality of the River Uruguay and the areas affected by the river.

In interpreting the joint treaty between Argentina and Uruguay, the ICJ held that states had an obligation to conduct EIAs where there was a risk that the proposed activity "may have a significant adverse impact in a transboundary context, in particular, on a shared resource" (footnote 4). States must also conduct the EIA prior to project implementation. However, the court "held that the content and scope of EIAs had not yet been defined by either general international law or by the statute" (footnote 4). Therefore, the court considered that each state should determine the content of EIAs in its domestic legislation (footnote 4). In reaching its decision, the ICJ reasoned that the practice of undertaking an EIA where there was a risk of transboundary harm was so accepted by states that it was now a matter of customary international law.

(See Part Two, Section I.A.2.a. Transboundary Litigation in South America for further discussion of this case.)

In another landmark decision that bears on state responsibility for transboundary harm, the Inter-American Court of Human Rights issued guidance for states under its jurisdiction in *Advisory Opinion OC-23/17 of November 15, 2017 Requested by the Republic of Colombia*.[5] The advisory opinion gives all states—and citizens thereof—who recognize the Inter-American Court of Human Rights' jurisdiction the right to file claims where environmental harms impact their human rights. The court will assess the claims against three types of obligations, including an obligation to cooperate and an obligation to provide information, justice, and public participation.[6]

Under the obligation to cooperate, states must notify potentially affected states when a proposed activity under their jurisdiction could generate a risk of significant transboundary damages. They must also negotiate with states potentially affected by significant transboundary harm. Under the obligation to provide information, justice, and public participation, the court noted that persons potentially affected by transboundary damages must have access to justice without discrimination based on nationality, residence, or the location of environmental damage.

The landmark Advisory Opinion opens the door to potential transboundary climate change litigation.[7] First, the court acknowledged climate change's adverse impact on human rights (footnote 6). Second, the court expanded

---

[5]   Advisory Opinion OC-23/17 of November 15, 2017. Series A No. 23.
[6]   Footnote 6, pp. 75–85.
[7]   M.L. Banda. 2018. Inter-American Court of Human Rights' Advisory Opinion on the Environment and Human Rights. *American Society of International Law*. 22 (6). 10 May.

the jurisdictional scope of the American Convention on Human Rights, a key international human rights instrument in the Western Hemisphere. The court explained that under the American Convention on Human Rights, a state was responsible for people whose human rights were affected by transboundary harm caused by that state's polluting activities.

The court's framing of a state's duty to prevent transboundary environmental damage that undermines human rights is sufficiently broad to include climate-related harm (footnote 6).

(See also Part One, Section II.A.1. The Right to a Healthy Environment in Colombia; and Part One, Section II.A.1. The Right of Nature in Colombia for further discussion of this case.)

The ICJ has also shown that states can be liable for money damages for causing climate-related transboundary environmental harm. In *Certain Activities Carried Out by Nicaragua in the Border Area (Costa Rica v. Nicaragua)*, the court awarded Costa Rica compensation for the loss of environmental goods and services the country sustained due to transboundary impacts—in particular, the loss of carbon sequestration services because Nicaragua excavated two channels on Nicaragua's territory.[8]

(See Part Two, Section VIII.A.1.b. Lost Sequestration Services in Nicaragua for a full case summary of Certain Activities Carried Out by Nicaragua in the Border Area [*Costa Rica v. Nicaragua*].)

II. Asia and the Pacific Approaches

A. European Carbon Dioxide Impacts on the Pacific

The Federated States of Micronesia (FSM) sought consideration of transboundary harm by requesting a transboundary EIA for a power plant in the Czech Republic. On 3 December 2009, the FSM formally requested the Czech Republic to conduct a transboundary EIA for the proposed expansion and modernization of the Prunéřov II coal-fired power plant.[9] The Government of the FSM asserted that the lignite-fired power plant was one of the biggest industrial sources of CO_2 emissions globally and would contribute to global warming. Such global warming would lead to the destruction of FSM's entire environment.[10]

---

[8]   *Certain Activities Carried Out by Nicaragua in the Border Area (Costa Rica v. Nicaragua)* and *Construction of a Road in Costa Rica along the San Juan River (Nicaragua v. Costa Rica)*, Judgment, ICJ Reports 2015. p. 665.

[9]   The Government of the FSM sought this review under the Espoo Convention and the Czech Act on Environmental Impact Assessment. Collection of Laws No. 100 of 2001.

[10]   A. Yatilman. 2009. Letter request for a transboundary environmental impact assessment (EIA) proceeding from the plan for the modernization of the Prunéřov II power plant. 3 December.

Although the Czech Ministry of the Environment accepted the request, the minister later approved the Prunéřov II expansion EIA.

The Government of the FSM made the request in the context of the Convention on Environmental Impact Assessment in a Transboundary Context (the Espoo Convention), to which it is not a party.[11] Hence, triggering formal legal procedures under the Espoo Convention was not open to the Government of the FSM. The government also did not pursue action in the International Court of Justice (ICJ) or seek to mount an argument founded on the principles established in *Pulp Mills on the River Uruguay (Argentina v. Uruguay)*.

The government's decision to request reconsideration of the Prunéřov II expansion occurred in the aftermath of the Copenhagen Accord, which set a goal to limit global warming to 2°C above preindustrial times.[12] Disappointed by the "weak United Nations climate deal," the FSM looked for another avenue to prompt stronger mitigation action.[13]

(See Report One, Part Two on climate change for a discussion of the impacts of 2°C of global warming.)

The Paris Agreement changed the legal and political climate change landscape, including on the issue of how countries might question other states' climate action. At the 24th Conference of the Parties to the UNFCCC in 2018 (COP24), the parties completed aspects of the Paris Agreement Rulebook. The rulebook guides the 5-yearly global stocktake—a process to review and take stock of parties' progress toward their pledges—and compliance with the agreement.[14]

At COP24, parties also agreed to establish a facilitative, non-adversarial, and nonpunitive expert compliance committee.[15] Assuming that countries remain committed to the Paris Agreement, these forums might provide a useful avenue for questioning other countries' decisions to permit coal-fired power stations.

---

[11]   *Convention on Environmental Impact Assessment in a Transboundary Context*, Espoo, Finland, 25 February 1991, *United Nations Treaty Series*, Vol. 1989, No. 34028, p. 309 (as amended by ECE/MP.EIA/21/Amend.1). The convention focuses on transboundary EIA issues in the EU and is open to members of the United Nations Economic Commission for Europe. There are 47 parties to the convention, including Poland, which ratified the convention on 12 June 1997.

[12]   Conference of the Parties, United Nations Framework Convention on Climate Change. Copenhagen Accord. Decision 2/CP.15. Copenhagen (18 December 2009), art. 1; and T. Brookes and T. Nuthall. 2009. What Did the Copenhagen Climate Summit Achieve? *BBC News.* 21 December.

[13]   M. Kahn. 2010. Pacific Islanders Bid to Stop Czech Coal Plant. *Reuters.* 12 January.

[14]   UNFCCC. 2018. Proposal by the President: Informal Compilation of L-Documents. 15 December; UNFCCC. 2018. Draft decision -/CMA.1.

[15]   *Carbon Brief.* 2018. COP24: Key Outcomes Agreed at the UN Climate Talks in Katowice. 16 December.

B. Rivers in South Asia

The National Green Tribunal (NGT) in India directed the government to pursue diplomatic efforts to resolve transboundary river pollution in *Madan Lal v. Ministry of External Affairs & Ors.*[16] Although this case does not deal with climate change, it presents a novel approach to responding to transboundary environmental pollution.

The applicant sued over severe pollution of the Churni River, which caused a large fish kill and made the water unsuitable for irrigation and bathing. He asked the NGT for directions requiring the Ministry of External Affairs to initiate a dialogue with the Government of Bangladesh regarding pollution emanating from factories in Bangladesh.

During consideration of the matter, the Ministry of External Affairs reported that it had raised the issue of transboundary pollution before the Government of Bangladesh. It had instructed the High Commission of India in Dhaka to raise the issue of pollution of the Churni River continuously. As part of that dialogue, the Government of India had offered to pay for an effluent treatment plant at Churni River.

After considering the report from the Ministry of External Affairs, the NGT reminded the national government that the constitution obliged it to make the environment pollution free. The NGT closed the matter by directing the Ministry of External Affairs to continue negotiating with the Government of Bangladesh on setting up an effluent treatment plant funded by India.

---

[16] *Madan Lal v. Ministry of External Affairs & Ors.*, Original Application No. 15/2014/EZ (National Green Tribunal, 21 September 2016).

The Turpan Depression, Xinjiang, People's Republic of China.
The depression is a mix of salt lakes and sand dunes, and is one of the few places on Earth that lie below sea level. Sea level rise threatens many parts of Asia and the Pacific (photo by the United States Geological Survey).

CONCLUSION

To see a World in a Grain of Sand
And a Heaven in a Wild Flower
Hold Infinity in the palm of your hand
And Eternity in an hour[1]

Decisions that allowed rampant and unchecked development misunderstood the immeasurable contribution of every living part of Earth's ecosystems and contributed to climate change. Humanity's choices this century (good or bad) will affect Earth's climate for thousands of years at least—an eternity for the human species. To solve climate change, we may need to focus on the seemingly tiny matter in the palm of our hands—protecting forests, grasslands, or mangroves, for example.

This report highlights examples of judiciaries from Asia and the Pacific valuing rights, protecting ecology (large and small), and requiring sustainable outcomes. Such cases have either explicitly or implicitly contributed to global climate change governance. Defending the rule of law is in the hands of judges and other quasi-judicial bodies. Demanding ethical conduct and balanced and sustainable action may seem small and mundane, but their value is immeasurable.

The people of Asia and the Pacific are some of the world's most exposed to anthropogenic climate change. They need climate action urgently.

Humankind sits at a crossroads and must pick a path. Unless we take urgent action by reducing global carbon emissions by 2030 and achieving net zero emissions by 2050, our path could see the loss of countries in the Pacific, ecosystem collapses, and the submergence of many of Asia's coastal megacities.

As Report One in this series explained, the path to 1.5°C warming is not safe for everyone. But it is the path that gives the future generations the greatest prospect of thriving in 2100 and beyond. Either way, when impacts grow and people suffer, some will look to the courts for justice. Climate change is coming soon to a court near you.

What can judges do? Prepare, of course. This paper seeks to aid judges in that preparation.

---

[1]   W. Blake. 1803. Auguries of Innocence. Chicago: Poetry Foundation.

More than that, however, judges should ask what their role is in climate governance and the global discourse on climate change. And what does humanity have to lose if judges uphold the rule of law, fairly referee executive climate action, protect natural rights, and ensure that climate science underpins decisions? Indeed, we stand to gain.

Each branch of government has a unique function. Legislators make the law, the executive sets direction and policy for governance and implements the law, and the courts protect rights and ensure that the government is acting lawfully. In common law jurisdictions, judiciaries also expand and write law.

ADB has worked with judiciaries across Asia and the Pacific for 10 years under its Law and Policy Reform Program. Judiciaries are crucial partners for achieving sustainable, equitable, and inclusive development. But judges need to be inspired and to have access to ideas and resources. This need prompts ADB to publish this report that aims to

(i) showcase excellence in judicial decisions across Asia and the Pacific; and
(ii) support judges in responding to climate change.

The authors organize this report into six broad topics and provide a comparative review of recent litigation trends. The discussion covers approaches in Asia and the Pacific, compared with those from other parts of the world. With this report, ADB hopes that

(i) judges will be able to find regional and global approaches to common types of climate litigation; and
(ii) the rest of the world can learn from some of the judicial innovations across Asia and the Pacific.

Our review of judicial decisions showed that judges are gravely concerned about climate change. They have also consistently accepted that climate change is real; humans are causing it; and without widespread and prompt action, humankind is heading to a world that cannot sustain civilization as we know it.[2]

While there may be knowledge gaps in climate science, particularly about future impacts, the field is improving as technology advances.[3] Greater scientific certainty stands to boost judicial decision-making.

---

[2] Intergovernmental Panel on Climate Change (IPCC). 2018. Summary for Policymakers. In V. Masson-Delmotte et al., eds. *Special Report: Global Warming of 1.5°C*. Geneva: World Meteorological Organization; and Noam Chomsky, interview by R. Hackett. 2019. Noam Chomsky: 'In a Couple of Generations, Organized Human Society May Not Survive.' *Canada's National Observer*. 12 February.

[3] IPCC. 2014. In R.K. Pachauri and L.A. Meyer, eds. *Climate Change 2014: Synthesis Report. Contribution of Working Groups I, II and III to the Fifth Assessment Report of the Intergovernmental Panel on Climate Change*. IPCC: Geneva. p. 56, Box 2.1: Advances, Confidence and Uncertainty in Modelling the Earth's Climate System.

Judicial acceptance of the scientific conclusions about climate change likely reflects the courts' emphasis on facts, veracity, and integrity.[4] Lawyers and court officers are bound by ethics, and courts require litigants to act in good faith and prove their case. Such a setting makes it challenging for lawyers to categorically deny the existence and causes of climate change during a trial.[5] Courts are also "among the most respected and trusted of public institutions," hence judicial decisions and findings of fact carry weight in society.[6]

Given judicial probity and societal esteem for courts, a recent report by the Environmental Law Institute concluded that judicial fact-finding on climate science should influence public discussion on climate change (footnote 4). These factors also demonstrate how judges may contribute to the global discourse on climate change.

A few circumstances hinder climate action in Asia and the Pacific. The majority of countries in the region have not been large GHG emitters and, hence, have not contributed to the problem. Consequently, their focus is mainly on climate change adaptation, and they rely on large emitters to do their part in reducing carbon emissions and also to share resources enabling climate adaptation. Asia and the Pacific also has a history of weak environmental governance, resulting in damaged ecosystems and biodiversity, diminishing resilience to climate change. Biodiversity and ecosystem regeneration and protection should be prioritized now to enhance adaptive capacity.

Courts in Asia and the Pacific have risen to the challenge posed by slow executive action and ordered their executive branches to do their part. Faced with poor implementation of environmental laws, South Asian judges have created continuing mandamus orders, enabling them to keep a matter open for monitoring. Other courts have directed the executive branches of governments to establish commissions on climate change when there is failure to implement legal and policy commitments on climate change. Asian courts have also demonstrated a willingness to expand the meaning of constitutional rights and relax standing for public interest litigants seeking to protect their climate and environmental legal rights.

The judicial trend of environmental constitutionalism is possible because the region's countries have relatively young constitutions that enshrine rights such as the right to life, the right to equality before the law, and environmental rights. These constitutions were largely adopted after the Universal Declaration of

---

4   M.L. Banda. 2020. *Climate Science in the Courts: A Review of U.S. and International Judicial Pronouncements*. Washington DC: Environmental Law Institute.

5   See for example Exxon Mobil Corporation. 2018. Exxon Mobil Corporation's Response to March 21, 2018 Notice to Defendants re: Tutorial. 4 April, in *City of Oakland v. BP*, No. 3:17-cv-06011-WHA (N.D. Cal. Feb. 27, 2018). Exxon Mobil Corporation conceded that the climate is warming "in part" due to increased GHG emissions and that human activity has contributed to those increased atmospheric GHG emissions. Also see footnote 4, p. 109.

6   Footnote 4, p. 110.

Human Rights; the International Covenant on Economic, Social and Cultural Rights; the International Covenant on Civil and Political Rights; and other international instruments, which expanded the human rights lexicon in the 20th century.[7] (For a discussion of the region's constitutional rights, see Report Three of this series.) By incorporating international environmental principles into national constitutional rights, judges in Asia have acted creatively to uphold environmental justice, an approach that lends itself to the climate context.

This report aims to showcase some of these judicial innovations.

Above all, the authors want judges to know that judicial action on climate change is not misplaced activism. Judges have a unique role to play in climate governance. Decisions requiring adherence to international or national climate change commitments signify that society's trusted institutions protect rights and hold governments accountable for meeting their commitments.

Climate change is the greatest challenge of our time. Now is the time to work for a just future, not to give in to inertia. Climate science (briefly discussed in Report One of this series) paints a dark vision of our future world if appropriate responses do not occur, and only collective and urgent action can mitigate the worst suffering and keep millions of people safe.

As Mary Robinson (former United Nations High Commissioner for Human Rights) says, "grim scientific prognoses must not paralyse civil society.[8] With this knowledge we must unite and take action. "Feeling a complete inability to do anything – 'This is too big for me, I give up' – that's no use to anybody. [With] despair, all the energy to do something goes out of the room" (footnote 8).

To this, we say to judges in Asia and the Pacific, uphold the law, protect rights, balance interests, and rely on science. Be vigilant and watch for the day when climate change comes to your courtroom. Tomorrow will dawn and in it our children must build their lives in the world that we create. Let them stand on the shoulders of those who advocate for integrity, justice, and fairness.

---

7   General Assembly Resolution 217 A (III), *Universal Declaration of Human Rights*, A/RES/3/217 (10 December 1948); *International Covenant on Economic, Social and Cultural Rights*, New York, 16 December 1966, *United Nations Treaty Series*, Vol. 993, No. 14531, p. 3; and *International Covenant on Civil and Political Rights*, New York, 16 December 1966, *United Nations Treaty Series*, Vol. 999, No. 14668, p. 171.

8   R. Carroll. 2018. Mary Robinson on Climate Change: 'Feeling "This Is Too Big for Me" Is No Use to Anybody.' *The Guardian*. 12 October.

Photo by Gerhard Jörén/ADB.

GLOSSARY

The terms presented in the glossary table have been adapted or taken from a number of sources listed under the Glossary References at the end of this section.

Abatement remedy	a legal action demanding a specified lower level of emissions (Latham, Schwartz, and Appel 2011)
Adaptation	the process of adjustment to actual or expected climate and its effects, in order to moderate harm or exploit beneficial opportunities in human or natural systems (Intergovernmental Panel on Climate Change 2018)
Adaptive capacity	the ability of systems, institutions humans, and other organisms to adjust to potential damage, to take advantage of opportunities, or to respond to consequences (Intergovernmental Panel on Climate Change 2018). See also adaptation
Atmospheric trust	a concept which requires governments to act as trustees of the atmosphere, with members of the public as beneficiaries (Hulac and Gilmer 2018)
Anthropogenic	of, relating to, or resulting from the influence of human beings on nature. (Merriam-Webster anthropogenic)
Anthropogenic carbon emissions	the emissions of various forms of carbon—the most concerning being carbon dioxide—associated with human activities, including burning of fossil fuels, deforestation, land use changes, livestock, and fertilization, that result in a net increase in emissions (Stenhouse et al. 2016)
Biomass	living or recently dead organic material (Intergovernmental Panel on Climate Change 2018)
Black carbon	(or soot) operationally defined aerosol species based on measurement of light absorption and chemical reactivity and/or thermal stability; mostly formed by the incomplete combustion of fossil fuels, biofuels, and biomass but also occurs naturally (Intergovernmental Panel on Climate Change 2018)

Cap-and-trade system	caps the amount of carbon emissions a given company may produce but allows it to buy rights to produce additional emissions from a company that does not use the equivalent amount of its own allowance. (Merriam-Webster cap-and-trade)
Carbon capture	a way of collecting the carbon produced by the burning of fuel or other processes, so that it is not released into the air (Cambridge Dictionary carbon capture)
Carbon capture and storage	(or carbon dioxide capture and storage) a process in which a relatively pure stream of carbon dioxide (CO_2) from industrial and energy-related sources is separated (captured), conditioned, compressed and transported to a storage location for long-term isolation from the atmosphere (Intergovernmental Panel on Climate Change 2018)
Carbon credit	a tradable credit granted to a country, company, etc., for reducing emissions of carbon dioxide or other greenhouse gases by one metric ton below a specified quota (Merriam-Webster carbon credit)
Carbon sequestration	the process of storing carbon in a carbon pool (Intergovernmental Panel on Climate Change 2018)
Climate change litigation	(or climate change case) any case that (i) raises climate change as a central issue; (ii) raises climate change as a peripheral issue; or (iii) does not explicitly raise climate change but has ramifications for climate change mitigation or adaptation efforts (report series definition)
Climate justice	Climate justice links human rights and development to achieve a human-centered approach, safeguarding the rights of the most vulnerable people and sharing the burdens and benefits of climate change and its impacts equitably and fairly. Climate justice is informed by science, responds to science and acknowledges the need for equitable stewardship of the world's resources. (Mary Robinson Foundation—Climate Justice Principles of Climate Justice)
Climate migration	human settlement patterns in response to changes in the climate (International Organization for Migration 2008)

Climatic habitats	the bioclimatic range within which a species or ecological community exists due to emissions induced by human activities of greenhouse gases (Government of Australia, Department of Agriculture, Water and the Environment Loss of terrestrial climatic habitat caused by anthropogenic emissions of greenhouse gases)
Compressed natural gas (CNG)	a natural gas mainly comprised of methane stored under high pressures (while remaining in its gaseous form), mainly as a means to transport it, or as storage for later use as vehicle fuel (Stenhouse et al. 2018)
Cumulative emissions	the total amount of emissions released over a specified period of time (Intergovernmental Panel on Climate Change 2018)
Disgorgement of amounts	the act of giving up something such as the profits obtained by illegal or unethical acts on demand or by legal compulsion, with the goal of preventing unjust enrichment (USLegal Disgorgement Law and Legal Definition)
Downstream emissions	those generated by a product or service when they are used and disposed of by a consumer (Timlin 2011)
Ecosystem services	ecological processes or functions having monetary or non-monetary value to individuals or society at large. These are frequently classified as (1) supporting services such as productivity or biodiversity maintenance, (2) provisioning services such as food or fibre, (3) regulating services such as climate regulation or carbon sequestration, and (4) cultural services such as tourism or spiritual and aesthetic appreciation (Intergovernmental Panel on Climate Change 2018)
Environmental constitutionalism	a relatively recent phenomenon at the confluence of constitutional law, international law, human rights, and environmental law; embodies the recognition that the environment is a proper subject for protection in constitutional texts and for vindication by constitutional courts worldwide (May and Daly 2017)
Environmental impact assessment	an examination, analysis and assessment of planned activities with a view to ensuring environmentally sound and sustainable development (UNEP 1987)
Environmental impact statement	a government document that outlines the impact of a proposed project on its surrounding environment; meant to inform the work and decisions of policymakers and community leaders (Middleton 2018)

Fossil fuels	carbon-based fuels from fossil hydrocarbon deposits, including coal, oil, and natural gas (Intergovernmental Panel on Climate Change 2018)
Gigaton of carbon dioxide equivalent (GtCO2e)	unit of measurement for carbon dioxide, which is the measure used to compare the emissions from various greenhouse gases based upon their global warming potential (OECD 2013)
Greenhouse gases	those gaseous constituents of the atmosphere, both natural and anthropogenic, that absorb and emit radiation at specific wavelengths within the spectrum of terrestrial radiation emitted by the Earth's surface, the atmosphere itself and by clouds (Intergovernmental Panel on Climate Change 2018)
Greenwashing	expressions of environmentalist concerns especially as a cover for products, policies, or activities (Merriam-Webster greenwashing)
Holocene	the current interglacial geological epoch (Intergovernmental Panel on Climate Change 2018)
Intergenerational responsibility	a legal concept which says that every generation has a responsibility to the next to preserve the rhythm and harmony of nature for the full enjoyment of a balanced and healthful ecology (*Oposa v. Factoran* G.R. No. 101083, 30 July 1993)
Intergenerational equity	the principle that states that every generation holds the Earth in common with members of the present generation and with other generations, past and future (Weiss 2013)
Intragenerational equity	relates to fairness among the present generation; primarily concerns the relationship between developed and developing countries (Shelton 2008)
Intergovernmental Panel on Climate Change (IPCC)	the United Nations body for assessing the science related to climate change (Intergovernmental Panel on Climate Change About the IPCC)
Kyoto Protocol	Adopted on 11 December 1997, entered into force on 16 February 2005, this international treaty operationalizes the United Nations Framework Convention on Climate Change by committing industrialized countries to limit and reduce greenhouse gases (GHG) emissions in accordance with agreed individual targets (United Nations Framework Convention on Climate Change. 2020. What is the Kyoto Protocol?)

Mandamus	a writ which issues from a court of superior jurisdiction, and is directed to a private or municipal corporation, or any of its officers, or to an executive, administrative or judicial officer, or to an inferior court, commanding the performance of a particular act therein specified, and belonging to his or their public, official, or ministerial duty, or directing the restoration of the complainant to rights or privileges of which he has been illegally deprived (Black 1968)
Mitigation (of climate change)	a human intervention to reduce emissions or enhance the sinks of greenhouse gases (Intergovernmental Panel on Climate Change 2018)
Paris Agreement	Entered into force on 4 November 2016, this agreement builds upon the United Nations Framework Convention on Climate Change to strengthen the global response to the threat of climate change by keeping a global temperature rise this century well below 2° Celsius above preindustrial levels and to pursue efforts to limit the temperature increase even further to 1.5°C (United Nations Framework Convention on Climate Change. 2020. The Paris Agreement)
Particulate matter	very small solid particles emitted during the combustion of biomass and fossil fuels. PM may consist of a wide variety of substances. Of greatest concern for health are particulates of diameter less than or equal to 10 nanometers, usually designated as PM10 (Intergovernmental Panel on Climate Change Definition of Terms Used Within the DDC Pages)
Perpetual easement	type of easement which is to last without any limitation of time; a right which a person has on the property of another person which to an extent is permanent (USLegal Perpetual Easement Law and Legal Definition)
Precautionary principle	where there are threats of serious or irreversible damage, lack of full scientific certainty shall not be used as a reason for postponing cost-effective measures to prevent environmental degradation (United Nations 1992)
Public trust doctrine	a doctrine asserting that the state holds land lying beneath navigable waters as trustee of a public trust for the benefit of its citizens (Merriam-Webster public trust doctrine)

Renewable energy	energy from a source that is naturally replenishing but flow-limited, and is virtually inexhaustible in duration but limited in the amount of energy that is available per unit of time (US Energy Information Administration 2019)
Reverse environmental impact analysis (REIA)	analysis of how the environment and climate change may affect a project to understand how the project will, in turn, impact the environment (Gerrard 2012)
Right to a healthy environment	the interaction between human rights and the environment; encompasses the environmental dimensions of the rights to life, health, food, water, sanitation, property, private life, culture, and nondiscrimination, among others (Human Rights Watch 2018)
Rights of nature	the recognition and honoring that Nature has rights; the recognition that our ecosystems—including trees, oceans, animals, mountains—have rights just as human beings have rights; about balancing what is good for human beings against what is good for other species, what is good for the planet as a world; the holistic recognition that all life, all ecosystems on our planet are deeply intertwined (Global Alliance for the Rights of Nature What is Rights of Nature?)
Sink	a reservoir (natural or human, in soil, ocean, and plants) where a greenhouse gas, an aerosol or a precursor of a greenhouse gas is stored (Intergovernmental Panel on Climate Change 2018)
Solar array	a combination of several solar panels forming a system that produces solar electricity (Sunrun 2018)
United Nations Framework Convention on Climate Change	Adopted on 9 May 1992 and entered into force on 21 March 1994, this international treaty ultimately aims to prevent "dangerous" human interference with the climate system (United Nations Framework Convention on Climate Change. 2020. What is the United Nations Framework Convention on Climate Change?)

Vulnerable groups or people	(or vulnerable persons) minors, unaccompanied minors, disabled people, elderly people, pregnant women, single parents with minor children, victims of trafficking in human beings, persons with serious illnesses, persons with mental disorder, persons who have been subjected to torture, rape or other serious forms of psychological, physical or sexual violence, and indigenous peoples (See European Commission vulnerable person)
Waste-to-energy	the conversion of waste into energy in the form of steam, electricity or hot water; a hygienic method of treating waste that reduces its volume by about 90% (Confederation of European Waste-to-Energy Plants What is Waste-to-Energy)
Water justice	Water justice refers to the access of individuals to clean water. More specifically, the access of individuals to clean water for survival (drinking, fishing, etc.) and recreational purposes as a human right. Water justice demands that all communities be able to access and manage water for beneficial uses, including drinking, waste removal, cultural and spiritual practices, reliance on the wildlife it sustains, and enjoyment for recreational purposes (*Leghari v. Federation of Pakistan*, PLD 2018 Lahore 364)
Writ of kalikasan (nature)	a remedy available to a natural or juridical person, entity authorized by law, people's organization, non-governmental organization, or any public interest group accredited by or registered with any government agency, on behalf of persons whose constitutional right to a balanced and healthful ecology is violated, or threatened with violation by an unlawful act or omission of a public official or employee, or private individual or entity, involving environmental damage of such magnitude as to prejudice the life, health or property of inhabitants in two or more cities or municipalities (Supreme Court of the Philippines 2010)

GLOSSARY REFERENCES

H.C. Black. 1968. Black's Law Dictionary. St. Paul, Minn.: West Publishing.

Cambridge Dictionary. carbon capture.

Confederation of European Waste-to-Energy Plants. What is Waste-to-Energy.

European Commission. Vulnerable Persons.

M. Gerrard. 2012. Reverse Environmental Impact Analysis: Effect of Climate Change on Projects. *New York Law Journal*. 247 (45). 8 March.

Global Alliance for the Rights of Nature. What is Rights of Nature?

Government of Australia, Department of Agriculture, Water and the Environment. Loss of terrestrial climatic habitat caused by anthropogenic emissions of greenhouse gases.

B. Hulac and E. Gilmer. 2018. Kids' Case Tests 'Hail Mary' Climate Argument. *E&E News*. 5 October.

Human Rights Watch. 2018. The Case for a Right to a Healthy Environment. 1 March.

Intergovernmental Panel on Climate Change. 2018. Annex I: Glossary. In V. Masson-Delmotte et al., eds. *Global Warming of 1.5°C. An IPCC Special Report*. In press.

Intergovernmental Panel on Climate Change. About the IPCC.

Intergovernmental Panel on Climate Change. Definition of Terms Used Within the DDC Pages.

International Organization for Migration. 2008. Migration and Climate Change. IOM Migration Research Series No. 31. Geneva: International Organization for Migration. p. 21.

M. Latham et al. 2011. The Intersection of Tort and Environmental Law: Where the Twains Should Meet and Depart. *Fordham Law Review*. 80 (2). p. 760.

Leghari v. Federation of Pakistan, PLD 2018 Lahore 364

Mary Robinson Foundation—Climate Justice. Principles of Climate Justice

J. May and E. Daly. 2017. Judicial Handbook on Environmental Constitutionalism. Nairobi: United Nations Environment Programme. p. 1.

Merriam-Webster. anthropogenic.

Merriam-Webster. cap-and-trade.

Merriam-Webster. carbon credit.

Merriam-Webster. greenwashing.

Merriam-Webster. public trust doctrine.

T. Middleton. 2018. What is an Environmental Impact Statement? American Bar Association. 17 December.

OECD. 2013. Glossary of Statistical Terms—Carbon Dioxide Equivalent. 4 April.

Oposa v. Factoran G.R. No. 101083 30 July 1993

D. Shelton. 2008. Equity. In Bodansky, D., J. Brunnée, and E. Hey, eds. The Oxford Handbook of International Environmental Law. Oxford: Oxford University Press. pp. 32, 53.

K. Stenhouse et al. 2016. Anthropogenic Carbon Emissions. University of Calgary Energy Education. 18 February.

K. Stenhouse et al. 2018. Compressed Natural Gas. 25 June.

Sunrun. 2018. Solar Array. 1 March.

Supreme Court of the Philippines. 2010. A.M. No. 09-6-8-SC Rules of Procedure for Environmental Cases. 29 April. Rule 7 Section 1.

L. Timlin. 2011. Carbon Emissions Downstream—Are You Measuring Yours? *NewStatesman*. 21 November.

UN Doc. A/CONF.151/26 (vol. I), 31 ILM 874. 1992. Principle 15.

United Nations Environment Programme. 1987. UNEP—United Nations Environment Programme Goals and Principles of Environment Impact Assessment: *Preliminary Note*. 16 January.

United Nations Framework Convention on Climate Change. 2020. The Paris Agreement.

United Nations Framework Convention on Climate Change. 2020. What is the Kyoto Protocol?

United Nations Framework Convention on Climate Change. 2020. What is the United Nations Framework Convention on Climate Change?

United States Energy Information Administration. 2019. Renewable Energy Explained. 27 June.

USLegal. Disgorgement Law and Legal Definition.

USLegal. Perpetual Easement Law and Legal Definition.

E. Weiss. 2013. Intergenerational Equity. *Oxford Public International Law*. February.